D0205498

REVOLUTION FROM THE HEART

REVOLUTION

from
the Heart

NIALL O'BRIEN

New York   Oxford
OXFORD UNIVERSITY PRESS
1987

Oxford University Press

Oxford   New York   Toronto
Delhi   Bombay   Calcutta   Madras   Karachi
Petaling Jaya   Singapore   Hong Kong   Tokyo
Nairobi   Dar es Salaam   Cape Town
Melbourne   Auckland

and associated companies in
Beirut   Berlin   Ibadan   Nicosia

Published by Oxford University Press, Inc.,
200 Madison Avenue, New York, New York 10016

Oxford is a registered trademark of Oxford University Press

Library of Congress Cataloging-in-Publication Data
O'Brien, Niall.
Revolution from the heart.
Bibliography: p.   1. Philippines—Politics and government—1973–
2. Philippines—Politics and government—1946–1973.   3. O'Brien, Niall.
4. Negros Island (Philippines)—Politics and government.
5. Missionaries—Philippines—Negros Island—Biography.   6. Missionaries—Ireland—
Biography.   7. Catholic Church—Philippines—Clergy—Biography.   I. Title.
DS686.5.026   1988   959.9′046   87-14312
ISBN 0-19-504950-0

The author's royalties on all sales of this book will be used to help
the invalid children of Negros Island, the Philippines.

9 8 7 6 5 4 3 2 1

Printed in the United States of America
on acid-free paper

923.6
C'BC
1989

DUN. 822.50

8-28-07

For

TULLIO FAVALI   †
ZACHARIAS AGATEP   †
NILO VALERIO   †
PITES BERNARDO   †
RUDY ROMANO   ?

FOREWORD

This book is the story of Father Niall O'Brien, an Irish Columban priest who has spent most of his life as a missionary on the island of Negros in the Philippines.

At one of the busiest times in my life, when I was concluding my thirty-five years as President of Notre Dame, Father O'Niall wrote to ask if I would write this Foreword. When I saw the 576-page typescript, all of my instincts said, "No." But here was the sincere account of a priest who had worked for justice and suffered for it, too. After struggling with my better judgment, I agreed.

When all the farewell lunches and dinners (each requiring a speech) and my last commencement exercises were done, I was going to spend a week on retreat in Northern Wisconsin before taking off for Moscow and a meeting on nuclear peace. I decided to read Father Niall's manuscript and write the Foreword as part of my retreat. I was sure that I would learn from his experience; I have always been concerned about justice worldwide and believe that concern to be an integral part of my priesthood.

So I found myself in a cabin on an island in the North Woods, sitting before a roaring fire, with that fat manuscript on my lap, growling with myself for being a soft touch—hardly in the proper mood to begin a retreat. But I began to read.

The early chapters spoke of a young priest assigned to the Philippine island of Negros, which lies between the northern island of Luzon and the sourthern island of Mindanao, and is noted mainly for growing and processing sugarcane. His was the usual missionary story—learning a new language and customs, assigned to one parish and then another—the story of parochial missionary activity everywhere, with the usual small successes and failures that attend every young priest's life in the early years of his ministry.

Then the story began to come into focus. Vatican II was beginning to change the centuries-old face of the Church in the early 1960s: there was a new role for the laity, a new view of the world, a place where the new Church must become involved and share the joys and sorrows and hopes of the people, not to reject the world, but to save it.

All of this was an added burden for the new young priest. He was now living in a highly structured feudal society, the fruit of the Spanish conquest with an overlay of a brief period of American conquest and Japanese occupation. His new people were passive and oppressed, overworked on sugar plantations from dawn to dusk, underpaid and undernourished, badly housed and without any adequate medical care. Add to this the burgeoning corrupt regime of Ferdinand Marcos, which supported the few wealthy landowners by a growing brutal military presence, an utterly dishonest judicial and governmental regime, a total structure for all the multiple forms of organized injustice that have inflicted misery on the poor in so much of the Third World.

I began to meet dozens of humble parishioners who suffered the most blatant injustices without any recourse, except to tell their story to Father Niall, who was torn apart by his inability to do anything but plead their causes, mostly without effect, with the rich and powerful people who were also his faithful parishioners.

Now the story begins to find its powerful theme: how to react to structural injustice. Some turn to violence and revolution, but Father Niall, who is a disciple of Gandhi, Dorothy Day, and Martin Luther King, cannot bring himself to follow that path, which so often leads to more injustice, suffering, and harm to innocent people. On the other hand, nonviolent resistance seems quixotic in the face of heavily armed and corrupt governmental forces. What then to do? This is the true drama of Father Niall O'Brien's story. He remains faithful to his convictions and refuses to meet violence with violence. It lands him in jail facing a death sentence.

Every story of the struggle of a people for justice is gripping, but this one is even more so because all of us witnessed via television the downfall of the corrupt Marcos, the drama of poor women, men, and children kneeling in the street, praying the Rosary and actually stopping the tanks that were trying to bring down Cory Aquino as she was bringing down Marcos. Nonviolence did unseat violence for once!

There is an ecclesial sub-theme that is just as exciting and, in the long run, perhaps more important than this drama.

Father Niall, with the urging of Vatican Council II, rouses his people from their fatalism, their passivity, their total dependence on him. He becomes a new kind of missionary who makes the people and their natural leaders, rather than himself, the true center of Church activity. They learn this lesson with great reluctance and great difficulty and multiple failures, but they do learn, and a new Church is born: the people of God. Then *he* begins to learn from *them,* and the drama of his religious experience and growth becomes exciting indeed.

I was reluctant to read this book. Now I confess that my retreat was better this year because I did read it. I found that Father Niall, who has been a priest just half as long as I, is indeed a brother. I have never met him, and maybe never will, but I resonate with his most basic conviction that we cannot be priests, or even pray, if we are not consumed by hunger and thirst for justice—doing whatever we can, even unto death, to change the structures that support injustice and oppress the poor. I hope that Father Niall returns to his new resourceful people in Negros, from which he was expelled, and writes another book—in which they will go from success to success. That will be a happier book, but not as gripping as this one.

(Rev.) Theodore M. Hesburgh, C.S.M.
President Emeritus
University of Notre Dame

ACKNOWLEDGMENTS

This is the story of the journey of a people toward their own freedom and of the author who straggled along. I am grateful to the people of Negros for allowing me to accompany them.

The names of certain people and one place have been altered in this book to protect the safety and confidence of some and because of the feelings of the families of others. Hence there will be one place not visible on the map.

The monetary value ascribed to the peso is the value it had in dollars at the time of a particular event. Since the dates of those events differ, so do the values ascribed to the peso.

For help in producing this book I should like to thank Carmel Murphy, Pat Noble, Rayna Paz, Tadgh McDonnell, and Jorge Emmanuel. For reading the manuscript and making helpful suggestions I would like to thank Eve Donoghue, Stella Bates, Mary Ann Ganey, Leslie Wearne, Cynthia Read, Laura Brown, Joan Bossert, Joellyn Ausanka, Marie Zarowney, and fellow Columbans Paddy Bastable, Cyril Lovett, and Donie Hogan; for help in theological background, John O'Brien, Regina Bectle, and Robert Imbelli.

This book tells only part of the story; space did not allow me to introduce you to so many people who have been working to make Negros a better place from long before I arrived and who are still quietly working away without any fanfare. Their story is written not in books but in the lives of the people.

Negros, Philippines   N. O'B.
May 1987

REVOLUTION FROM THE HEART

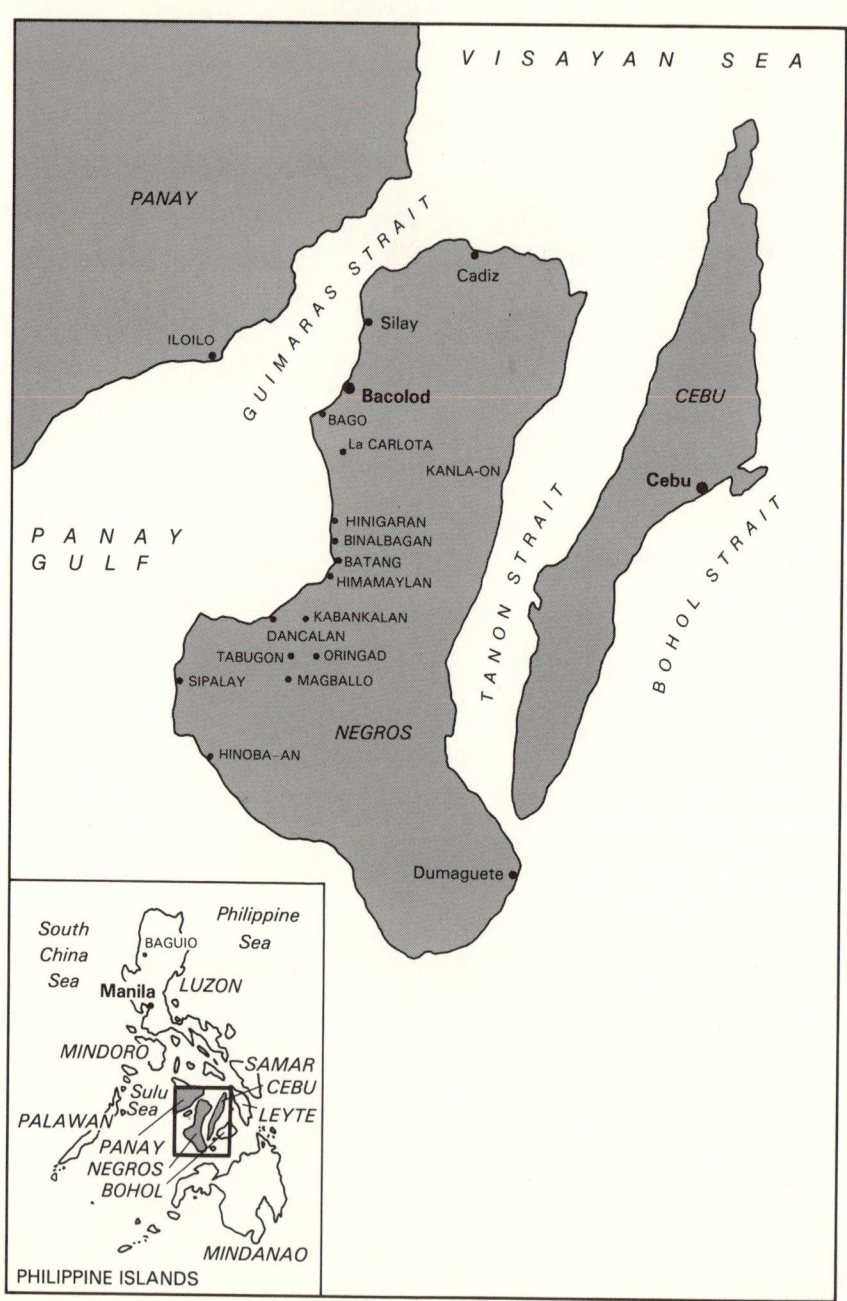

Chapter 1

EVENING was coming in the city of Bacolod on the island of Negros. It was Holy Week. The day was Holy Thursday. The year 1984. The dying light concealed the squalor of the prison yard. As the darkness advanced the prison itself seemed to disappear, leaving only a glow from behind the bars of each cell . . . like a stage set from *Carmen*. From our cell looking west I could see the last blue of the sky. To me it seemed to reflect the waters of the nearby bay. My thoughts traveled back to Dublin Bay where in my boyhood, sitting on the shore at the end of a summer's day, I would watch the gentle approach of evening over the waters. For a moment I was free again.

Our cell gate was open. Presently, I stepped out and walked quietly to Cell 9 and peered through the bars. The prisoners were sitting on the floor in silence. Nene the Bosio, or "Boss," of the cell was on his hunkers awkwardly washing the feet of one of the prisoners. One of the others was reading out loud the words of St. John: "I have given you this example so that you may copy what I have done to you." I had feared our suggestion that each cell perform the Maundy ritual would meet with ridicule. I was wrong. The other prisoners were listening in silence; the sense of something sacred going on was tangible. I thought again of how presumptuous I had been in coming to the Philippines thinking only to teach. The truth was that most of the time I was the one who was learning and in these last months in prison, more so than ever.

I used to slip away each day from the babble of our cell to say my breviary in the prison yard. The other prisoners gradually learned to leave me alone for those minutes. As I read the Psalms, they took on a meaning they never had before. I had always seen them as hyperbole, poetic exaggeration, a little unsuited to our age, maybe any age. All this about being falsely accused, pursued by enemies, ensnared, hungry, sick, abandoned and forgotten. But now as I read them and looked around me I could see that they were literally true, word for word, and syllable for syllable:

> Reach down from heaven and save me
> Draw me out from the mighty waters
> From the hands of foes
> Whose mouths are filled with lies
> Whose hands are raised in perjury.

So many of the prisoners waiting for me to finish could have written these very words. It was as if I were praying them now for the first time since I had come to the Philippines, twenty years before.

* * *

I arrived in Manila in 1964. I remember the heat hitting me like a slap in the face as I got off the plane, the milling crowds on the streets, the conspicuous Mercedes automobiles everywhere. The clapboard slums for miles and miles. The crowds of laughing children, the smiles, the welcome, the solid quiet of our own Columban house.

St. Columban's was the headquarters of the Society of St. Columban, the largest foreign missionary society in the Philippines, with some two hundred and fifty priests. We were the latest arrivals, twelve young men just ordained, straight from the seminary in Ireland.

Almost immediately we were fitted out in long white soutanes, which we were to wear even downtown—in fact everywhere except indoors. On a green baize bulletin board in the foyer of our house was posted a list of names opposite a list of places. Our assignments were already out. I read "Niall O'Brien . . . . Negros."

If you look at a map of the Pacific, you will see the Philippines just below China and well north of Australia—an archipelago of more than seven thousand islands. Within the archipelago there are three clearly discernible areas: the large northern island of Luzon, the large southern island of Mindanao, each about the size of Great Britain, and in between a bunch of smaller islands called the Visayan Islands. Negros Island is one of these.

In charge of our papers was Paul Richardson, a quiet-spoken American with red curly hair. He had been working in Negros, and I plied him with endless questions, pushing him to tell me about the island and to give me examples of the language.

It was a custom here to treat the new arrivals to a film. Not every diocese allowed us to go to the films, but Manila did, so priests in from the rural areas for a break took advantage of the opportunity. I do not remember what the film was now, probably because a little incident on our way home knocked it out of my head. We were walking through what I now realize was a sort of red-light district. Pimps of various sorts called out to the strange band of foreign priests walking in white robes through their territory; the night was sultry and I felt threatened by what were really friendly cries from doorways and women calling. The older fellows were amused at our discomfort; we moved at a clip. Suddenly something in a doorway caught my eye. It was a little boy, maybe seven years of age, fast asleep on the cold cement. I hestitated . . . but we moved along and I said nothing. In a moment we had left the little fellow behind. But that night I lay sleepless in the safety of my room as the image of the small boy came back to me and, unexpectedly, I was overcome with grief such as I had never experienced before, as if I was that child and I had lost my mother and father. I knew I should not have walked on by.

In 1964 the Second Vatican Council was in full swing. It was a time of great excitement and optimism. The Mass was to go into the vernacular and bring about miracles of ecumenism. The priests' own prayerbook, the breviary, was to go into the vernacular too. Altars were to be turned around toward the people, and that turning toward the people was to be the theme of all theology. The third session of the Council was now opening in Rome. Apart from launching the Council, and thereby swinging open the windows of the ancient Church, Pope John had issued two startling encyclicals— first *Mater et magistra* (*Mother and teacher*) in 1961, and then, a few weeks before he died, *Pacem in terris* (*Peace on the earth*). Both were full of optimism. Both had taken the side of the poor and were hopeful about doing something about poverty—so much so in fact that *Pacem in terris* was mocked by a rightist Milan newspaper with the headline "Siklo in terra" ("Sickle on the earth"). Both encyclicals had also seen the search for world peace as an integral part of the Church's mission. I was excited about the changes and frustrated that I could not get any information on what was now happening at the Council. Here in Manila no one seemed interested.

In a few days I flew south to the island of Negros. Negros is shaped like a boot, the toe facing south away from Manila. Down the length of the boot runs a line of mountains dividing Negros Oriental from Negros Occidental, where the Columban Fathers have worked since 1949. Oriental, the east, speaks Cebuano, the language of the island nearest it—Cebu, while Negros Occidental, the west, speaks Ilongo, the language of Panay, the island nearest it. In 1964 the island of Negros had about two million people, most of them situated in the western half where the Columbans had been working.

As our airplane circled to land I was struck by the contrast between the deep turquoise of the surrounding seas—you could see right down to the bed of the sea—and the rusty down-at-heel look of the corrugated iron roofs of Bacolod City.

When I alighted from the plane, I saw two large figures in conspicuous white soutanes waiting on the tarmac. They greeted me matter of factly as if they had known me for years, and we set off on our journey south in a Volkswagen van. Gerry O'Connor, the older of the two and an old China hand, said to me: "Bacolod may seem lousy to you now, but believe me as the years go by it will look better and better!" I began to understand what he meant as our journey continued; the road got so bad, potholed with large craters, that the van had to maneuver slowly down into them and out again in first gear. We went at a snail's pace and at times were hanging onto the seats, as if in an airplane hit by turbulence. I was soon to learn that south of Bacolod a properly paved road was a rarity.

All the way down south, the mountains were on our left and the sea was somewhere over to our right. From the mountains to the sea was a green coat of sugarcane through which our road cut a channel, so that sugarcane was on either side—sometimes newly planted, sometimes ten feet tall enclosing the road like walls, sometimes being cut by men dressed in tattered denims wielding broad-bladed knives with a little hook at the end. In some fields women and children were planting cane points or spreading fertilizer. At one point our van stopped for the driver to check the tires, and I jumped out and smelt the strange heady aroma of the ripe, newly cut sugarcane. Years later I would still associate that smell with my first arrival.

As we moved on, gradually a beautiful peak appeared amid the mountains, eventually towering over everything else. It was the cone of Kanla-on volcano, Gerry said, and it could be seen from most anywhere on the island. This mountain was the home of Manaul, the ancient guardian spirit of Negros. Kanla-on had been dormant for a long time now.

We passed through four towns. At one point the road passed right along the seafront where small fishing skiffs were drawn up on the roadside. In the distance I could see some islands and thought of home. I had grown up on the shore of Dublin Bay, and Howth was just about that distance out to sea, looking just like that on a good summer's day. I felt a pang and never failed to think of home every time I passed the spot from that day on.

Outside the towns, we passed very few houses, except for some dilapidated shacks and a few stately plantation dwellings. In the distance we saw smoke from the chimneys of sugar mills and, at one point, almost choked with the stench from the effluent of one of the sugar factories. We passed a few fish ponds where milkfish were being cultivated in brackish water, and we crossed many bridges spanning the rivers that flowed to the sea from the high spine of the mountains to our left.

We got to the town of Binalbagan as darkness fell at around six o'clock: this was headquarters for the thirty Columbans who worked in southern Negros Occidental. In the *convento,* as the priest's house is called, several Spanish friars had lived in the old days. Downstairs were offices, upstairs were cubicles for the priests with much mosquito netting and a large dining-cum-living room called the *sala.*

It is hard to describe the welcome we got from the men who were there. They were a brotherhood and I was a member, immediately accepted; nothing needed to be said or proved. I would work alongside them maybe for the rest of my life. We would maybe have different methods, but we had the same goal and that overcame all the other differences—in temperament, age, and nationality. Some were Irish, some Australian, some American, but all were priests and Columbans, a bond as strong and sometimes stronger than that of natural family.

I was the first young priest to arrive in Negros since the Vatican Council got under way. While in Manila I noticed that hardly any news from the Council had reached the house there. I had no recent news, but I did know quite a bit about the new constitution on the liturgy, which had appeared in Latin. I had read up carefully on the changes that were now around the corner. I knew they were going to revolutionize almost every aspect of Church life. I liked them.

One of the older priests asked: "What's all this we hear about dropping Latin in the Mass?" His disapproval was evident. But I had no notion of the passion that such a loss would arouse in many for whom the medium was almost inseparable from the message. I answered glibly: "I am in favor of retaining Latin." "For what reason?" "Why," I said, "because of the *argumentum ex turismo,* the advantage it gives the tourist: no matter where you go in the world, when you hear Mass it's in the same language . . . which you don't understand." My sarcasm won a laugh, but there was hurt silence from the man who had raised the topic. The conversation turned to other things, but I sensed a lingering uneasiness in the air.

A young Australian priest, John Stratton, arrived from the town of Isabela. He understood the disorientation I was going through. "Why don't you come home with me tonight?" he said. "I'll drive you in again in the morning, and you can get the bus south to Kabankalan where you will be beginning at the language school." So off we went in his war-surplus Eisenhower jeep.

As we neared the town John observed: "Seems as if we'll have no lights tonight. The town lights are off." But it was a moonlit night, and we could easily see our way into the large old *convento*.

Once into the *sala* he offered me a beer, and we sat down in the dark. "Things are going to seem very strange to you. My advice is to observe but say nothing for a year, then say all you want. But you'll see that lots of things are deep into the culture and sometimes there's a surprisingly sane reason behind what seems pointless or bad custom. The Columbans have tried to change some things, but if you push too hard you open a can of worms."

I mentioned that the new document on the liturgy had a lot about adapting the Mass to the culture of the people.

"What document?"

"The first document from Session One of the Vatican Council."

"Is that still on?"

"Yes, it's in full swing. It's only beginning."

"Look, Niall, I don't want to dampen your spirits, but you must have noticed the negative reaction of a couple of the men to your remark about the Latin Mass. Rome is a long way away from here, and a lot of the stuff that has come down from above in the past has been pretty irrelevant. The Manila Synod of '56 came up with resolutions that we should not go to the cinema and that we should all be tonsured."

I argued that this Council was a pastoral Council and that the new insights had really come from below.

"Maybe so, but what can they know about Isabela? You see that church there?" In the moonlight the bulk of the Spanish church stood out. "When John Holloway, the pastor, took over here in '50 that was only a ruin. Perhaps a dozen people went to Mass downstairs in this *convento*. People hardly knew what extreme unction was. A great number were not properly married, and almost no one was confirmed, and you could forget about confession and Communion. He rebuilt the church, put up a school on a shoestring, got Sisters to come here, brought the Mass out to the *barrios,* and put catechists in all the public schools. And on Saturday night now you'll be several hours hearing confessions and, on Sunday, that church is packed three times. And it's the same story in most of the other parishes we took over. So naturally you can't blame the men for feeling that they're doing O.K. I mean, the way they look at it is, 'Why change the rules of the game when you are winning?'"

That night as I lay under the netting, listening to the whine of the mosquitoes in the darkness all around, I thought about the events of the day. I liked John. He wanted to save me some difficult times. People seemed to have hardly heard of the Council, not to mention that new document on interpretation of the Scriptures. Theologically an earth-shaking document, and no one had even heard of it. Not to mention all the other documents filled with changes. I remembered what John had said: "Why change the rules of the game when you are winning?"

Chapter 2

IT MUST have been *siesta* when I arrived at Kabankalan. My first memory is of waiting on the church steps because the doors of the *convento* were closed, as they always were during the noon heat. I sat on the steps looking out at the town *plaza*, a large *plaza*, the type found at the center of most old Filipino towns built in Spanish times.

I was shaded by the façade of the church behind me. The church was cement, built in 1935 in the Odeon Cinema style. Soon someone opened the doors and I went inside. In the distance I could see a red light flickering beside the tabernacle which dominated the main altar. I knelt and prayed for a moment. No matter where I was in the world, it came naturally to pray when I saw the tabernacle and the light signifying that the Sacrament was there. Now in the disorientation of change it was a point of permanence and warmth.

The church was cruciform. Behind the altar was a huge, round, stained-glass window—St. Francis Xavier by the looks of it—and, underneath him in large letters, "Donated by Doña Granada Viuda de Ruiz." On the left, an altar with a statue of Mary over it. On both side walls, confession boxes. There was a balcony high up at the back.

I began mentally reconstructing the church in the spirit of the new ideas from the Vatican Council. I pulled out the altar so that I could say Mass facing the people. I removed the altar rail to lessen the distinction between the priest and the people. I brought down the organ from the loft and put it up front, and I brought the choir with it so that they could sing with the people and not just for them. I took a few statues away for painting, but I didn't return them all!

I was in the middle of a sermon, fluent in the local language, when I felt a tap on the shoulder.

I turned around. "Welcome to Kabankalan! I suppose you're the new fellow. Mike Doohan is the name." With a big grin on his face.

"I'm Niall O'Brien."

"I know. Come on up. You'll have plenty of time to see the church."

The *convento* was beside the church. It was the same arrangement as at Binalbagan: downstairs offices and meeting rooms, upstairs the priests' quarters. We climbed the stairs to the *sala*, a large room for eating in and sitting around in, where Mike offered me a Coke. I was hardly a week in the Philippines and I had already drunk more Coke and Pepsi than in my whole previous life.

Later Mike took me around town in his blue Volkswagen. We circled the *plaza*, a huge sward of green grass which Mike assured me probably really belonged to the church but was lost when the Spaniards were expelled at the turn of the century. In the center was an octagonal bandstand.

"That's where the great political rallies are held. We have two parties here, the Liberals and the Nationalists. There's no difference between the two of them. Votes are bought almost openly and whoever gets into power shares out the jobs to their own people."

On one side of the *plaza* was the *municipio*, or city hall, built in 1935 like the church, but in American colonial style—it must have been a good year for sugar.

"That's where the mayor's office is," said Mike, "and the court, and where you get your residence permit, and marriage licenses. That's where the jail is too—it's an awful hole."

On the church side of the *plaza* was the parish school. On another side of the *plaza* was the public school.

"There are one thousand two hundred children in our school and two thousand children in this public school, not to mention another thirty smaller public schools spread throughout the municipality. You can imagine what a job it is providing religious instruction. There are about seventy thousand people in the parish, and a lot of the time I've been here on my own."

We passed some beautiful houses in off the road, which Mike said belonged to the sugar planters. The planters are *mestizos*, he explained, mixed Filipino and Spanish or Filipino and Chinese descent. "They own ninety percent of the land in the municipality of Kabankalan. Many of the owners don't live here at all, but live in Bacolod or Manila and have an administrator, or *encargado*, looking after the land."

We passed some large hardware stores. "Those belong to the Chinese. They are great business people. They come here from places in mainland China like Canton and inland Macao, and they work like blazes in a small buy-and-sell operation. By the next generation they are big stuff and ready to marry into the *mestizos* and the land, and from there they can launch into politics. But sometimes things go wrong and in the third generation they lose everything again. Gambling is to the Chinese what drinking is to the Irish."

When we got back to the *convento* Mike laid out the plan. "You're supposed to learn the language, and I've been warned not to inveigle you into helping in the parish. But you're free to help when your study is done. I've set up three teachers for you—three hours in the morning and two hours in the afternoon. It may seem a lot, but believe me it's worth it."

The language lessons began on Monday of my first week. I was delighted to be getting down to work. Not only did I enjoy the classes, but after class finished at five and the heat was going out of the day, I spent the last two hours before supper going from house to house with a notebook, introducing myself to the people and learning the language from their own lips. One by-product of this language force-feeding was that I got a firsthand look at the poverty of the surroundings. A lot of the poorer houses had little or no furniture. The family sat on the floor which was made from bamboo lattice. Walls were made from bamboo matting, called *sawali,* and the roof thatched with the fronds of the nipa palm. Roof, walls, and floor often had gaping holes, so one had to step carefully. In many of the houses a sick person was lying inertly in a dark corner. None of them had electricity, water, or sanitation, but no matter how poor, most dwellings had planted flowers around—bougainvillea, canna lily, even roses.

I was taken aback by the poverty, but it did not disturb me deeply since I saw my work as being somehow "spiritual." To me that meant exclusively concerned with the "soul," which I pictured as a sort of invisible second heart, like a flame. My questions focused on whether the people were going to Mass, saying their prayers, or properly married. If there was a sick person, I would ask whether they had received the sacrament of the dying, the last anointing, and frequently as a result of these visits I found myself coming back to "fix up" a marriage or anoint the sick. I made sure to leave in every house a copy of the formula for baptism in danger of death. If there was a sick person in the house, I got them put on the list for our weekly Communion rounds, when the priests of the parish brought the Eucharist to the sick. I do not recall people asking me to help in medical matters or with problems of civil injustice.

I really threw myself into the language. My teachers were good and conscientious. And apart from visiting the houses, I performed any religious ceremony that came up, using the occasion to practice. They got a free sermon at every baptism and funeral—at first read, then learned by heart, and finally stumblingly spontaneous. Within three months I was able to speak Ilongo, though haltingly.

As soon as I had the language learned, I was appointed to the parish of Sipalay, down in the deep south by the sea.

The ride to Sipalay took eight hours. The roads were terrible, though not as bumpy as in the north and center of the island since many of them were gravel and had known no cement or asphalt at all.

The further south we went, the more the hitherto ubiquitous sugar gave way to coconuts, rice, and yellow corn. We got to Sipalay at two in the morning, and the bus dropped each one of us off at our separate houses. I was delivered to the *convento* where I woke up Tom Revatto, the parish priest. Tom laughed at the sight of me—covered in dust with all my cases, and at such an ungodly hour—his "new curate," the first and the last.

We went upstairs. The *convento* had the same layout as Kabankalan and Binalbagan, except that Tom had added a neat little balcony from which we could look out over the town. From the back window you could hear the waves, and that meant so much to me who had grown up beside the sea.

My time in Sipalay was to be very short, only a few months, but I was happy there, and they say a happy first assignment stays with you all your life.

In those days sugar had not yet engulfed Sipalay, with its monocrop monotony and inevitable sense of factory rather than farm. Tom was a gracious and easygoing host. He did not feel that souls would be lost if we took a long *siesta*. Moreover, he had a refreshingly maverick attitude toward what others would then have considered closed theological issues. Though we did not always agree on what the new should be, we frequently agreed that the old was inadequate. My contention was that what was constantly put forward as being the "old" theology and traditional pastoral practice was in fact relatively new, frequently no earlier than the Counter-Reformation and sometimes as recent as the First Vatican Council, in the nineteenth century. Tom was interested in this. In return he shared with me something about which I was totally ignorant—the history of the Columbans in Negros.

Fifty years before, two young Irish priests, Eddie Galvin and John Blowick, decided that China was it. Taking Columban, the Irish monk who re-Christianized much of Europe after the barbarian invasions, as their patron, they started out on the job of converting China. Through the twenties, thirties, and forties, the Columbans lived in the thick of it. Floods and plagues, famine and war and revolution. Eventually they were expelled by the communist government of Mao Tse-tung. Many of the "old China hands" then came to the Philippines, where other Columbans had already been working.

The Philippines was a special case. In 1521 Magellan had stumbled upon these islands in an attempt to find a passage to the Spice Islands. He was killed by the Filipino hero Lapulapu, but one of his boats managed to limp home across the western Pacific, down around the Cape of Good Hope and up again by West Africa, and back to San Lúcar, the Port of Seville. His expedition had put the Philippines on European world maps.

Still looking for those spices, the Spaniards reached the Philippines again half a century later, this time under Legaspi. On the boat was the veteran soldier-turned-friar, Urdaneta. During the intervening years Spain had learned some moral lessons from her early excesses in the Caribbean and Latin America, and her policies in the Western Isles (as the Philippines were first called) were comparatively enlightened compared with other contemporary colonizers. Slavery, which lasted into the nineteenth century in the rest of the world, had by this time been outlawed by Spain, and special laws defended the land rights of native populations. Whereas the Indians of North America hardly survive today, the *Indios* of the Western Isles have grown into a great nation of nearly sixty million people.

Spain came in search of spices and gold: a voyage unashamedly commercial, funded by banking houses of Europe such as Fugger's. They found neither spices nor gold in quantity, but stayed to propagate their faith—the personal decision of Philip the Second, after whom the islands are named. Letters to Philip are still extant, in which the first priests, who came on the Spanish galleons, vehemently attacked the oppression of the native population by the soldiery and corrupt government officials.

As time went on, however, the Church was co-opted into the new ruling body and became almost identified with it—an important part of the colonial means of control. When the people rose up in 1896 and overthrew Spanish colonial rule, the Spanish Church fell with it and a great number of the friars were expelled. Rome called on other mission groups to come to the aid of the beleaguered Filipino Church, which now had to contend with a militant anticlericalism, a breakaway native church called the Aglipayans, and a vigorous American Protestant missionary movement. Along with the expulsion of the friars, the lack of priests was aggravated by the fact that for centuries the Spaniards had blocked native ordinations.

This was the situation when the Columbans, now in nearby China, were urged by the Pope to come to the Philippines. A mission not to convert but to revivify.

Each evening after supper, Tom and I used to walk up and down along the side of the town *plaza* in front of the *municipio* discussing all these things. Tom had a wealth of stories and anecdotes. The Columbans in those early days had to contend with a legacy of anticlericalism. In fact the first priest back to Sipalay had been stoned! Compared with fifteen years before, giant steps had been made. It really did seem to be a case of why change the rules when you are winning.

After only a few months, just as I was getting to know the people and our new catechetical program was beginning to get off the ground, our superior moved me. It was a disappointment, and Tom was annoyed. But that was the way we did it in those days. We were to be sort of shock troops of the Church, ready to answer the call. Looking back now, it seems to me that the disregard for the relationship between priest and people reflected an unconsciously mechanistic theology. The Church, the parish plant, provided the sacraments, education, grace. The people—who were not the Church but the objects of her care—received. The parish was like a filling station where one went to get these graces. A priest must be in each parish to attend the pump. The product and the method of delivering it were beyond question. As yet I was not questioning the product, but my sudden change in post raised doubts about the delivery.

Chapter 3

AFTER lunch one day we packed my books into the parish jeep and set off north for Kabankalan. This time the sea was on our left and the mountains on our right. Fifteen years before there had not been even one priest in all this one-hundred-mile stretch, but now we had a Columban priest in each town all along the way. Each had built a *convento,* a church, a school, and had organized catechists, parish organizations, and a schedule of yearly or monthly Masses in the far-out *barrios.*

As we moved north we left the rice and coconuts behind and, after the town of Cawayan, sugar began to appear again in quantity. We then swung inland to Kabankalan. It looked like a city to me after the quiet south.

We pulled into the *convento* at about 6:30 P.M. It was getting dark. The lights were going on upstairs.

Up I went, expecting to find Mike there and hoping he had been told who his new curate was. (It wouldn't be the first time if he hadn't.) But when I got upstairs I had a surprise. It was not Mike; it was Paul, Paul Richardson, the quiet-spoken American who had looked after my papers in Manila. Paul was happy to see me and explained that Mike was in Iloilo getting teachers for the school.

Paul felt in no way threatened by the Vatican Council. His father was a Protestant and for years Paul had felt the need for ecumenism, in a very personal way. Many Columbans were Irish-American, but Paul was a "Yankee" like his father. He used to say that while I only had to adapt to the Filipino culture he had to adapt to the Filipino and the Irish culture simultaneously. He complained that on his last leave his family in Boston said he had developed a brogue! He was as stubborn as any Irishman, but he kept abreast of catechetics and liturgy and had a particular interest in Jewish theology, which gave him an open mind.

When I said, "I wonder will Mike agree to pulling out the altar and saying Mass facing the people?" he said, "Maybe if *you* ask him. From me it would sound like Protestantism but from you it's the Vatican Council again." He sensibly suggested that rather than try to move the massive marble altar we should place a simple wooden altar on a lower level, closer to the people.

Mike was glad to see me when he got back from Iloilo. Paul was appointed to the school, so I was Mike's only help for a very large parish.

"Well, what have you been plotting in my absence?"

"Oh, nothing. . . . Well, not exactly nothing." And I explained the idea about the altar.

"Who'll pay for it?"

"Well, I have a little money." Actually I did not have any at all, and I had made a promise to myself not to accept Mass offerings if I could do so without fuss. But I decided I'd have to break my promise—for a good cause!

Mike himself was busy all the time. He administered the three parish schools—a high school, an elementary school, and a college. He was constantly adding new classrooms, which meant contracting for lumber in the mountains and fighting with Chinese merchants over the price of cement and steel strengthening rods. He was an expert builder. He also took his share of Masses and confessions. He put me in charge of catechetics—that is, providing religious teachers for the public schools.

I toured the villages and contacted young women who would be willing to teach. They would have a small salary because I felt that otherwise the teaching would only be haphazard. Then I got them all to come into the *convento* every month for training. It was soon clear that the books available were useless: all in the old question-and-answer style, concerned with information rather than inspiration. Paul came to my rescue with a new conciliar religion book, which I got down to translating, trying to adapt it to the local circumstances. Money had to come from somewhere, so I began to tour the parish to solicit pledges from the richer parishioners. Mayor Sola pledged two hundred pesos a month, and members of the Catholic Women's League made pledges. I got a first glimpse of the more opulent side of parish life during these "collection" visits.

Mike asked me to give retreats to various groups: teachers, students, tricycle drivers, household help, of which there were many. We had contracted a very common ailment of priests: we were running so fast we hardly had time to think and ask ourselves where we were going.

I eventually got the chance to make a journey to Carolan, the furthest *barrio* we had in those days before the roads. No priest had been there in living memory, and I knew it would be a couple of days' walking. I prepared some food to tide me over along the way, but not enough for the whole journey. I had the mistaken idea that I could pick up some food on the road. Many things happened on that trip, but one simple incident, small in itself, has remained with me because it caused me to make a decision.

I had taken shelter from a passing tropical shower in a shack several hours into my journey. In the hut were some adults and some children. The children were bloated from what I now know was lack of food and probably infestation with intestinal worms. The children had no clothes except for T-shirts.

I took out my food and was thoughtlessly beginning to eat it when I noticed all eyes upon me. It dawned on me that they were all hungry and there was no food. I shared what I had, regretting that I had not brought more. The adults refused, allowing the children to take it, and the children wolfed down the little I had to offer, making me ashamed that I had begun to eat without thinking of them in the first place. When we finished I was still hungry. I had often fasted, but this was the first time in my life that I had experienced hunger because there was no food.

I was profoundly disturbed by this incident, more than I realized. On the next Sunday when I began to share it with the people of the town, the memory of the hungry children suddenly overwhelmed me, my voice cracked, and I could not go on speaking. I was reduced to tears in the pulpit. I was embarrassed by my show of emotion, but afterward said to Paul: "If we Columbans don't manage to come to grips with the poverty of the people, I am going to have to think about looking elsewhere." Since being a Columban meant so much to me, I was troubled by the implications of what I had said. Was I really serious about that? The thought of how hurt John Blowick, our co-founder and my own close friend, would be if I left kept coming back to me. So I postponed thinking about it in earnest. But unconsciously I had made the decision from that moment to support anything that would bring us Columbans closer to the poor.

Some months later, someone invited me to the city of Cadiz in the north of the island to do a retreat seminar. It was organized by a group called the Barangay Sang Virhen, the Family of Mary. Now most parish organizations either originated in Spain, the United States, or Ireland. Here was one that was native, and native to Negros. The founder, Antonio Gaston, was a Negrense who told a touching story of a promise made to the Virgin at the moment when the Japanese were about to shoot him. He was saved and so decided to start the Barangay, or Family of Mary. At this time the organization was not in our parish, but I felt attracted to it because it was a homegrown product. The Barangay people had set up this retreat seminar to revitalize flagging members. They called this retreat the Sa-Maria.

The Sa-Maria took me by surprise. I had not realized just how native it was. The songs were old native love songs I had never heard, but with the words changed. I found the music haunting. Those doing the retreat were all peasants, not at all your middle-class school-connected churchgoers, the backbone of our church in Kabankalan. Here they had a chance to stand up and share their opinions. Almost all the talks were given by a band of devout laypeople. The talks were inclined to be strongly Counter-Reformation in tone, and certainly not Vatican Council. But the simplicity and devotion of the little band who gave them were attractive. The purpose of the retreat was to promote the Barangay of the Virgin. By the time the retreat was over the seventy-two participants were deeply affected and were obviously going back to their parishes to raise a spiritual storm.

Tony Gaston invited me home to his house in Silay when the retreat was over to meet his family, and that was another pleasant surprise. Although from what in Ireland would be called the ascendancy class, or aristocracy, Tony was very consciously proud of being a Filipino and knew a lot about the suffering of the poor—and did care. He called them "the little people" and was personally prodigal in his charity toward them. Because of his own wartime experience of being saved by sincere prayer, he tended to see that as a universal solution, and he was persuasive when he spoke. He liked the native music, the native dress, and spoke beautifully in Ilongo. His English was also impeccable. Tony was very open to the changes in the liturgy if it would help the people and felt they could be introduced into his seminar. I asked him if he would consider bringing his team down to Kabankalan. He said he would, and had me driven all the way home in his Volkswagen—120 miles!

On the way I had a chance to think and weigh the pros and cons of the Sa-Maria. On the contra side, the theology was inclined to encourage more devotions and religious practices, to emphasize what we should *not* be doing, rather than the things we *should* be doing. It was determinedly otherworldly and quite unchallenging of our social situation. In fact injustice was not an issue at all. However, on the pro side, it was the first group I had seen that was geared to the poor. It was determinedly Filipino and Ilongo and proud to be, which was very unusual at that time when most of the middle class and many of the aristocracy looked to the United States as the mecca of genuine culture. If the Sa-Maria tended to be emotional, maybe the imported European liturgies erred in the opposite direction. Also in its favor was that it was totally a lay group. And finally, it aimed at interior change rather than just external conformity and a joining of the Christian parade. In a word, it had possibilities, especially if the talks could be rewritten in the spirit of Pope John and the Second Vatican Council.

Mike was quite agreeable to having a Sa-Maria in Kabankalan, and we fixed a date. It was held in the school, and we had so many applications that we had to turn many away.

When it was over, Tony suggested we build a permanent Sa-Maria retreat house for the south in Kabankalan. We called a meeting of the Columbans in the south to discuss the idea. The most prominent objection was that it would probably die out in a few years anyway. Gussie Rowe, a Columban who had pioneered our schools for the poor, answered that that was probably so, but if it would do good while it lasted why not use it while we could? He added that this is the way with many organizations. His perceptive remark was to help me again later on. And it swayed the group, who agreed we should go ahead with the Sa-Maria house. I was to build it and find the money! They would support it.

Building the Sa-Maria house was one thing: Columbans had done so much building I could get lots of advice on what not to do. But rewriting the *rollos*—as the lectures were called—was another. I would need not only theological advice, but such advice would have to be within the cultural context of Negros. I needed a collaborator.

In the city of Bacolod was the diocesan seminary. The rector was a tall, athletic, Filipino priest named Edgar Saguinsin. He was a good theologian, a scholar, and had a deep interest in the poor, and therefore in labor unions. We made friends early on—he got me to give retreats in the seminary, while I asked him to speak in the parish. Edgar recognized the possibilities latent in the Sa-Maria, and together we proposed to Tony that we rewrite the *rollos*. From the Vatican Council we would take the theology, with an emphasis on Scripture, on liturgy, on justice. From the Barangay we would take the orientation to native culture, respect for the devotions of the people, especially their devotion to Mary, and an orientation to the poor.

We hid ourselves away in a plantation house in Cadiz and got to work. It was not easy. The catechism of the Council of Trent—that staunchly Counter-Reformation document—had been in use for four hundred years. It had plenty of time to develop a lot of "stories" with which to illustrate its points—sometimes medieval miracle stories, like the one of the host dripping blood during Mass offered by a priest who doubted the real presence of the Lord in the Eucharist. To illustrate the Vatican II theology, we turned to the Scriptures for our examples, but much of the new theology was "orientation," "dimension," "perspective," . . . so hard to express simply and forcefully. It lacked punch, and as yet we had no "stories." That is no longer true. Since then, the stories have been lived—all over Negros crosses mark the places—and a new martyrology has been written.

But at that time Edgar and I could not know just how deep the renewal would go and where it would lead or that one day as a consequence he would have to flee the Philippines in fear for his life.

Just then we were working on introducing the *panimbahon* into the Sa-Maria and so into Negros. Let me explain about the *panimbahon,* because it will become very important later on.

It must have been my first village Mass, a monthly Mass in this case, in the *barrio* of Hilamonan. I was immediately struck by something. After Mass the people had been complaining that it was some months since they had had a priest. I explained that there just were not enough to go around. "But why don't you meet yourselves and have the first half of the Mass? The people can do that, you know." They looked at me askance. I was speaking directly from the new document on the liturgy of Vatican II, which proposed just this. It emphasized the division of the Mass into two sections—the liturgy of the word, the teaching section, and the liturgy of sacrifice, the worship section. In putting the Mass into the local language the Council Fathers hoped to bring back the teaching section. The problem went back to the Reformation. The Reformers had gone for the word and deemphasized the sacrifice. The Catholics had gone for the sacrifice and deemphasized the word. Only the priest, in Catholic theology, could perform the sacrifice, so without a priest there could be no real worship. I could see that the people grasped the value of having their own worship without a priest. But as yet there was nothing I could do. The time was not ripe, and we had no "vehicle" to introduce it with.

But now the time seemed right because we had so many graduates coming out of the Sa-Maria anxious to help, and others going home to *barrios* where they would not be able to have Sunday Mass. We decided to launch our *panimbahon,* a "worship service." Paul helped to put it together, and soon we had it going in some of the mountain *barrios.* Now that we were revising the Sa-Maria we thought of incorporating the *panimbahon* into the Sa-Maria. Edgar agreed, and Tony and the Barangay council agreed. And since the Sa-Maria had now spread all over Negros and even Panay, the new worship service spread with it. Hundreds of *barrios* which formerly had only a monthly or yearly Mass now had their own weekly worship service.

It was just at this time that Mickey Martin arrived. Mickey was as strong as a horse, and the other Columbans soon called him Mickey the Muscle. He had a forceful mind and the gift of being able to situate a particular pastoral practice within the overall theological picture.

Mickey and I had been close friends in the seminary and had followed the developments of the Vatican Council together. Together too we had "discovered" the French theologian Paul Hitz. Though he never became famous, his little book *To Preach the Gospel* was considered ahead of its time in Catholic circles and was to profoundly affect the teaching of Paul VI, who was aware of Hitz's research. It affected our outlook as well and was now behind the sort of vision I had for the Sa-Maria.

Hitz's thesis was this: Christendom is now gone, we are back in the days of the early Church when the apostles had to announce simply and starkly: *Jesus is alive!* Preaching must return to this "kerygma," this proclamation. For years the Church had been concentrating on catechesis, or education, and *presuming* belief. But belief could only be brought about by evangelization—literally translated, the "announcing of the good news." One of the results of this inversion was that in many places the faithful were baptized, catechized, sacramentalized, but not evangelized. And so priests in their pastoral practice were continually tempted to use pressure of one sort or another instead of the joyful invitation to discipleship.

We now faced the task of reversing this process. The Sa-Maria could supply the basic evangelization that had been skipped, and I knew that Mickey would understand and support this approach.

Our shared insight bonded Mickey and me together. I couldn't believe my luck when he was appointed to the Philippines and not to Korea, where big fellows like him, it seemed to me, were frequently sent.

Mickey was immediately sent to Kabankalan to learn the language. Knowing him, I knew he would not confine himself to learning the language but would help us to get the Sa-Maria and the *panimbahons* off the ground.

Chapter 4

MICKEY brought news of the Council, in particular the document *Gaudium et spes*—the Pastoral Constitution on the Church in the Modern World. That was only one of a score of documents, each of which slightly altered the direction of the Church and all of which together amounted to a revolution. We could not find enough time to digest all there was, and then we had to try to interpret it in the light of the strange world around us. Every few months these documents would appear, modifying, expanding, deepening some Church teaching. They came first in Latin, then a translation from the Latin, then a commentary, and finally we had to make the application. There was an air of euphoria, as if there was nothing we could not do.

When time for my yearly vacation arrived, I went to Manila hoping to get into the International Liturgical and Catechetical Congress taking place at the Ateneo de Manila, the Jesuit university. To my disappointment, Father Johannes Hoffinger, the organizer, said that only two participants could be accepted from each country, and that the Irish and Filipino quotas were filled. I waited till the last moment to see if someone would fail to turn up, but they all came. I could not just walk away. The famous Austrian liturgist Josef Jungmann was taking part, Father Clifford Howell from England, and so many others. I hung around until the registration closed and then I went back to Father Hoffinger. "Do you need a secretary, because you have one here if you'll take me." He agreed, and in I walked, secretary to the very group that Jungmann was in. I got a bird's-eye view of the discussion.

On the last day, we all met in the large hall where conclusions and statements and joint petitions to Rome for this and that were read out. The world's greatest liturgists and pastoral theologians were represented. I had enjoyed the Congress and learned a lot, but as it was ending I suddenly realized that no one, not one speech or petition or statement, referred to the fact that so many of the world's people were hungry. My mind went back to the little shack in the mountains and the bloated hungry children gobbling my sandwich. I realized that among all the scholarly representatives I was probably the only one actually in daily pastoral work.

I put my head down and let the others leave. I had no heart to move. So much suffering, and the best and the brightest had not even touched on it. Once again I was overcome by grief like the night I had seen the little boy in the doorway. It came on me like a storm, and now I was ashamed to lift my head in case anyone would see.

Presently I felt a hand on my head. I looked up. I was alone in the great hall with an old bearded Greek archimandrite, wearing a sort of miter.

"They never mentioned the poor," I said to him. Then I repeated it in French.

He nodded compassionately again and again. He understood. His threadbare clothes said the same thing.

We remained there silently, understanding each other, anguished and shamed that the churches we loved so much should take so long, so long, to notice that Lazarus was at the gate.

One result of my attending the seminar was that when I returned to Negros I got a letter asking me to join the National Liturgical Commission and another letter from Rome in Latin. Paul could not believe this one till he had read it himself: it appointed me to experiment with the sacrament of baptism in many different ways and to report on them.

Many Columbans used to pass through Kabankalan on their way north to our central house in Binalbagan. Jack Hynes from the next parish south was one of them. He threw up his hands at the organized chaos of our parish. Mike was out building classrooms. Paul was teaching in our college. I was in the midst of building the new Sa-Maria house. The newly arrived Mickey Martin was constantly having to drop his language studies to do the baptisms, marriages, and funerals which lined up outside the *convento*. Some Saturdays we had fifteen weddings!

As the buildings continued to go up, I had to find money somewhere. One of the ways was to go around the wealthy homes and ask them to donate a number of sacks of sugar. I had a form they could sign and I would collect it from the sugar factory when their crop was milled. That took a bit of the pain out of giving. I hated the job of asking and kept telling myself I was not ordained to the priesthood for this. I hated waiting outside the door, I hated the moment of asking, but what I did not know then was that these "hat in hand" visits to the planters would be very valuable years later.

I got to know many of them whom I would never have met otherwise. They came to me with family problems, and I persuaded some of them to take retreats. I knew them as persons, not just as plantation owners—the pinnacle of the Negros social pyramid, the liege-lords of a semi-feudal system, the bourgeoisie. In the not-too-distant future when the battle would be raging between the Church and the landowners, the planters could never be just a social category to me, one side of the contradiction in a dialectical clash between classes. In my mind's eye I would see this particular planter with her children and her personal problems, a human being. The day would come when I sorely needed this.

The mayoral elections arrived. It was the custom of the Columbans to keep resolutely out of party politics and not to let the Church be used. I told the lectors at Sunday Mass and the catechists to resign until after the elections were over if they were going to be involved in the campaigning. I thought I was being very careful, but I managed to put a foot wrong. It happened like this. Someone persuaded me that if I came with him on a certain day a wealthy businessman in Bacolod probably would be prepared to donate to the building of the Sa-Maria house. Off we set. This businessman's house was palatial and the huge reception room resembled the morning levee of a duke because a large number of clients were seated around, obviously waiting for favors. In the center of the room a group of well-dressed men surrounded the "duke" on his seat. Tied under his chin was a white sheet. He was being shaved, shorn, and his nails attended to as he held court. My contact brought me toward the inner circle, where I stood in my soutane, feeling distinctly ill at ease. We were interrupting a conversation.

"Burn their houses, burn their houses," the duke was saying.

"But Papa, we are asking people to vote for us."

The duke noticed me. My contact introduced me. I was allowed a couple of sentences in which to explain my visit. The duke interrupted, speaking to me and the courtiers generally: "I told the bishops that if they wanted money for social upliftment I'd organize . . . but not for more religion."

He turned to a man who was about to leave.

"Yes, go ahead, buy that helicopter." Then, back to me: "I told them I'd help and they haven't asked. . . . Look, if we don't put more money into the hands of the workers how will they afford to buy the products we are manufacturing for them? It's as simple as that." And he turned away to the next client.

When I got back the news was out that I had been refused. The Liberals in the town let it be known that they were hurt that "their" priest had been treated like that. And they used it.

As if that weren't enough, one night I was walking around the *plaza* in the dark saying my rosary when I noticed a blaze of light and noise in Colosso Street. I came closer, and from the shadows I watched what appeared to be a political rally. It was Pablito Sola, the Liberal candidate for mayor. To my chagrin someone saw me, and Pablito was soon saying: "And I'd like especially to welcome tonight to our gathering our beloved priest, Father O'Brien." I moved away as soon as courtesy would allow, but next day the story was going around that I had sung at the rally.

To make things worse, the male choir I had painstakingly built up for the community liturgy suddenly began to appear at rallies for Pablito, their name changed to "D' Grey Hounds"!

A couple of days later I had a visitor. It was the campaign manager of the Nationalist party from Bacolod. He was stony-faced. His message was simple: "Keep out of these elections."

It was a dirty election and Pablito won easily. He would have won anyway because he was an exceptionally popular candidate, possibly because he had one very unusual qualification: he did not want to run. And to the day he died he always believed that I had supported him.

That election of 1967 was to be the last genuine election in the Philippines for a long long time.

We worked too hard in Kabankalan. Maybe it was inevitable, being so few and having to carry all of the traditional work at the same time we were experimenting and introducing new forms of pastoral action. We did not have enough time for each other or to enjoy the hospitality of the people. Filipinos are famous for hospitality, and the townspeople of Kabankalan exceeded even the national average. We were welcome everywhere, and they were continually thinking up ways to make sure we would not feel homesick. This very hospitality and kindness would make the crisis that was around the corner all the more anguishing when it came.

The second anniversary of my appointment to Kabankalan had not arrived when I was suddenly moved again.

When we became members of the Columbans we made a promise that when we were commanded to go somewhere we would "set out without delay." Our term between furloughs was now six years, but in the early days it had been ten, and frequently much longer. In fact, to set out for bandit- and fever-ridden China in the twenties was like leaving home forever. If you ever did get back, your brothers and sisters would be grown up, your parents old, and the friends of your youth scattered. But we had a tradition that doing the hard thing was sanctifying. And we borrowed from the Jesuits the motto "*Agere contra*" ("Fight your inclinations"). So we accepted it all in that spirit.

The Council, however, had begun to reaffirm the value of human things, and our superiors in Ireland had now sent us all a questionnaire asking such questions as: Did we want to elect our local superiors (who up to now were appointed from Ireland)? Did we feel we should be consulted on our appointments? And how long should our working term be between furloughs? The very questionnaire itself struck a blow at the old system whereby wisdom was handed down from above rather than collected from below.

I had been uneasy when I was moved so soon after being appointed to Sipalay, and now was devastated to be suddenly told I would be moved from Kabankalan. I had not yet been there two years, the Sa-Maria house was half-built, and money for it half-collected. And I had incurred debts in buying the hollow blocks, the wood and cement, and the steel rods for its completion. I was still writing the new Vatican II *rollos* for the seminar retreat. The *panimbahon* was just getting off the ground. And I was to be moved to the parish of La Castellana, as far north as I could be from Kabankalan.

Most of my fellow Columbans had been moved frequently. One told me he was moved nine times in fifteen years. It was accepted. Now we were questioning it, and yet the old system still remained in force. I did not know what to do. When I discussed it with one of our councillors he did not feel the change was unreasonable. I felt angry with him for not seeing my point. On the other hand there was the set-out-without-delay tradition. It was a solemn promise I had made.

I prayed before the Blessed Sacrament, and finally I sat down and wrote a letter to the Negros superior asking for six months' grace to finish the Sa-Maria house.

The answer came in a roundabout way. Mark Kavanagh, who had now taken over as parish priest from Mike, was on the superior's council. I knew he liked me and I knew he would speak up for me at the upcoming meeting, although I also knew he would never speak to me about it. He went to the meeting, but before he came home he made his monthly shopping trip to Bacolod City, from which he always brought back a package of powdered milk for me.

When he arrived I waited anxiously for any word of what my fate was to be. My deadline for leaving was the end of the month, which was in a few days' time. I was hoping Mark would give me a hint. When we unloaded the box of groceries he took out not one but two boxes of powdered milk: "Well, that should do you for a couple of months." And he said no more. But I knew the reprieve had been granted. I felt it was the beginning of a reasonable change in the system.

When Paul VI's extraordinary encyclical *Populorum progressio* (*The*

Development of peoples) came out, we were busy straining to get the Sa-Maria finished. The *Wall Street Journal* called the encyclical "warmed-over communism." I was too busy to notice it too much, and while I saw it was an impassioned plea for the poor and that it pushed the idea of development, I failed to see that it was opening us up to the idea of structural injustice. I think that at this time I was not ready to consider structural change. I felt that the Sa-Maria was the answer to all the problems of poverty: it would teach the people to share; it would make them see how precious the sacraments were and that we could not receive them unless we were just in our dealings with others. Of course it was the poor who were attending the Sa-Maria retreats, and to preach to them about justice seemed to me a little like preaching at Sunday Mass-goers about the absentees.

Looking back now, I think that I was more than a little seduced by the apparent success we were having all over, the growing numbers at Mass, the number of catechists, the number of First Communions, the numbers at our schools, the numbers doing retreats, the number of *panimbahons* in the *barrios*—"the numbers game" some call it, an ever-present trap for religious professionals.

As soon as the Sa-Maria house was finished, I took up my new appointment. It had been changed again: now I was not going to La Castellana but to Isabela, the parish I had slept in when I first arrived.

I was hardly there when stronger waves of the Council hit us. As a result of that questionnaire, two things happened. We were asked to elect our new superior, and our work term was shortened. I was told to prepare to go home for a furlough at once, though only four of the six years were up. We elected Mark Kavanagh, my second parish priest in Kabankalan, as superior, and he immediately appointed me to full-time work with the Sa-Maria and in charge of two Sa-Maria retreat houses—the one I had built in Kabankalan and one in San Ramon to the north. As I set off for Ireland on my furlough I was in great form. I was seeing my family years sooner than I had hoped and I would be returning to work I liked, free of the constant fear of sudden reassignment.

I was feeling self-contented and was completely unmindful of the warning that an old Columban had given me: "It's usually not the first term in the Philippines that breaks a man. It's the second."

Chapter 5

I WAS ON my way back to Negros after my first vacation, about to take up my job working full-time at the Sa-Maria retreats.

The passport control at Bangkok Airport was looking at my yellow card. "Your shots for yellow fever are out of date. Would you please join the line over there." I found myself in a line of Vietnam GIs queueing for shots. It was done in a moment, but my life was profoundly affected by the consequences of that simple needle-prick.

When I arrived in Negros, I was asked to stand in for the chaplain at the Blanco sugar mill in the town of San Ramon, who was on vacation. I could continue my retreat work with the sugar mill as my base, because there were now two Sa-Maria houses, one there and one in Kabankalan. I would be chaplain to both of them.

The sugar factory at San Ramon was enormous. Built at the beginning of the twenties, it was one of almost a score of centrifugal mills introduced by the Americans when they took over the Philippines. It produced nearly three million *piculs* of sugar a year. (A *picul* was the Spanish equivalent of a good fat sack of sugar—about sixty-two kilos.) The San Ramon Sa-Maria retreat house was nearby, which was handy for me.

The mill chapel needed remodeling, so I approached the manager, Juan Garcia, who agreed. In the process I got to know him and his Spanish wife Annie. They were thinking people from outside the province and, like me, interested in understanding their new surroundings. He explained that he wanted to break away from the old semi-feudal way of running the mill, where it was not what you knew but who you knew that mattered. He made it a point of not accepting invitations to be godfather at baptisms. He wanted the workers to live away from the mill, and he preferred that the mill not play a role in local politics as it had traditionally done. His model was drawn from the industrial West, and his aim was to make the mill cost-efficient. That had been the aim of the previous manager, an American, and the rock on which he had foundered because the local plantation owners ganged up on him when he attempted to reform things. Mr. Garcia, on the other hand, a Filipino, knew the dangers of approaching directly and moving too quickly. His view was that a contented labor force made for better results profit-wise. It seemed to make sense to me. I enjoyed visiting him and his wife and discussing issues with them.

I had only been at the Blanco mill a few days when I got to know Meding and Baby. Their husbands were both in upper management, each had a house full of exuberant children, and both were willing to help in everything connected with the Church and particularly the Sa-Maria retreat. Meding was so correct in her ways that everyone constantly pulled her leg about it. She stood for everything orthodox. Baby was far from orthodox; she loved to play the devil's advocate and ask awkward questions—nothing was too sacred to be questioned. Working with Meding and Baby made life much easier for me, and I was going to need that extra support very soon.

Every ten years the Columbans held a decision-making congress. We called it a "chapter," after the old monastic usage. Columban superiors and elected delegates came from all over the world and, when they met, apart from electing a new superior general, they were a parliament that decided the future of our society. Rome had put pressure on religious orders and societies like ours all over the world to push forward their chapters and get in line with the Vatican Council. Now we in the field were asked for the first time to meet and decide for ourselves what we wanted that chapter to do. The chapter would be held the following year. In Negros a special pre-chapter meeting convened.

We were very united. We wanted participation in decision-making at every level. We wanted consultation before new assignments. We wanted ongoing education for ourselves about the new liturgy, about catechetics and the new approach to Scripture. We wanted better language training. We wanted a new direction to our work. We wanted to start serving the poor.

I was one of those sent to Manila with all these enthusiastic recommendations. There we would meet with representatives from the other areas of the Philippines, and our recommendations would go on to the general chapter in Ireland.

In Manila, I became sick. I had been feeling irritable and had not been sleeping well. During the opening days of the meeting I found myself anxious for each session to end.

One night I felt so bad someone suggested I go to the hospital. As soon as

I got to the hospital I began to vomit violently. It was hepatitis. That needle in Bangkok had done it—so old Doctor Jesus Tan felt, a gracious and careful man. He said my hepatitis was the most serious he had seen: "It's a virus, not a bacteria, so there's no antibiotic for this. In fact there's no cure other than a lot of liquids and sugar and bedrest."

Something alarming began to happen to me while I was in the hospital. Mickey was in Manila, studying at the South East Asian Pastoral Institute. He would come and visit me and bring me the latest theological papers and lectures he had heard. Instead of being excited as I used to be, I found myself uninterested. And not just uninterested: I was afraid. I felt positively threatened by anything new. I could not have put words to it. But that was the reality. I could not tell Mickey . . . why, I don't know. Why did I not just say how I felt? I began to dread Mickey's appearances.

Lying in the hospital bed I was able to listen to the election of 1969. In U.S. style the Philippine presidential election was held every four years, with a maximum of two terms for any president. Ferdinand Marcos, head of the Nationalist party, was running for a second term. Since the war no president had ever won a second term. But Marcos was determined. Money had always flowed in the Philippines at elections, but there had still been enough popular will expressed to defeat the incumbent. This time there was an avalanche of money. Marcos was determined to win at any cost. He won in a landslide, becoming the first president to gain a second term since Quezon, the founding father of the Philippine Commonwealth.

After a month my skin and eyes were less yellowed and my urine was no longer the color of strong tea. I was restless, and when Doctor Tan went off to the United States on a lecture tour, I managed to get permission to leave the hospital. What I did not say was that I was going straight back to Negros.

Once back in Negros I became immediately involved in the chaplaincy work in the sugar factory and the two Sa-Maria retreat houses. The numbers applying for the retreats were increasing. I kept at it, but felt weak. Hepatitis is treacherous because after the yellowness has cleared up there are no obvious symptoms. I began to think I was being lazy or just needed exercise. The old "*Agere contra*"—"Fight against it"—syndrome was still with me, and it kept me going when I should have been lying in an air-conditioned room. The work was heavy, what with the parish duties and the retreats, and I began to feel weaker and weaker, but was not about to admit it.

One night when I had closed up the retreat house on the plantation and was walking back alone to the chaplaincy at the mill, I found I could not go another step. I sat down on the ground for an hour, and when I felt I had enough strength I shuffled home. I knew then I must take the rest I should have taken in the first place. I decided to ask to go home to Ireland to recuperate. There is no place like home when you are sick.

The visit home refreshed me, but when I returned to the Philippines I was still not strong. I hadn't as yet grasped the seriousness of the hepatitis and the limitations it would set on me. It was only later when my friend Lynn Whitely, an Australian Columban, died of it that I fully realized.

Back in the Philippines the spirit of the student uprising in Paris was reaching the streets, and students, up till now quiet, began to ask for political change. Christian groups of student activists, like the Khi Rho, took to the streets, as did the more left-wing Kabataan Makabayan. A new spirit of nationalism was emerging. Even Cardinal Santos was under siege, with the seminarians demonstrating and demanding that he get rid of his bank.

I had to find a place to live in Negros. Still without stamina, I knew I could not do both the retreats *and* parish work. Either was exhausting on its own, especially in those days when nothing could proceed without a priest. I also wanted space and time to work on a translation of the Latin missal into Ilongo. There was as yet no definitive translation, and I had met with Bishop Jaime Sin, who agreed that I should work with others on such a translation. If I wanted to avoid parish work I would have to live away from a *convento*. But where?

The land for the San Ramon Sa-Maria house had been donated by a planter named Juan Ramirez and was located on one of his sugar farms. The same man had helped to build the town church and the Sisters' convent. I thought I might approach him to get him to do up a room for me there beside the retreat house. He was a quiet self-effacing man who was respected by the laborers on his three farms, although they rarely saw him because he did most of his business through an *administrador* who managed all three plantations, an overseer who ran each plantation, and a gangman who was the immediate boss over the workers. But it was not just his distance that made him seem likeable. He was pleasant and a good listener, and he did not go in for any conspicuous consumption. He agreed that I should live there and paid for fixing up some rooms for me. I would actually be living on a plantation—unusual for a priest.

I had not been on the plantation a week before I knew it was a completely different reality from what I had known before. The people were thin, sickly, and in rags. Most nights coming home I would see lights burning in one of the houses. It was usually a wake. There were always wakes . . . so rarely for the old. One night my Volks was waved down by Tia Carmen, a widow and herb healer. She asked me to drive a young couple home. They got silently into the back, carrying a white bundle—their dead child. They had not been able to afford the hospital, and Tia Carmen had done what she could. We drove in silence toward the plantation where they lived with their grandparents, about ten miles away near the sea. I drove the Volks right under their house which was on stilts. They got out and went up. At first I remained below, but then I followed them up. No one noticed me, as I stood in the shadow of the outside awning. The young couple broke down when they saw their grandparents. The faces of the old people crinkled up as if to cry, but no tears came—only spasms of pain and distress. The grandmother took the little bundle in her arms, and looking in at the face, addressed the dead child: "Inday, little one, we went into debt, just to keep you alive." The desolation was overpowering. I backed away and went quietly down the stairs. We priests were often there before death, and afterward, but rarely at moments like this.

This farm was a sister farm of the one I was living on. They belonged to the same owner. The owners of such farms frequently lived far away in Bacolod, in Manila, or even in the United States. Ramirez, for example, lived in Manila. And, in effect, the administrator had the power of life and death over the people. In a grave illness they depended on him for immediate loans and for the use of the *hacienda* transportation. In fact a situation like this arose not long after I first arrived; Esteban, who had driven the tractor for the last twenty years, got an acute pain in his side. It seemed serious. His family went for help to the administrator, but he refused to loan the truck. By the time they got back, precious time had elapsed. Finally they came to me and asked for the Volks. Esteban died in my car on the way to the hospital.

As I drove away from the shack by the sea I realized that this penniless couple who could not pay for medicine to keep their grandchild alive had in some way paid for the comfortable rooms I was living in.

Chapter 6

IN NEGROS the word *sacada* conveyed a certain sense of mystery. The *sacada* was the symbol of the darkest side of the sugar industry. The *sacadas* were immigrant workers brought on contract from other islands. They were paid an advance at a time when they usually needed money, and they spent the cane-cutting season in Negros paying this debt. It was common for them to go home to Antique or Bantayan Island after eight months of backbreaking cutting and loading of cane, with only the equivalent of twenty dollars in their pockets. We priests rarely had anything to do with them since they didn't come to our churches. On Sundays they were working or exhausted or did any marketing they might have to do. If they wanted the sacraments they waited till they went home. A few years before, a young Jesuit seminarian, Arsenio Jesena, had posed as a *sacada* and worked with them for a season. His report revealed the labor camp conditions in which the *sacadas* lived and told of old men who had spent their lives working in the cane fields of Negros, who broke down in tears as they shared their stories.

The report shocked us all, but it stirred anger among some of the planters, who felt it was biased and that Jesena had unfairly tarred all the planters, the good and bad, with the same brush. We talked a lot about the *sacadas* but could never get near them to do anything.

Now I suddenly found myself living right beside a whole barracks of *sacadas*. The *sacada quartel,* as it was called, was like an old wooden warehouse, fifty yards long. Twenty families lived there. The living space in each "cubicle" was not much bigger than the size of a sleeping mat and, sometimes, only sacking stood as the partition between married couples. No running water, no kitchen, no toilets.

A constant complaint was that the price they paid for food from the *cantina* (the company store run by the contractor) was exorbitant. Between deductions for food and the deduction for the loan they had received, they took almost nothing home.

At dawn a bell called them to the cane field. A bell that was really someone battering away on a rusty acetylene cylinder. One Sunday, as I drove off before dawn to say Mass in Kabankalan, I was astonished to hear the swish swish slash of the cane cutters already at work in the dark.

Yet some people claimed that the *sacadas* were better off than the *duma-ans*—the permanent laborers—on some farms because the *sacadas* went home to the island of Panay or Bantayan where they often had a little piece of land, while the *duma-ans* faced six months without work in which they depended on a rice ration doled out by the *hacienda*. This dependence kept them permanently in debt, passive, lethargic, spiritless, like the humid tropical weather they lived in.

Ever since I was sick I had become uncharacteristically conservative. I felt that there had been enough changes and now it was time to implement the ones we had. Before I was full of optimism, now I was anxious about the future. When I revisited Doctor Tan he said to me casually: "Some people get depressed, you know, after having hepatitis. But it passes." So that was what was wrong with me! I was not myself with all this fear of change. I determined to stick it out, but I felt homesick and melancholic and drained of energy. I found the ordinary asceticism of being a priest more difficult and was dispirited at my own failings. The depressing surroundings of the *hacienda* challenged me, but I had no energy to do more than the retreats and the translation work, which I had now started. It helped to write, and I tried to put down on paper how I felt.

> I'm a newly starched shirt
> Got damp;
> I'm a flow of candle grease
> Beside a candle;
> I'm a spilt glass of water;
> And I'm a little fire
> Smouldering away
> Waiting for a day.

How shall I put it? Before I felt I could do anything. Now I was so weak that if there was no chair in the room I would sit down on the floor. I could not stand for long. I could not listen or concentrate for long, and for the first time since my student days I began to hear what my colleagues were saying, if they said they were tired, lonely, feeling down. I just had not experienced these things before. I could feel more, too, for those colleagues who felt threatened by the changes. Whereas before sitting around having a drink seemed for me a waste of time, there was so much I had to do, now I sought opportunities to sit and chat. Nor was I so certain about everything theological. Now I was insecure, and the old ways, the accustomed ways, gave me security. I had put my hand to the plow but was now looking back. One day I said to Mickey as we were driving to Bacolod: "Mickey, what is most important to you?" He had just finished his pastoral theology course in Manila. He thought, and replied: "That human beings should be given a chance to grow and develop and that we all should have this chance. . . . And for you?" "The Church, loving the Church and being faithful to it."

Now as I look at both our statements I realize that he was talking about launching out into the deep, while I was talking about battening down the hatches. Doctor Tan's remark had helped me a lot. I knew that the cloud would lift.

Gradually—very gradually—it did. One day I was driving toward Batang, where we had recently built our new headquarters. As I drove along I caught myself whistling a snatch from an old song I used to like: "I want to say hello, I want to see your smile, I want to hold you in my arms again." I stopped short and said out loud: "I am better," and I flew along the road singing, whistling, chuckling to myself.

My new conservatism did not all go away with my gradual return to health because some of it was grounded in more than a need for security. The aim of the Council, I felt, was a radical renewal and this was to come about by a return to the sources of Scripture and tradition, coupled with a real engagement with the modern world. But I was aware that in some instances the changes were more liberal than radical. Millions had heard about the things they were no longer bound to do; few seemingly had understood how the released energies were to be spent. The abolition of the Friday abstinence is an example. Overnight an ancient tradition disappeared, a tradition for which many had been prepared to sacrifice, and it was not replaced in the popular mind by the urgent need to fast and offer money to the poor. Liturgical changes were often introduced mechanically, without "soul." People missed the old ways of prayer and found the new barren. Some beautiful liturgical practices were lost—in my home diocese of Dublin the traditional visit to the seven churches on Holy Thursday, a great day for old friends to meet, simply disappeared.

I accepted, however, that these were growing pains and was consoled that in the Philippines, in general, the changes had been for the best and made something like the Sa-Maria possible. In the Sa-Maria the talks and the liturgy, the catechetical method, were inspired by the Vatican Council and done in the context of the local culture. The result was thousands of people returning to the sacraments. In every retreat I witnessed husbands and wives reconciled, parents and children forgiving each other. It was visible in the churches too. Before, when you looked down from the altar, you saw a sea of women's veils and rarely would a man come to the communion rail. Now the men were almost half the congregation and eager to help in any way they could. Every other organization was getting a fillip of new life. The Vatican Council was having an effect, and it was hoped that these people were becoming more sharing with their fellows. In this way we seemed to be answering the material needs *indirectly* and dealing with the social problem in a peaceable way. It all seemed to fit together. So when new arrivals like Brian Gore from Australia and John Brazil from Dublin began to criticize things and call for radical structural change, now *I* felt they were moving too fast and did not realize the changes that had already taken place in such a short time.

The Blanco sugar factory was due for a union certification election. That is, another union could challenge the existing union, and the employees would vote for which union they wanted. The National Federation of Sugar Workers, called the N.F.S.W., the sugar union started by Hector Mauri, a Jesuit priest, and now guided by Edgar Saguinsin, was going to do battle with the existing union.

In the run-up the dirt came out. The existing union was a "yellow" union, a union which did exactly as management asked. That was normally to the ultimate detriment of the workers, though the basic wages in the mill were not bad. The National Federation of Sugar Workers were surprisingly well-organized, and out in public came all the scandals that had been tolerated by the other union: the workers waiting for years to be put on the permanent roll, the jobbery, the kickbacks. The fight became very bitter. Workers were clearly threatened with being sacked if they did not vote for the company union.

The N.F.S.W. asked me for use of the Sa-Maria house for their assembly. I refused. Shortly after a letter condemning the mill was circulated and signed by a great number of the priests. I would not sign. On the one hand the N.F.S.W. accusations were mostly true, but on the other I had been recently chaplain to the mill and had made friends with all of the management. Most of all, Baby and Meding were my right-hand aides and close friends. Their husbands had pressured the mill to get concessions for the Sa-Maria house. Free electricity was one. In my mind the Sa-Maria was more important than this labor fight. And I felt the Sa-Maria cut across the two unions and it would not be fair for me to take sides. At the back of it was my basic assumption that the message we brought was "spiritual" not activist, and that it was possible to remain neutral even though serious human rights violations were taking place. But as the actions of management became draconian, my "neutrality" became an embarrassment. I felt guilty and confused as to how pure my motives really were.

Nearing the certification election, I attended a meeting of the local justice committee. An N.F.S.W. union leader, Ed Tehada, also attended.

Looking at me, he spoke about the need for courage. He was obviously implying that I lacked it. His remark stung me. I was hurt that the conflict I was going through should be reduced simplistically to a problem of courage.

At supper a few days later, a get-together of the priests in Kabankalan, John Brazil asked: "Niall, why weren't you prepared to sign that letter?"

"Look, John," I replied, "I acted as chaplain in the mill. I knew all the management. I was accepting help from them all the time. I was so often in their houses. Humanly speaking it was impossible for me to sign. Can they not rightly say, 'Father O'Brien, you have eaten with us, you have talked with us so many times, yet you never mentioned anything to us about abuses in the factory. . . . Then suddenly without any warning you sign a petition condemning us for being unjust.' If I had had any warning of what was coming I could have distanced myself, but even when I was in the mill as chaplain I had no idea of the abuses, and no one had said that things were so bad."

I was happy that John had given me the chance to explain. There had been some awkward silences whenever the Blanco mill topic came up. I knew, too, that Mickey understood, and that was important to me. But I still was not sure that I had done the right thing. Had I put my own human feelings before the "just thing"? And to what extent was I putting "the Church" before the welfare of the people?

I determined not to be caught again like that. I began to distance myself from powerful people and to make a point of not receiving gifts from anyone in power. I became closer to Baby and Meding, who were suffering from the other side because they were so close to the priests—the mill management regarded the Sa-Maria as being the original "bonder," the unifying force, which made the insurrection against them possible.

It was a Sunday night, the closing night of the women's Sa-Maria retreat, when we heard on a transistor radio that President Marcos had suspended the writ of habeas corpus, which is the right to be accused before being arrested. He imposed a nationwide curfew. He closed down the media and put the army in charge, he being commander-in-chief. Martial law had been declared. His second and final term was due to run out the following year—1973. Marcos had found a way to stay in office. Arrest orders were now said to be out for people like Father Luis Jalandoni and most others in the front line of justice work.

The Philippines is a land of rumors, and you are often taken by surprise when a rumor comes true, you become so used to discounting them.

Father Jalandoni now went underground, as did many other of our friends—people all over the Philippines who were pushing for social reform. Marcos had made many reformers into revolutionaries and, of course, that suited him, because now the revolutionaries became retrospectively one of the reasons for his grabbing power in the first place.

The new Philippine constitution was nearing completion when Marcos seized power. It reflected a lot of the reformist movements in the Philippines and was supposed to be a process independent of the government in power, done by elected representatives throughout the country. In spite of the usual interference it had been coming along well. Marcos now suspended it. He appointed what he called an "interim constitutional convention," and his delegates rewrote the constitution to Marcos's liking. Under this bowdlerized constitution Marcos was president or prime minister, or neither or both, as it suited him. He no longer had a limited term of office. And he ruled by decree. Behind the scenes as co-architect of the takeover was Juan Ponce Enrile, the new Minister for Defense.

When the shameful history of this era is written, the venal members of the interim constitutional convention will bear the greatest burden of blame. They prostituted themselves to Marcos and gave birth to a constitution that allowed him to cause the deaths of tens of thousands. The hypocrisy of people like this drove thousands of outraged students to the hills, and many priests too.

One of the first things Marcos did through his labor minister Blas Ople was to declare labor unions tantamount to illegal. Later he reinstated unions, but they were not permitted to strike in the sugar industry. The constabulary, troops under General Fidel Ramos, so intimidated the people that, whatever the official statements, "labor union" became dirty words. Naturally farm people were scared to join unions and an uneasy quiet settled over the plantations, including the one on which I was now living. Only after a long while did union recruiting resume . . . this time secretly.

Many things now had to be done in secret. Father Jalandoni was on the run, and he arrived in the dead of night on my doorstep. I put him to sleep in a secluded room where I thought he would never be seen. But Meding and Baby, always putting the house in order, came upon him fast asleep and recognized him immediately. Soon a continuous stream of letters between Baby's husband and Luis started, in which each put his side of the revolution-versus-reform debate. I took the chance to ask Luis about my dilemma over having planter friends. Did he feel I should break with some of them? "No, not at all," he said. "In fact, all my relations are planters and they are the ones who funded so much of the legal work I did. They gave their land in bail security for so many accused peasants. My policy is, do what is right, do the just thing, even though it goes against their class interests. If they don't drop you, you've found a real friend." That formula saved me many good friends.

Chapter 7

MEANWHILE, I was making friends on the plantation. One of them was Padot. She was a widow with six young children. Her husband had been killed by a neighbor. The *hacienda* settled the matter by allowing Padot to cut the swamp reeds and weave them and sell them for roofing; the neighbor was let off. Both of them were now in debt to the *hacienda*.

Tony, Padot's eldest boy, was seventeen years old. He helped his mother to weave the reeds and so to feed and school the others. Tony worked quietly all day. He often passed my room on his way to the swamp to cut reeds. On the other side of the swamp was the scrapyard of the sugar factory. One night a boy called Jimmy and some other boys persuaded Tony to go with them to steal scrap from that scrapheap. Tony agreed to this to help his mother buy rice for his younger brothers and sisters. But now the scrapheap was guarded day and night. The factory guards sighted the boys, and Tony and Jimmy were caught, while the others got away. The guards beat Tony so much that they thought he was dead. Then they shot him to cover up the beating and left him there. Padot waited up all night for Tony and at dawn she went to look for him. She found him dead under a tree near the scrapyard.

That justice might be done was out of the question. However, with a bit of follow-up, there was a hope of getting some compensation from the mill. I helped in this. Finally it arrived. It was a very small amount, the equivalent of about a thousand dollars, enough I reckoned for Padot to buy a motorbike and side-car (used in San Ramon as a taxi) which could earn an income for the family. When I heard that the money had come, I sent an urgent message to Padot to try and see me. When she was seated I said, "Padot, many people around here are in need and I know you will be tempted to help them, but really I feel that you should buy a motorized side-car or something like that to help support your family. Please let me keep the money in safety until then, and if anyone wants to borrow it, let them deal with me."

But I was too late. She had already given the money as bail for Jimmy. Seeing my dismay she said simply: "What good is the money to us if Jimmy is in jail?"

That was the end of her money and her little hope of security. This woman who had never been to school or studied or indeed read the Scriptures was telling me that people are more important than things. For me, who had done twenty straight years of schooling, seven of them in an intense quest to know and do what is right, it was profoundly disturbing to meet someone like Padot.

My room was at the back of the retreat house. Attached to my room I had built a reception room made from bamboos with a thatched roof, high pitched and curling at the edges, a bit like the roof of a pagoda—a recognizable style in the Muslim south. The people called it the *bahay kubo,* the native house. Baby and Meding furnished it with whatever I needed and the people of the *hacienda* felt free to come in and shelter there from the sun. They seemed to be determined not to abuse my presence; they never asked for food or money, but as a last resort they would come in sickness.

Late one night, shortly before Christmas, there was a knock on my bedroom door. Nanding, one of the laborers on the plantation, wanted me to drive his wife Clarita, who was about to give birth, to the small hospital run by the Blanco sugar mill. The town of San Ramon had no hospital and not even an ambulance. I obliged.

The next day when I visited the hospital I found that Clarita had given birth to two baby girls. I baptized them Margarita and Benilda immediately because they were premature and seemed unlikely to survive. The hospital had only a makeshift incubator, heated by an electric light bulb. The twins had to take turns at the oxygen. Nanding had bought a small tin of the cheapest milk for the twins—all he could afford.

The following day I sent over a large can of special baby milk, and that night I visited them again, only to find Margarita dead. The milk was untouched. Benilda now had the incubator and the oxygen to herself. But it did not help. She too died. I tried to console Nanding and Clarita: they could not even cry.

That night I went for the first time to Nanding's house at the edge of a large sugarcane field. The thatched nipa-palm roof and the matting walls were so full of holes as to be well-nigh useless as shelter. Inside, Margarita and Benilda were laid out in dainty pink dresses on top of a wooden box.

When I came nearer I realized that they were not really wearing dresses: it was crêpe paper. I prayed for a short while, then sat on the floor with Nanding. There was no table or chair.

He broke the silence. "Father, we have a problem. Some say we should bury them in one coffin and some say in two. What do you think, Father?"

"What do you think yourself?"

"I think they should be buried in two coffins, and in two graves, because they are two."

In the midst of this sorrow and poverty Nanding's understanding of the dignity of the human being was far above what society had taught him.

"Look, Nanding, we're having the Misa de Gallo [the Mass in preparation for Christmas] at dawn. You might like to come?"

"No, I'm afraid the *aswang* [bad fairy] will take the children."

I must have looked disapproving because immediately he added: "Do you believe in the *aswang*, Father?"

"I don't know what I believe about this, but I believe in your love for Margarita and Benilda because you will stay up all night watching them."

Nanding watched the dead babies all that night, and the next day they were buried in separate graves.

Two nights later I visited the hospital to see how Clarita was doing. It was about 11:00 P.M. I was sitting by the bed and I took Clarita's hand. She grasped mine tightly and said, "Father, it's very painful. Don't go away."

I saw that the dextrose intravenous fluid had stopped flowing. The nurse did not seem to have noticed, so I looked for her, and then I looked for the doctor and asked him to examine Clarita. He wrote out a prescription and gave it to Nanding, who hurried off.

"Where's he going? Don't you have medicine in the hospital?"

"No," the nurse said. "If we kept medicine here we'd never be paid for it. He has to go back to the *hacienda* to get the administrator to O.K. the prescription. Then he can take it to the drugstore and wake them up and get the medicine."

"But that'll take two hours!" I ran after Nanding, signed the prescription, and sent a messenger over to the drugstore to get the medicine.

The medicine did not ease Clarita's pain at once. Her womb had ruptured with the twins. The doctor promised he would try and operate in the morning. Meanwhile, Nanding and I sat on the bed, each holding one of Clarita's hands.

"Father, if I die please give advice to Nanding whenever he needs it."

Nanding was bent over Clarita. His tears began to fall down on her face.

"Don't worry, Nanding. I won't die."

Finally, the medicine reduced the pain, so I slipped away, as I had a Christmas Novena Mass at four that morning.

At 1 A.M. Clarita took off her ring and asked Nanding to wear it. Around 2 A.M. she died.

After Mass I hurried back. I saw the faces. I broke down and cried bitterly.

Clarita was laid out in the hospital morgue with a five centavo piece on each eyelid to keep them closed.

I said to Nanding, "I'll leave and get a few hours' sleep. I hardly slept at all last night."

"I'm very tired too, Father. I haven't been to bed since Monday." It was Friday morning.

Belasyon—the nine-day vigil after burial—was held in Clarita's father's house because, though poorer than any house you have ever seen, it was far better than Nanding's. Everyone sat on the floor. The married women played *pan-ginggi*, a card game, using old Spanish-style cards so thick from use that they could stand on their edge. The boys and girls played *bordon*, a sort of truth-or-consequence game: they sat in a circle, boys and girls alternating, and a ring passed from hand to hand; whoever was caught with the ring had to sing a song or else propose marriage to someone in traditional verse style. At the bottom of the stairs that led into the house, a large slate served as a table on which the men played *corona hari* ("crown or king"), a form of pitch-and-toss which takes its name from the long-gone Spanish coins. In the midst of the noise and laughter, Nanding lay on the floor, face down, totally unconscious to the world.

Everyone except me was in rags. These were the laborers on a 220-acre sugar plantation that earned over $76,000 the previous milling year. Each of the fifty-two families employed there received a little over $200 each for the whole year. And this was not in the category of bad *haciendas*.

Later I asked Nanding why Clarita had not had a prenatal checkup. They were supposed to do that free of charge in the town.

"Well, you see," he said, "she had no clothes to go to town in, and we had no money for the fare. I owe a lot because of my baby who died last year, so the *hacienda* deducts from my earnings gradually to pay that debt, and the rest they take for our rice ration debt which built up during the off-season. So we had no money in our hand at all, except what Clarita earned by washing clothes for people in town, and that's why she kept working till the last moment."

"And I suppose that's why her womb burst. How much do you owe now?"

"1,400 pesos [$213.50]."

I reckoned that if he and his surviving child Nenita did not fall sick it would take him several years to pay off the debt, but he would have to make his working clothes from fertilizer sacks and keep to the bare rice and dried fish ration.

Nanding was deeply attached to Nenita. During the height of his troubles he entrusted her care to his in-laws. After the funeral he came to me worried lest, having left her with them for a time, he had forfeited his right to the child.

"Of course not," I said, although I was not too sure. "Does Nenita remember her mother?"

"Oh, yes, because when anybody asks, 'Where is your mother?' she says, 'She's in the graveyard covered in sand.'"

The death of Clarita and the twins affected me deeply. My living on the *hacienda* in a house open to the life around me made it possible now to be in hour-to-hour contact with the people as they suffered. Before, in the parish *convento*, I was shielded by custom, by the layout of the *convento*, which had an upstairs-downstairs style that kept poor people at a distance—the parish clerk, whose job was to protect the priest a bit, sometimes overprotected us.

Now I was in the midst of it in a way that few priests have a chance to experience for any length of time. Gradually my understanding of injustice began to take on an added dimension. I knew the owner of this *hacienda*. I knew him to be a quiet, unostentatious, pious man who paid the minimum wage according to law. He knew the older people by name. His unfair treatment of Esteban's widow Rena notwithstanding, he was way ahead of most of his neighbors. The people did not blame him, but instead blamed the administrator and the *encargado*, fate and "the will of God."

But this was not good enough. Somehow this landowner must be ultimately responsible. On some level I had begun to grapple with the mystery of the evil that good people do.

Juan Ramirez had inherited these *haciendas* and their system. He was faithful, more faithful than many, to his recognized obligations. But the systems themselves were deeply tainted. The system that encouraged him not to live on the farm also encouraged the abuses of the administrator. It reminded me of the absentee landlord system that bedeviled Ireland in the last century, placing all power over the peasants' lives in the hands of ruthless agents. The system of contracting labor from Panay and paying the contractor, leaving him free to deal as he wished with the laborers, promoted their reduction to debt-slaves. Within the *sacada* system, the *cantina* system invited fraud. There were so many corrupt systems circumscribing the lives of the workers: the system according to which the minimum wage was set by representatives of the owners, not the workers; the system that had effectually outlawed labor unions; the system that "solved" labor disputes by means of a pro-owner labor court. Now the ultimate system of martial law had been mobilized precisely to ensure that none of the other "systems" were dismantled.

I was beginning—only beginning—to understand structural injustice and how important it was to its perpetuation that at the head of these unjust systems there should be a face, a good face, a friendly face, a human face like that of Juan Ramirez, to mask the real nature of the system.

When the encyclical *Populorum progressio* came out I had been so busy I had had enough time only to note that it favored the poor and the oppressed. I now asked a friend, who was lying low after the martial law crack-down on unions, to translate it into Ilongo so that I could have it printed. When I went over the translation I saw that *Populorum progressio* was a more powerful document than I had realized. It reemphasized the primary Vatican Council insight that we must listen to the hopes and fears, the yearnings and deepest wishes, of the human heart because in some way God is speaking to us through these voices. It insisted that human development be holistic, or, to use Paul VI's favorite word, integral. We must look to the spiritual *and* the material welfare of human beings. Paul's vision of development harked back to the early Hebrew vision of humans as not divided sharply into body and soul, but as soul embodied and body ensouled. Paul touched on structural injustice and its global nature and dared for the first time in a major Church document to say that there were times when a people would be justified in revolting; it was the just war theory applied within the boundaries of a nation, whereas up till now it had only been applied "between" nations.

This was the part of the encyclical that gave me problems. For years I had been inching toward a pacifist philosophy. I felt that the Jesus I knew would rather be killed than kill, even in self-defense. On the other hand, what I was witnessing on the farm was a whole system of injustice, a system which fitted, in the judgment of many, the conditions under which Paul VI said violent revolution was justified. In fact, all around me good people were making that decision, including many of my friends. They said that revolution was now an act of legitimate self-defense, of counter-violence against violence so deeply institutionalized within our society that, for example, in a parish like Kabankalan, half of the funerals were of children under the age of one, killed by this society. If I pushed my pacifism too far I would be going against my own experience, against the testimony of my friends and fellow priests, and now against the explicit teaching of the Church.

I did what I have done so often before in this type of dilemma: I picked my way carefully, determined not to lose either of the apparently contradictory poles of value. For myself I would cling to the pacifist way, not sure how I would react in a crisis; for others I would respect their opinion, acknowledging the weight of common sense behind their position. I told myself, "I'm like a Filipino priest in Ireland in 1916, the year of our armed revolution. This visiting Filipino priest thinks the Irish are crazy in rising up against the British Empire. No one has ever succeeded. He also thinks it's immoral. But he knows nothing of what the Irish have been through—the great famine, the emigration, the rack rents, the land wars. He should sit back and listen, and maybe he'd learn something."

But in the back of my mind was a dream that someday the Church would ban all war, all nuclear weapons, all chaplaincies in armies, all carrying of arms, in a burst of prophetic faithfulness to her vision and faithfulness to her Lord . . . and take the consequences.

The part of *Populorum progressio* that most caught the attention of the public when it first came out were the final words: "Development is the new name for peace." To work for development was to work for peace. Behind it was the profound truth that war and violence are rooted in the unjust poverty which so many suffer. And of course Paul VI always meant "integral" development—development of body and spirit. But the statement was taken up by neocolonial investors, who saw their overseas investments, no matter what the ultimate effects, as "development" work . . . and therefore equivalent to "work for peace."

It was this part of the encyclical that attracted me too. It was nonconfrontational. It allowed me to put off the inevitable conflict with structural injustice and turn to "development projects."

Chapter 8

*T*HINGS sometimes seem to simply fall together, and that is how it happened with the *kibbutz*. The first of those things was a random visit I made to the house of the plantation bookkeeper. I saw the account books on the table and asked him to explain them to me.

"We have 220 hectares here, Father. It's the best land because every now and then the river floods and leaves a new coat of rich mud. The topsoil here is a couple of meters deep. Sometimes we get one hundred tons of cane on one hectare."

"What do others get?"

"Well, they could get as low as thirty tons in the mountains. Though it's not merely the tonnage that counts, but the amount of sugar per ton, and that's where we score again. We get as high as two and a half *piculs* of sugar per ton, which gives us nearly two hundred and fifty *piculs* per hectare. In the mountains they get as low as one *picul* per ton of sugar and therefore sometimes only thirty *piculs* a hectare."

I asked how he could be sure that someone in the mill was not tampering with their sugar content.

"They dare not. Our master is a member of the board of planters. But they do tamper with other people's. That's well known. If you know who to pay, you can get your sugar content raised. Of course someone else's gets lowered."

He told me that thirty percent of the sugar went to the factory in payment for milling the cane and making the sugar. Additional expenses included labor, the fertilizer, the gasoline, and the *sacadas*.

"The *sacadas*? Are they not included in labor?"

"No. We pay the contractor a fixed sum and he sees to them. They do the cutting and the loading."

"And the *duma-ans,* the permanent laborers?"

"They got about ₱1,400.00 each this year [$200]. I don't know how much the other two *haciendas* made, but the administrator gets a bonus if it's a good year."

"And the workers?"

"Yes, at Christmas Señorito comes here and gives gifts and his wife gives T-shirts. Their parents used to live here before the war," he said, pointing to a burned-out mansion which had only the Ionic pillars of an ornate porchway still standing. "Things were much better then, when the old people lived here. They knew what the people were suffering, and no one would really go hungry. Tio Esteban would never have been refused the truck to go to the hospital."

"Did the Japanese burn the mansion?"

"No, the *guerrilleros.* They burned a lot of *haciendas* around here. Many of the planters were more afraid of the *guerrilleros* than the Japanese. Some *hacenderos* joined the *guerrilleros,* but a lot took refuge in the city under the protection of the Japanese, and when the Americans came back they reclaimed their farms . . . but most of them never returned to live here. Before the war I went to school with the master's father in the local elementary school. That's why he had a soft spot for me. But all that has changed. His children hardly know where the money comes from and don't even know our names."

When I got home I wrote down the figures he had shown me and worked out the percentages. Fifteen percent of the net profit went to labor.

The second part of the falling together happened when four of the *duma-ans* from the plantation came to visit me. They had brought along some one-year-old. "One-year-old" is the local name for a lethal rum made from sugarcane. Even as a cleanser it is probably dangerous.

The four were Tuting, Ireneo, Naldo, and Utay, all in their twenties and among the hardest working of the *duma-ans.* Ireneo was married to Alice and had three children. Tuting and Utay were newly married, and Naldo was single. Naldo held the plantation record for the amount of cane points planted in a day. He was the one who broached their request.

"Can we plant rice on the land beside the Sa-Maria house? You are not using it."

"I might be using it. If I did give it to you where would you get the water?"

He said they would plant upland rice which needs no water other than the rain.

I was not sure I owned the rights, but said I would speak to the overseer and think it over.

I took this opportunity to ask why we had *sacadas* here on the farm all the way from Antique. It seemed to me that the *duma-ans* could do the cutting and loading as well as the cultivating.

"We could by stretching it out and doing a little every week and in between doing our other jobs, like fertilizing, and planting the cane points. But that would mean lengthening the work season. The *sacadas* usually begin cutting in September and finish cutting on this farm by February."

"What's wrong with stretching out the season? Surely it would mean you would have work for a longer time, and a shorter off-season, a shorter hungry season. No?"

"The overseer says it's best to cut the cane early, when the sugar content is high. If we delay after February the quantity of sugar per ton goes down. The overall profits would be less. He might lose his bonus."

Ireneo interrupted: "If we owned the farm ourselves it would be different."

"Of course. In that case we would do the cutting ourselves," said Tuting. "We'd have no need for *sacadas*. We'd have a longer season. The quality of the cane and the sugar content would suffer a bit, but the cane would be ours and so we'd have more than double our income."

The third part of the "falling together" was a letter I received from Father Bob Burke, a Chicago priest who had helped pay for the Sa-Maria house. He had been left ten thousand dollars in a will. Had I anything in mind? I had. Ever since seeing those account books I had been thinking, what if a group of laborers owned a sugar farm themselves cooperatively? Couldn't they have twice or three times the present income, work most of the year, and still bring others in to join them? A piece of land like this could support one hundred families in comfort, instead of forty on the edge of desperation.

Meantime the men began to work the land outside my door. But I was in for a shock. I saw another man, not one of the four, doing the plowing. He said that Naldo and Ireneo had sent him.

"So you are getting a share of the harvest?"

"No. They're paying me twenty-five pesos."

Others arrived to plant the rice seed. They were also on contract.

Naldo and the boys were going to run this little bit of rice land on the same principle as the *hacienda*. Others would do the work and by virtue of ownership they would take the profit. The example seemed to come straight from Paolo Freire's book *The Pedagogy of the Oppressed*. His theory was that the "oppressed" internalize the values of the "oppressors" and implement them when they get on top. I had some rethinking to do.

A reply now came from Bob. He liked the idea. Say the word, and the money would be on the way. But I was now having second thoughts. What if the same thing happened if a farm was bought for Tuting and Co.? What if they just put other men to work there and collected the profits? It would have to be set up so that only those who worked on the farm could take a profit from it. The ownership would have to be in the name of the working group. If you ceased to work, you ceased to own.

Many long evenings and much rum later, a group of six, carrying iron plows on their shoulders, set off for the mountains, where we had purchased a ten-acre sugar farm with Bob's donation. Land in the lowlands was too expensive and, in any case, no one would sell to us. That forced us to look in the mountains, which had its advantages. Monsignor Fortich, our bishop, had put up a secondhand sugar mill for small farmers there. The six could join the mill without fear of being locked out for political reasons. Meantime we had come to the decision that the land would be worked communally and that only those who worked on it would have a right to the profits. Without having planned it, we found ourselves with a *kibbutz*, and that was what we called it.

Chapter 9

ALL THIS time the Sa-Maria retreats were growing. This was because of a new program we had started, the *maharlika*—a training program for lay leaders. We asked each parish to send their leaders and gave a month's course to these men. The hope was that they would help the priest to pull the parish into the age of Vatican II, so we tried to give them a whole sackful of skills—Scripture, group dynamics, liturgy, social teachings of the Church, how to run a *panimbahon,* and in particular how to run a mini Sa-Maria. One result was that hundreds of these mini Sa-Maria retreats were held in remote areas of Negros by these leaders, and we were being invited to attend their special functions. By "we" I mean me and Dondoy, the husband of Meding, for he was coordinator of the *maharlika* leadership course and had taken the burden off me. I was the chaplain.

With Meding helping me in the Sa-Maria and Dondoy doing most of the work for the *maharlika,* I came to spend a lot of time in their house. I knew I could always walk straight into it and feel immediately at home. It was the same with Baby's, but her house was not so close. Meding worked in the pharmacy in the sugar factory hospital, and since a great number of sick people would come to the Sa-Maria for help, I would channel many of them through Meding to the doctors of the mill hospital. These doctors would not charge for their services if they knew the patients were recommended by me. Meding would look for sample medicines, and so we kept the cost down.

Apart from all that, Meding and Baby had become my dear friends. I relaxed when I was in their company. During my first few years in Kabankalan, though I mixed a lot with the people, my relationships had been functional and I avoided the vulnerability of being a true friend. In those days it was an unwritten code that once you left a parish you left it. Going back to visit friends was frowned on. So real friendship was not on the agenda. This was part of a practical pastoral principle, so that you would not interfere in the new priest's attempt to run things his way. But it was also a reflection of a spirituality that saw human friendship as competing with the divine. We were to strive for detachment. Life was merely a journey. It was the destination that mattered.

Here again the Vatican Council had something to say. It redeemed an earlier Christian tradition when it insisted that the truly human was good, to be striven for, and was the only sound basis for other Christian values. In rediscovering the human Jesus the Council helped us to rediscover the goodness of our own humanity.

Looking back, I realized that in my first term I had acted as if the work was more important than the people I was working with. The "detachment" spirituality suited me just fine. It allowed me to avoid being emotionally involved, to be practical, to be efficient and even close to hardhearted. I recognized this in myself now and was determined that it would not happen again.

And it would have happened if it were not for Baby and Meding, who insisted on being real friends by sharing their feelings and teaching me to share mine. They would open topics others wouldn't mention. For example, when a priest would leave the ministry to get married, that was always a big blow to Meding, who had a staunchly traditional view of the priesthood. She might have been an Irish mother for that. Naturally when a priest friend left it was a blow to me too. I would feel down, and even threatened, but I would keep a stiff upper lip, cover up my feelings with a wisecrack, and say no more. Not so Meding. She would share her disappointment and tell me she had seen signs of the priest falling in love, and she would make specific recommendations to me if she felt I was in the way of danger. One thing she was certain of—it was always the woman's doing, never the priest's.

Meding was very strong on not giving people handouts. She felt it destroyed them, demeaned them, and turned them into beggars. She insisted that work be done for anything given, even if she had to invent a task. She considered me an easy target and warned me continually. But it was not so simple for me to follow her advice.

In the Sa-Maria I often talked on the subject of love. I would try to explain that love must show itself as concrete help for those in need. Many of those who did the retreat reckoned that since I was so strong on concrete help, in grave necessity I was the one to come to. A stream of people, even from neighboring towns, came to me. Medical help there was no refusing. I gave this through Meding. Requests for straight handouts I refused. But for a long time I helped in schemes and "projects" that I hoped would help people to help themselves. A sewing machine for Maria, a widow, to help support a big family. An ice grinder for José, to make ice cream and sell it. A pig whose future piglets would be shared with neighbors. A small store for Ramona to support a large family since her husband was sick. Unfortunately, these schemes rarely came to anything, and the weak link was always where I least expected it. In the case of Ramona, she had just got the store stocked when her previous creditors descended on her and demanded payment. Goodbye store. I thought I had been smart by telling her not to stock rice because I knew that it is difficult to refuse rice to hungry people. The sort of people I was trying to help were the type who did not refuse.

Meding would always find out about my failures and chide me with an "I told you so."

I used to feel so desperate when people came for help. I knew that whatever I gave them would be quickly swallowed up because of the abyss of poverty all around them. You got Juan started in some little business and it was just beginning to take off, when one of the many members of his extended family would get sick. Should he help now, or postpone help until his business strengthened? He always chose to help now. People were always more important than possessions.

I tried to think of anything other than handouts. It was not just that concerned people told me again and again that it was not a good thing. It was not just that I could see from experience that it did harm. And it was not just that I was aware of the dangers of playing God. More than all these factors, it was clearer and clearer that by these handouts we were in a way covering up the wounds created by an unjust society and, by helping, were perpetuating that society. And yet sometimes to refuse would be inhuman. When I felt there was a case that could not be refused I struggled to reduce the ill effects. In the case of Nora, in my determination to insist on cooperation from the recipient, I made a serious mistake.

It was Christmas night 1974, the last Christmas I spent on the plantation and a few months before I left for Ireland on furlough. I returned home from our own party to find Nora and five of her children in our *sala*. They were huddling in a corner. She was obviously relieved when I arrived.

"What's wrong, Nora?"

She started to cry and told me that her daughter Tina, a deaf-mute, pregnant and unmarried, had threatened to kill her and the children with a cane machete. They had fled and taken refuge in my house.

Nora's husband drank and beat her and he also molested Tina. Everyone said that it was he who made Tina pregnant.

They hadn't eaten all day. So I took out food, of which there was lots left from the Christmas lunch. The children were so hungry they forgot their fears and wolfed down what was put before them.

I brought them some blankets and then let them be.

In the morning I talked with Nora. When she spoke she wheezed and coughed piteously.

"You have T.B., Nora. You know that?"

"I do. I've had it a long time."

I told her that she must get medicine, but that first she would have to go to the hospital and see Doctor Rivera so we could get a full prescription. I said that she should bring it to me and I would get Meding to look after it.

Nora would need a full course of drugs not available through Meding, but I didn't want her to know I would be supplying them.

Nora did not travel the five hundred yards to the hospital to get her prescription and I did not do any more for her. Several times I asked her, but each time she had not yet gone to get the prescription. I felt I should not take it completely into my own hands. I had done this too often before. I must ask some cooperation on the part of Nora.

I did not realize, however, just how bad things were for her. Nora must have had no time to go to the hospital, spending the day searching for food for the children: after a long day she would have no energy left. She had no clothes to wear to the hospital. Then again, I do not know what fears the hospital held for her. I should have broken my rule and gone and got the medicine myself; from so many other cases, I knew it by heart. Thirty to sixty vials of streptomycin, a year's supply of isoniazid and multivitamins. Or I could have driven her over to the hospital to see the doctor.

Nora got worse and worse. Unbeknownst to me, her eldest daughter Lilly, who worked in Manila as a prostitute, sent her boat fare so that she could come up to Manila where Lilly could look after her.

Next time I looked for Nora she was gone. When I realized she had had to leave behind her five children, the youngest of whom was only four, and leave Tina at the mercy of that feckless husband, I was crushed with the thought of her sorrow and my own failure.

Chapter 10

SINCE September of 1972—the declaration of martial law—the labor unions had been under relentless attack by Blas Ople, the Minister of Labor. His job was to castrate them and to do it with the appearance of helping them. Most unions succumbed. But not the National Federation of Sugar Workers. It kept its head above the martial law waters by using what limited freedom it still had. They were not allowed to strike, so they devoted more time to raising the consciousness of the rank and file to the injustice they were suffering. Although they were strongly supported by the Church, some unions had picked up an anticlerical rhetoric. I found the anticlericalism hard to take, but felt it was a time to be patient. The N.F.S.W. was one of the few unions faithful to the workers, which was why they were so heavily attacked. Union leaders had worked mainly in the sugar mills, but now were moving into the *haciendas* to organize the field laborers. They started in the one next to me, where conditions were very bad.

I remember one day being called to baptize a baby on this particular *hacienda*. As I began to perform the ceremony, I saw the eyes of the baby rolling back in its head, so that only the whites were showing. I stopped and strongly suggested to the mother that we go immediately to the hospital. She had no money, she said. I assured her not to worry about that but to hurry because the child looked very bad. She went over to a cardboard box in the corner of her hut to try and find a respectable cloth to wrap around the child. I watched as she went through the rags in the box. She was trying to hurry, but she would take out an old cloth, look at it, and, seeing it was too much of a rag, she would reject it. There was panic on her face as she neared the end of the box with nothing at all to wrap the child in.

"Come on," I said. "Anything will do. Don't mind what anyone thinks."

And off we went to the hospital.

What happened to this infant is lost amid the memories of so many similar cases. But the look on that mother's face as she searched through her box of rags remains with me. This incident was typical of the conditions on that farm, and why the union took hold there so easily. When union members asked if they could use my house, the *bahay kubo*, to meet in (it was not too far away but in safe territory for them), I could only agree.

After one of their meetings they asked me if I would go to Doña Clarit, their *ama* (a term used in Negros by the laborers for a woman who owned and ran a *hacienda*). They wanted me to take their complaints to her. They would try this as an opening gambit.

I drove over to the villa of Doña Clarit a couple of days later. It was on the main road. A beep on the horn brought a guard out to open the gates. I drove in. A maid showed me into a large carpeted *sala*. Carpeting is very unusual in the tropics because of the upkeep it requires. Here it looked very well because it stopped short of the walls, revealing the marble floor beneath.

After a few moments Doña Clarit appeared. I introduced myself, and she asked me to be seated. Could she get me a glass of brandy? I declined. And we both sat down.

Gradually I worked around to the topic of the conditions on her farm. Growing alarmed, she explained that she took Communion daily and hoped that anything I had to say would not interfere with that. She had been unaware of the conditions and promised to have her *administradora* look into it.

When I was leaving she got up and said: "Wait a moment, Father, I want to get some money for you." I thanked her, explaining that at this time I was not in need. And we parted.

The *administradora*, Tia Cleming, came over to see me a week later. Apart from being administrator of the many farms of Doña Clarit, Tia Cleming herself owned the cinema in the next town.

I could not give away too much information, as I did not want her to know who the union leaders were, but I had been detailed to ask for a raise in the price of cutting and planting cane points. I also knew that she was paying much lower than the *hacienda* where I was living. And because of the *kibbutz*, I now knew my way around the farming vocabulary and slang. She put up some arguments about debts she had, and hard times, but agreed to look into it.

That night the leaders came over to my place; they'd been watching carefully and had seen Tia Cleming coming toward the Sa-Maria house. I reported to them, and we agreed to wait and see what would happen. When nothing did, we decided that all the laborers would visit the old lady together. I was for exhausting all other methods before thinking of taking "industrial" action.

We planned the visit to Doña Clarit carefully, because a sixth sense told me that a large group of people arriving would be taken as an assault and would never be let in. We borrowed the truck from the mountain *kibbutz,* and all the laborers from her farm hid in the back of it while Islaw, the head of the new union branch, sat in the front with the driver. I went ahead in the Volks. The truck passed into the compound after me. Islaw got out and came into the house with me. The workers remained in the truck. I introduced Islaw to Doña Clarit when she eventually appeared. She was nervous.

After preliminary greetings, she asked: "Who is this?"

"This is Islaw. He's been working for you for the last thirteen years. He'd like to talk to you."

Islaw with great deference began to tell Doña Clarit of the conditions on the farm.

When he finished she remained impassive and mumbled something about not knowing all the details of running the farms.

"Islaw, is that your best shirt?" I said, pointing to his threadbare polo shirt.

"Yes, it's my best. I bought it about seven years ago."

"Tia Clarit, I know you don't realize it, but the people on your farm cannot even buy clothes."

She started to weep as when one is being harassed. And it was clear that the discussion was at an end. We took our leave politely. I was glad now that the other workers had remained outside.

The union met that night in my house. It was clear that Doña Clarit had foiled the visit. Islaw gave several examples to show that she knew exactly what the administrator was up to. The workers could not strike, as strikes were illegal, so they decided to withdraw their labor on some other pretext.

But, as it turned out, Tia Cleming was ahead of them. She had moved first, borrowing *sacadas* from another planter. She dropped the *duma-ans* from the work roll, and had the *sacadas* do the cultivation, thus leaving all the *duma-ans* and their families desperate. They then had to go to other farms to look for work and, in a sense, became wandering *sacadas* themselves. And now some people—I don't know who, but I suspect it was some of the original workers—began to harass and make life difficult for the wretched *sacadas* who had taken their place.

A few months later Doña Clarit had a new fishing boat blessed. Beside the frail skiffs of ordinary fishermen it looked enormous. It had sonar for underwater detection of fish and cost one million pesos. I was not invited to the ceremony. The parish priest from the next town did the blessing.

Conditions in Negros were deteriorating under martial law, because nearly every economic move of martial law was ultimately aimed at making the rich richer. A simple example: motorized tricycles were a simple way that the poor could pull themselves up by their bootstraps. They drove these as baby taxis around the town. A man could work late and earn a living with one of these. I had managed to get one for Nanding and he was supporting himself and Nenita. Now a new regulation came out. The license fee for these tricycles not just doubled, but jumped more than five times, making it impossible for a poor man to pay. But the law now decreed that one license fee would do for *one tricycle or six.* Nanding would have to pay the same amount as the person who owned six tricycles. The big people were given a bonus and the little people were knocked out. Their only hope was to be employed by the owner of a fleet of tricycles. And this pattern was repeated throughout the economy. A land reform bill was passed, but sugar land and coconut land were exempt. The result was that people who had rice lands switched them to sugar to avoid land reform. In Panay ancient rice paddies were destroyed and gave way to sugar. A cash crop took the place of a food crop. Sharecroppers became day laborers.

The mini Sa-Marias being run by the *maharlika* leaders were spreading all over the island. I lost track of how many, but I calculated that nearly five hundred had taken place already. The parish priests were constantly asking me to come to their parishes to speak to their Sa-Maritanos. After a few years this began to give me pause. What effect was the Sa-Maria really having if I was always being called in to "rev" them up? The parishes themselves did not seem to have outlets that would allow the Sa-Maritanos to flex their new spiritual muscles. Everywhere it was the same. Prayer, Mass, and the sacraments to strengthen them to avoid sin. And no matter how much we talked of justice in the Sa-Maria, when it came back to the parish, sin was frequently and sometimes almost exclusively seen in terms of personal sexual morality and sacramental obligations. The concept of social sin, or sin as the neglect of talents we have and omission of good deeds, was not effectively present. Of course, the new Sa-Maritanos also joined parish organizations, but these usually had this same spirituality.

One thing the new graduates from the Sa-Maria could do was to help promote the mini Sa-Marias. But I could not help thinking that it was getting a bit like the school system which did not prepare students for a job but prepared students to be teachers, to teach more students, who could be teachers. . . .

Added to this, I was now coming under criticism for the Sa-Maria. Some priests said that as the vice of poverty closed tighter on the people justice issues demanded more courage. The Sa-Maritanos were not at the forefront where you might expect them to be. In fact, as some parishes began to take a prophetic role, denouncing abuses, the Sa-Maritanos often seemed to side with management, with government, and not with those who were struggling. I countered such charges with my own experience: the husbands and wives reunited; the families reconciled; peace for the heart of the woman who lost her only child; a joyful return to the Church for thousands. And some of the leaders of the labor movement had made their first steps into service through the Sa-Maria. I felt the fault was with the parishes, because a Sa-Maritano going back to his parish, "rarin' to go," was presented with no real program of social action.

However, I too was becoming unhappy with the Sa-Maria. Why were not more Sa-Maritanos getting their teeth into social issues in those parishes where the priests *did* have programs going? Was it because some of the speakers at the Sa-Maria were themselves status quo and that attitude was getting across? Our attempt to give all the *rollos* a new social relevance in line with the increased urgency had been scotched by those in charge of the *barangay* once martial law set in. We had trouble even keeping the talk on social justice in the program. The government propaganda and army threats were getting through if only by endless repetition. The phrase "social justice" was becoming tainted, almost subversive. There were many on the staff with whom I could not speak of these trends, but Baby and Meding remained courageously open and I could discuss them with them.

I gave more and more time to the *kibbutz*. I felt that it was in line with the development proposed by Pope Paul and that it went further because it offered an alternative model of ownership to the unadulterated laissez-faire capitalism of the government, or to the utopian commune-ism of the communist world.

I wonder now how much my enthusiasm for our *kibbutz* co-op sprang from the desire to avoid the looming confrontation with the whole system.

Four and a half years on the *hacienda* was coming to an end, and my next furlough in Ireland was approaching. I was determined not to leave the *hacienda* without in some way touching each family. I arranged a series of house Masses around the farm, and once again was shocked by the poverty I found. The people had no belongings. The little snack they would prepare for me was pathetic and touching. I would hear confessions in the house, say the Mass, and then take the snack as I chatted with them. I would think: "I have been here for nearly five years. Nothing had changed. So many sick and consumptive. Everyone in rags. People still sit outside their doors, thin and listless like cloth dolls which have lost their stuffing. And what have I done for them?"

I began to feel that one of the best things I could do for them was to make sure that the union was started there before I left. One day at Mass in our bamboo chapel a visiting group—members of the union—acted out the Gospel. It was the Gospel of the Good Samaritan. In the original Gospel a man is attacked by robbers and left to die; a priest, a Levite, and a Samaritan pass by; only the Samaritan helps the victim. In the acted-out version done by my visitors, the man attacked by robbers is a man who has been cruelly oppressed on a sugar farm. He is dejected and listless. Some people pass by: the first group suggests he should pray; the second group suggests he should accept the will of God; the third group invites him to join the labor union, and the man suddenly has hope.

The actors left the altar, and the lector finished the reading: "Which one of them then was neighbor to the man who fell among thieves? The one who helped him! Well, go thou and do likewise." In its simplicity it struck home to the people and to me. The union was on its way.

My memories of the *hacienda* are nearly all touched with melancholy. My favorite time was about five in the evening. The heat has gone out of the sun, which casts a golden glow on the sugarcane. To the northeast quietly, unexpectedly, the cone of Kanla-on volcano appears, silver, serene, sad. I stand there waiting for the vision. My thoughts are wandering. Today they go to Nora. Her last days spent in being taken from hotel to seedy hotel by her daughter Lilly, struggling to care for her properly. Her customers do not know that in the next room Nora is dying. And who is looking after Nora's other children now? And what of Tina, the deaf-mute? Someone said that she has gone to the red-light district of Bacolod City. What have I achieved here? I think of the words of the Gospel: "Woe to you priests. . . . The prostitutes will go into heaven before you."

I am on the plane home. My time is up at the Sa-Maria; its sheen is gone now as I see it in my mind's eye. The *hacienda* is way back there, the same as I found it five years ago. Some of my friends have made the decision to leave the priesthood. And me? What does the future hold for me?

I feel a bulk in my pocket. It is two unopened letters, stuffed in there in the rush of leaving. One from Baby and one from Meding. "Dear Father Obee"—that was what they used to call me. I read both letters silently. I paused and reread them slowly this time. I am surprised. My friends feel differently about my years in the Sa-Maria and on the *hacienda*. They feel they were good years. They feel I helped them and many others. They say I have a lot more to do. They want me to come back.

Did they see my doubt? I reread the letters yet again and hold them . . . thinking for an instant of how unaware the person beside me is of how much this moment means to me.

I still have those letters.

Chapter 11

WHEN I got on the plane at Manila Airport, bound for Hong Kong and home, my bag carried more than the usual souvenirs. I had the complete translation of the Roman missal into Ilongo, which we had labored over during the previous five years, and I had the signatures of all the bishops in the Ilongo-speaking dioceses approving the translation. It now had to be approved by Rome, so I would stop there on my way home. I also planned a stop in Israel and a stay on a *kibbutz* to see what I could learn for our own little experiment.

The stop in Israel came first, with a week on a *kibbutz*. This *kibbutz* was on the West Bank in sight of the Dead Sea caves where the Qumran scrolls were found. Strangely enough, there were no families on the *kibbutz*. It was occupied by students and soldiers, and seemed more like part of the Israeli defense system. Mounted machine guns were on the flat roofs of all the houses. Soldiers were much in evidence, and Shimon Peres, then Minister of Defense, paid us a lightning helicopter visit; he was on a defense inspection tour—presumably of the new perimeters of Israel.

We worked picking tomatoes and loading aubergines—the largest you could imagine, growing right in the desert. The system was simple and ingenious: the seeds were planted in the sand and the plastic pipe which brought them water also brought them all the nutrients they needed. Since the pipe only dripped water exactly over the seed, no weeds could grow at all. The results were spectacular. The tomatoes were as big as grapefruit, the aubergines as big as small vegetable marrows. The project seemed to have an open budget. The original *kibbutzim* were conceived as a way of shortcutting the road to socialism independently of the government. This one, however, seemed to be in the service of the government. Built on occupied and disputed territory, it looked as if this *kibbutz* had been used by the government as an advance outpost.

I did not get to know anyone and left disappointed, because this *kibbutz* didn't seem representative of the *kibbutzim* I had read about. But it was the one the government agency had chosen for me to see.

Rome was my next stop. It is a measure of how tired and wrung out I was that in neither Israel nor Rome did I make much attempt to see the famous or holy places. I delivered the translation of our missal to the Congregation of Rites, situated in a high-ceilinged Renaissance *palazzo* overlooking one of the Vatican courtyards. In addition to the translation itself and the signatures of the bishops, one had to submit the words of consecration in three languages: the new language in question (in this case Ilongo), a word-by-word translation in a modern European language, and one in Latin. While I was there, the Cardinal Prefect, Cardinal Knox, came out and checked the words himself. "Very good," he said and checked it off. I left the manuscripts with the secretary and took my leave.

One thing happened before I left Rome. That Sunday was Pentecost Sunday, and a couple of us went from the Columban house to Mass at St. Peter's. It was a warm sunny afternoon in May. When we got to St. Peter's Square it was evident that this was a special occasion. There was an air of *fiesta*. People were singing, and many almost dancing. Everyone was greeting everyone with "Praise the Lord" and "Alleluia." As we were soon told, we had happened upon the very first international charismatic Mass to be held in St. Peter's ever. It was an ecumenical event, and many different Christian churches were represented.

I separated from my companion at the great bronze entrance doors and managed to worm my way through the huge crowd right up to the front, so that I had a view of the altar. The Mass was being celebrated by Cardinal Suenens of Belgium, one of the architects of the Vatican Council and a man I much admired. He moved easily among several languages and was in tune with the congregation, who sang in Spanish, Italian, French, and English.

This was my first time attending a charismatic Mass. I found the spirit infectious and was prepared to give it a chance. At the Offertory everyone raised their hands together to sing "Les mains ouverte devant toi, Seigneur" ("With hands outstretched before you, Lord"), and for a moment we were so united it was a glimpse for me of what might be if the peoples of the world could let down their guard and love each other as the sisters and brothers they know in their hearts they are. After Communion there was a silence, in the midst of which a strange bird-like warbling broke out. First I thought that some people were playing reed pipes, and then I realized: "So this is what singing in tongues is." It seemed to me a very appropriate way of giving thanks after such a moving religious experience and it meant that the ecumenical and international congregation was sharing the same language.

When the Mass was over it was announced that the Pope would speak. After a while there was a stirring and a frail old man was led to the altar. It was Paul VI. He looked very weak, but his voice was unexpectedly strong and two sentences spoke straight to me: "You have tasted the fruits of the Spirit," he said. "Now you must do the *works* of the Spirit. The people of the world need life. They need bread!" Bread: he had said the vital word for me. Food: not just spiritual food, but bread, rice, beans, for hungry stomachs and outstretched hands. He was not going to be content with "joy in the Lord." That joy would be a sad and empty self-indulgence if it did not express itself in efforts to feed our sisters and brothers all over the world.

Those words of the Pope renewed my spirit and helped me to shake off some of the melancholy that had kept returning so relentlessly these last few years. That melancholy came from the conviction that all the magnificent cathedrals of the world, the stained glass windows of Chartres, the Book of Kells and all the illuminated manuscripts, the Cistercian monks singing the "Salve Regina" in their evening stalls, the nuns in perpetual adoration before the Holy Sacrament, the Sistine Chapel, and even the "Exultet"—all the great works of the Christian spirit—were but ashes, for one simple reason: we were Dives and Lazarus was at our gate, waiting and waiting for the crumbs from our groaning table.

In Hong Kong I had picked up a copy of Karl Marx's *The Communist Manifesto* and had read it on my journey. As a schoolboy I was taught to regard Marx as a devil incarnate. In the seminary they were more objective, but nevertheless he had been quickly dismissed. The man who comes through in *The Communist Manifesto* is a compassionate one who would have understood our rage that people were reduced to things, were objects of other people's lives rather than subjects of their own. A man who passionately cared about Nora and Padot and wanted to do more than shed a tear for them, more than say a prayer for them, more than offer them charitable assistance. In fact Marx felt that sentiment, prayer, charity stood in the way of what he wanted to do for the poor. What he wanted to do for them was to build a world in which they would not have to live such piteous lives, to change the world so that we would have a world in which Lilly would not have to sell herself to keep Nora alive. Was that so far from what *we* wanted to do?

Back in Ireland I stayed with my parents, visited old friends, swam and played tennis—things I had no time for in Negros. My parents remarked, when it was safe to do so, that when I had first arrived home I was very tense and restless. I had been unaware of it, though I do remember an outburst of uncontrollable anger over some social issue. I was ashamed of the incident, but they were understanding and seemed to realize better than I did where the anger was coming from.

As the months went by I learned to relax again and one of my favorite things to do was to spend time with my growing nieces and nephews. The complete change of scene helped me to stand back from what I had been involved in and look at it with a critical eye. I went on retreat with the Jesuits and tried to assess where I stood. I was sure I was going in the right direction, I was asking the right questions, but relying too much on my own solutions. I must begin to listen to the Filipino priests.

I was soon headed back to Manila. This time I was sure of one thing only—I had none of the answers.

I was a couple of days in Manila when Mickey Martin met me. He took me aside and told me that things had changed in my absence. The Filipino seminarians to whom he and I had given retreats were now priests and were running the diocese. They had an entirely new perspective; it was our turn now to listen and learn. The time for initiatives from us was past. We must follow and support.

I would have a chance to observe the new climate, he said, while I was doing my refresher course in Ilongo and waiting to receive a new appointment.

I, however, had decided not to do the refresher course, but to take Tagalog instead. Ilongo is very heavily influenced by Tagalog. It makes up a large part of the national language and is used in the schools. All the films are in Tagalog, as are the comics. I knew it would be a great help to me in my translation work.

A fringe benefit of doing Tagalog in Manila was that I got to know the capital. Manila is built on the Pasig River. A few years after the Spanish arrived in the Visayan Islands in 1565, they realized the importance of it and attacked the original fort of Maynilad, which guarded the Pasig River. The fort was defended by Raja Sulayman, but the Spanish with their superior firepower defeated him. This was in 1571, six years after they had first arrived in Cebu. They immediately built their own fort on the same spot—Fort Santiago, which still stands and which, until the Americans came in 1898, remained the nerve center of Spanish control on the islands. Of course the Spaniards expanded it into a much larger fort and finally built the city around that fort. The original city is today called Intramuros, meaning "within the walls."

The original walled city was unique, filled with old Spanish churches, houses, convents—a strange architectural anomaly in the Asian tropics. It survived from early Spanish times to the last days of World War II, when it was finally destroyed after suffering intensive shelling by U.S. forces who were attempting to dislodge the Japanese. The only thing left standing in the city was the Church of San Agustín, the oldest church in the Philippines. Its style is what they call "earthquake baroque" because of its huge flanking buttresses.

With the arrival of the Americans a new type of building appeared on the Manila skyline: American colonial architecture. After all, the Philippines was to be a U.S. colony. It was only fitting that some of the glory of the new mother country be reflected in the "islands." Great columned public buildings reminiscent of what can be seen along the Potomac rose outside the walls. Broad avenues and boulevards and streets built in straight lines, with names like Kansas, Texas, Dakota.

Manila was left in ruins by the war. Cheap Jerry-built corrugated-iron roofed structures mark the postwar years, but also a whole new city of sleek skyscrapers in the Makati district, which could almost be a part of San Francisco. It was now no longer America imposing her image, but the ex-colonized imitating the ex-colonizer.

After the war, too, the phenomenon of squatters appeared: homeless people building shacks out of old scrap material on land to which they had no legal claim. After martial law most of Manila seemed occupied by squatters. Miles and miles of hovels made from bits of election-board advertisements. No water, no sanitation, no sewage arrangements. What lights there were were strung around precariously. No paving. The surroundings a sea of mud in the monsoon season. Perhaps three million living this way, while marble palaces rose around the city.

After my class I would go out and try and get some practice at speaking Tagalog. One day I was sitting on the stone ramparts, which protect Manila from the waters of the bay. It was the afternoon of *Sabado de Gloria*—the eve of Easter Sunday. The streets were eerily quiet as so many Manileños had gone home to the provinces to celebrate with their families. I was sitting there listening to the waves lapping and thinking of home because the seafront of Blackrock where I come from has ramparts just like this, built in the last century to protect the coastal railway against the waves from Dublin Bay. I spent many happy summers as a boy playing around those granite ramparts. Now I just sat looking out at the horizon over the bay.

But as my ear grew accustomed to the sounds around me, I became aware of the sound of crabs—their rattle as they scuttled across the stone into a crevice—and my eye caught sight of ugly cockroaches that appeared for a moment to scan me with their waving antennae and disappear again to report the presence of an alien in their territory. Then I noticed at the edge of the water dirty bits of styrofoam, a condom, a lady's plastic shoe bobbing up and down. The pleasant smell of the sea became suddenly mixed with a smell of sewage. My mood was changing as I got up to go.

Just then I heard a voice. "Hello Joe." It was a smiling woman. In no way could I tell her age, but she seemed to have been through the wars. "Where are you going?"

"Nowhere. I'm just relaxing here. Where are you going?"

"Home." And she pointed to a couple of plastic sacks standing on stakes further along the ramparts.

"Can I see?"

"Yes. Come along."

She carried an oilcan of water, and as we got near the sacks, I saw that there was a fire lighted. On the fire was a piece of tin, and on the tin were some small crabs' legs.

As we approached she said: "Badoy, meet Joe."

And suddenly out from behind the sack a head emerged, and gradually a body. This was Badoy.

"Hello, Joe, how do you like our house?" He laughed and I looked over the sack and saw a hole in the ramparts big enough to shelter a couple of people. The huge granite rocks of the ramparts had fallen in, creating a half-cave. With the sacks on top some of the wind could be kept away. They both laughed at my amazement.

"You live here?" I said, looking at the hole.

"Yes, this is our home," replied Badoy.

"But how do you live?"

"I dive for crabs and we sell them." He pointed to all the cuts on his body from the sharp barnacles. "I used to be very big and strong"—and he cupped his hand over his arm muscle to show where it used to be—"but I got thin from giving blood."

"To whom?"

"People buy it from us. Eighteen pesos a liter. I can't give any now. I'm too thin."

The woman interrupted: "And I used to tell fortunes with cards at the clubs. But the police arrested me twice." A note of having been done ill by was in her voice.

"Why did they arrest you?" I asked angrily.

"Oh, they have no compassion."

"That is true: they have no compassion!"

We lapsed into silence.

"Joe, taste some crab. It's very tasty," said Badoy, offering me the largest piece.

"Yes I will, but give me that small piece of leg."

They watched my face. "Mmmm . . . this is tasty." And they immediately offered more.

By now the water was boiling. The woman made some coffee from a paper packet. I reckoned it was some sort of coffee substitute. They poured it into a pickle jar and offered it to me. They shared a second jar, laughing.

We drank in silence as the sun went down behind the sea. It moves so fast that you would almost expect to hear a sizzle as it touches the water. Suddenly in the distance we heard the sound of singing and the clacking of bamboos.

"What's that?"

"It's the procession of the Lonely Virgin."

I recalled that on Holy Saturday, the day after Good Friday, in the Philippines the Virgin Mary, when everyone else is gone, retraces the steps of her Son's last journey. Men were not allowed to participate in the procession.

It was getting dark. I thanked them and took my leave.

The streets were empty. The procession of the women was gone. Why were no men allowed in that procession? Was it because only women had remained by him at the end?

As I made for home, I thought of Badoy, his body cut all over from the barnacles, and of his life living in that hole. They had not asked me for anything. They had shared what they had with a complete stranger. Nor was I surprised.

Back in our house that evening I sat down to a meal with my fellow Columbans. We had lamb for supper and our conversation was about quartz watches, I remember.

One of my favorite trips in Manila was down to Quiapo Church. It was a church that had defied the changes in the liturgy, or should I say in which the new liturgy and a totally native inculturated liturgy went on side by side. The church was packed from early morning till it closed at night. Worshippers kissed the feet of the black Nazarene or, to fulfill some sacred vow, moved in waves on their knees up the center aisle till they got to the altar, praying as they went; then they knelt with arms outstretched before the tabernacle, or knelt in groups saying the rosary here and there; and all the time the low murmur of prayer from young and old, men and women, could be heard. A priest would appear at the altar and Mass would be celebrated "at" the praying people; a few voices would answer the responses, but the majority would take no notice and go on with their devotions. A young boy and girl kneel before a statue and a candle they have lighted; oblivious to all around them, they are praying fervently for some desperate need.

Many of these people feel no need for Mass. This public liturgy is their faith's expression and it all goes on without any priest. Outside the church native medicines are sold, and holy images—the sort that appear to religious art connoisseurs in nightmares but which after many years I was beginning to accept.

Just as my language course was ending I got news that I would be going temporarily to the parish of Candoni to take the place of Eugene McGeough who would be on vacation. It was a mountain parish and one of our toughest. John Brazil was in Manila at the time, and when he heard the news he told me that the perils of Candoni had earned it the sobriquet of "Jaws." I asked where *he* would be going.

"Myself and Brian Gore have asked to start an experiment not far from you, in Oringao. While you were away we went around the Philippines looking at what's happening in other places. We think these new Christian communities have a lot to offer."

"Well, I don't know the answer, but we need something more effective than the parish. It doesn't touch the mass of the people."

My departure for Negros and Candoni was delayed by the opening of our pre-chapter convention. This was a convention held in each country where we worked prior to the general chapter, which was coming around again after six years. In the 1970 chapter we had broken ground and tried to adapt to Vatican Council. It was a special chapter summoned by Rome, and we had concentrated on internal reform of the Columbans, like introducing democratic procedures for appointing superiors. Now we were ready to look outward. I hoped it would help in answering the question of how our work related to the plight of the poor and what I should be doing in Candoni.

At this pre-chapter convention we were to prepare the Philippine contribution to the general chapter, which for the first time ever would take place not only outside Ireland but in a Third World country—the Philippines.

Delegates for the pre-chapter convention came from the two hundred and fifty Columbans stationed all over the Philippines. Each area had a different approach to the different concerns, but all were agreed that the issue of justice must be faced and must become central to the aims and nature of the Columbans as a society. And in the light of this, the renewal of our whole purpose of existence must be examined at the chapter. Some had feared that this would be a move away from the intentions of our founders, who had gone to China to save souls. Most felt it was a fulfillment of their creative spirit and that as things had turned out, most of their work in China had been in battling famine, flood, and disease. They had answered the signs of their times. This new direction was an answer to the signs of *our* times—signs Pope John had pleaded with us to heed. Now after weeks of discussions and prayer we had come to a unanimous agreement. The signs were clear. Hunger and oppression were everywhere. We must do something about them, not only as individuals and as crisis intervention, but as a society and as an integral part of our mission.

But would the other members from all over the world feel the same way as we did in the Philippines? The chapter would tell. It was due to begin in the autumn. It was now May. Meantime I was on my way to "Jaws."

Chapter 12

THE JAPANESE occupied Negros during World War II, but not the whole of it. They never controlled the mountains. Neither did the Spanish before them, nor the Marcos regime after them. Into those mountains had fled the guerrillas and those who felt they could not live under Japanese rule. There they met two groups of people: the first were the Negritos, a proto-Malay tribe of wandering people, now dying out; the second were the descendants of Filipinos who had fled into those same mountains to avoid the law in Spanish times. Unlike the Negritos, these *tumandoks* (natives) tilled the land, using the slash-and-burn method. They moved from place to place and never filed legal claim to the land.

When the war was over, the lowlanders came home to the lowlands but they did not forget those times in the mountains, nor the lands they had seen. Many lowland families, mainly upper and middle class who knew something of legal matters or had relations in the Bureau of Lands, filed claims to land in the mountain valleys. One law allowed them to file claims to thousands of acres, provided they raised cattle. These claims were called *ranchos*. Another law allowed logging companies, controlled by the same families or Americans, to cut down the mountain rain forests. Finally a third group, known as settlers, "small" people, usually landless peons from the *haciendas*, followed on the heels of the loggers and started to plant rice and corn, hoping someday to make a claim. The *tumandoks* usually moved on to new places, sometimes accepting a little money for the land they cleared.

After the war a group of settlers from the sugarlands of the town of Isabela decided to start a new life in the Tablas Valley, a fertile valley inside the Kabankalan mountains. They left behind the plantations and sugar factories of the lowlands and became small farmers themselves in the heart of the mountains at the source of the Tablas River. The little town they started was called Candoni.

On my first day in Candoni I walked around the town. It was bleak: a row of unpainted wooden houses along one side of the *plaza*, the down-at-heel *municipio* on another, the church and school and *convento* on another, and the fourth side empty—a sign that the town had stopped growing when the logging in the mountains ceased. Now they had no work, no wood, and irreversible erosion of the sloping land was destroying many of the farms.

I was only scheduled to be in Candoni for eight months, since Eugene McGeough would be coming back after his furlough. I was "holding down," as we said, a time for not starting anything new other than gardens, a time for learning; though indeed I already knew something about Candoni and in particular about Jimmy, the sacristan who served the Mass and looked after the church there.

Jimmy's father, Miguel, was a small settler. He lived with his wife and seven children. One day a very wealthy man from the lowlands, a banker—a millionaire in fact—acquired the rights to a large ranch. He employed armed cowboys to ensure that "his" land was not encroached upon. Frequently cows from the ranch would damage the crops of the small farmers, but to get compensation was impossible. As a consequence, there was ill will between the cowboys and the local settlers. On one particular occasion someone killed one of the rich rancher's cows. It was probably not the first time. The rancher decided to settle this once and for all. A group of settlers was accused in court. The judge was totally compliant. The settlers were found guilty and so high a value was put on the cow that even together the men could not find the bail money. They all went to prison, among them Jimmy's father.

Once the men were in prison, the cowboys went into action. One evening they arrived at Jimmy's house. Now in Jimmy's house there were a total of thirteen children because Jimmy's mother had taken in the children of the other men who were imprisoned. The cowboys asked for Jimmy's mother, and when she appeared they seized her and dragged her to a nearby copse. They threw her to the ground and each one of them raped her. Then they hacked her to death with a knife. Watching in terror behind the reeds, eleven-year-old Jimmy saw it all.

Eugene, the parish priest, took temporary charge of the children while Miguel took the case to the authorities, who were just not interested. This sort of thing was happening everywhere. What was strange was not that it was happening but that it was being reported. Eugene decided to try the courts. The case had now dragged on for four years. On his innumerable trips down to the city a hundred miles away, when Eugene would bring all the witnesses with him in his jeep, they would all sleep overnight at the Columban H.Q. in Batang. This was how I had got to know about the case.

The court case was now coming up once more in Eugene's absence. I dreaded the ordeal. The usual thing was that having got all the witnesses together from outlying areas and taken them away from their families for two days—the time it took to get down to the courthouse and back—you would arrive at the court to find the case had been postponed; but you couldn't afford not to go, because failure to appear by you would mean that the case might be dismissed.

I will never forget the day in court with Jimmy's case. Though the case had been going on for several years, Jimmy was only now getting to testify. The state prosecutor was a woman, and I had the hope that she would not be as inhuman as so many prosecutors seemed to be. But she kept a straight face, giving away nothing. So also the judge, overdressed for the climate in a coat and tie.

The lawyer for the defense plied Jimmy with questions about what he had seen the men do to his mother, point by point. I could not believe a lawyer could be so crass with a mere child. After a while Jimmy complained that he had a headache; his body was rebelling at the questions. Our lawyer asked for a break. The defense lawyer said there was no proof that Jimmy had a headache and that we should call a doctor to prove it. We got the break, but I was fit to burst by this time. The woman state prosecutor slipped five pesos to one of our group for a soft drink for Jimmy during the break. I hoped that meant she cared. I was clinging to anything.

The trial resumed. The lawyer for the defense pulled out a photograph. He pushed it up in front of Jimmy's face. "Do you recognize this?" It was a photograph of a woman lying on the ground, covered in blood—his mother.

"Yes," Jimmy said. Tears were spilling down his cheeks as he tried to control himself.

"What do you see?"

Our lawyer jumped up and protested. The judge counseled the defense lawyer to be more discreet. Then he turned and very deliberately said: "Jimmy, this is very difficult, I know. But answer the questions asked because, if found guilty, the penalty for the accused is death." Somehow I felt that the judge had been touched and there was a remote chance that we would not lose this in the way we lost all other cases.

But we knew the millionaire was backing the cowboys. In an effort to stop the rancher from abusing his influence I organized a petition that the rancher, who had received some sort of papal award, be stripped of this award, through the papal nuncio. A great number of priests signed, and I delivered it to the nuncio's residence in Manila. His Irish secretary received it, and I explained the details. Naturally I did not accuse the rancher—we had no tape recording of what went on behind closed doors. My argument was that by looking after the bail and defense of the killers the rancher was in effect aiding and abetting them, and protracting the case. The years of litigation were destroying Miguel's life; his farm and family neglected. The secretary was polite. He would process the petition. A while later I got a letter telling me that the nunciature could take no action until the court had decided.

The case dragged on for years and years and did more to disillusion the Columbans about the justice of the courts than any other single case. The fact that years later, in a rare decision, Jimmy did win the case, made no difference. It was clear to me that it was not the court system that had swung the decision, but that the embarrassing petition had reached the rancher and he had withdrawn support for the cowboys. They were last seen acting as drivers for military men.

In the parish of Candoni was a community farm started by Father Luis Jalandoni and Bishop Fortich. Its purpose was to give a practical example of land reform. They got a piece of land from the Bureau of Lands, distributed it among small settlers, put a full-time agriculturist on the farm, and some tractors, and started it off as a cooperative. The farm had fared well, but Luis was no longer around. While Luis had been in charge of social action, he had got involved in hundreds of cases like Jimmy's and used up a lot of the land titles of his wealthy family as bail bonds for the poor. But out of some four hundred cases he had nothing to show. He began to feel that legal action was tantamount to cooperation with a vast charade in which all the trappings of justice were meticulously observed while the reality was systematically denied.

One day Luis was conversing with a band of strikers in a *hacienda* when they were fired on by the *hacienda* guards with the full cooperation of local police. He had to dive for cover with the workers, and as he lay in the ditch with the bullets ripping over him, he thought, "Enough is enough." When he climbed out of that ditch his mind was made up. He would join the revolution.

Luis was a great loss to the diocese. He commanded such respect that his leaving us probably did more to legitimize the revolution for Church people in Negros than that of any other individual.

The truth of a lot of what Luis had been saying was brought home to me by living in Candoni. What had happened a hundred years ago in the lowlands was now visibly taking place here. The lowlands were almost all sugar. Up here, however, there was also rice and corn growing—farming on a smaller and more human scale, since these were food crops, not cash crops for export. Up here too the people kept much to their native ways, while on the plantations people suffered the poverty even of having lost their traditions. But now things were changing in Candoni. For one thing, the logging was coming to an end simply because the trees were now almost all gone. Erosion caused by the logging was carrying away the soil so that young people whose parents had come as settlers to Candoni twenty-five years before were now leaving to try their luck farming on the island of Palawan. As one of our leaders said to Eugene: "In ten years my land will be only stone because of the erosion." Moreover, sugar was beginning to appear in the mountains these last few years, since the price of sugar went up and new sugar factories opened.

But there was yet another cause of change in Candoni, and that was the land-grabbing which had always existed but was now taking place at an accelerating rate. With the arrival of sugar the price of land in the mountains went up. Lowlanders now took an interest in lands they had long ago gained title to but not tended and, in some cases, never even seen. Other lowlanders without such legal claims took advantage of the poverty of the mountain people and bought them out for next to nothing. Of course the mountain people did not know that new sugar factories were being planned or that roads were going to be improved or that the price of sugar was on the way up. The bishop and the priests kept up a campaign of "Don't sell your land," but poor people would sell anything if they had someone sick and needed money. People always came first in their minds. They didn't even have to think. Their land would be collateral for a loan. The loan would pay the medicine and hospital fees. Then, unable to repay the debt, they would lose the land.

There were also those vast ranches given for a nominal fee to influential people. This had been part of a government scheme to foster the cattle industry. In practice, sugar was often grown on these ranches. In the Candoni area there were four such ranches, each numbering thousands of hectares. And by most standards a man who had ten hectares of his own thought himself comfortably well-off. Our *kibbutz* with six families was occupying ten hectares. When these ranchlands were encroached on accidentally or deliberately, the ranchers, who were close friends of the constabulary, would ask for soldiers to go up into the mountains to protect their land. While on their "policing" calls, the soldiers would steal from the people and commit atrocities. But the people got no help from the law or its agents. Apart from the local parish priest—Eugene in Candoni, or Eamon Gill in the new parish of Magballo next door—the people had no one to go to, except the New People's Army, known as the N.P.A. These young idealistic students had gone into the mountains at the declaration of martial law and there gathered peasants around them. Their political philosophy was a sandwich made of nationalism and socialism with a filling of Marxist theory. They held out in the inner mountains and their numbers were growing steadily.

The constabulary sent liquidation squads up to the mountains to stamp out the small groups of rebels. One of these squads was commanded by Sergeant Jaime Rosano. He would roar through a village on his motorbike, followed by his men, and terrorize the people in the hope of deterring them from cooperating or fraternizing with the N.P.A. He killed and tortured civilians at will. We complained many times, but the provincial commander would give us the same answer: "He is not under my jurisdiction." The naked violence of Rosano justified the presence of the N.P.A. and drove people to join them.

While I was in Candoni I was floundering. I was more and more convinced that the whole system was rotten. I could see that our religious response was inadequate and at times added to the problem. For example, our school. True, it was a school for the poorer people, it was a community school, it made no profit. But now it was being twisted from its original purpose. Its curriculum was revamped by Marcos. All the schoolbooks had been rewritten (with the help of generous funds from international agencies) to incorporate the Marcos "new society" ideology. Our school had become part of the martial law apparatus.

The new curriculum trained students not for the farming life that most were destined for, but to fill posts in the bureaucracy which organized the schools. If a good student emerged, she moved up and Candoni lost her. And the school had another more subtle, but poisonous, effect: by its whole academic bent the school quietly "put down" the farming way of life, creating consumer aspirations among the students which they could only satisfy by going to the overcrowded cities. The students now saw farming as second-class labor, but they were unable to survive in the city.

It was easy enough to pick holes in our traditional methods, to show what we should *not* be doing—it always is. It was much harder to say what we *should* be doing.

Chapter 13

DURING *siesta* one sweltering afternoon a man came hurrying up the stairs of the *convento*. I knew something was amiss. Filipinos do not rush around very much, and particularly not at *siesta*. The man's name was Gregorio, and he told me his wife, Lina, was sick with cholera. She was also with child. He and a friend had carried her for eight hours from their mountain home, using a baby's hammock as a stretcher. But when they arrived in Candoni, they found no doctor. Though Candoni usually did not have a doctor, at the time a young doctor was doing his six months' obligatory rural training. He was not to be found, however, and Gregorio wanted to borrow our Landrover to take his wife to the hospital in Kabankalan, a two-hour drive over a rocky road. I told him that one of the other Columbans, Hilary Shannon, had borrowed it and that I didn't know when it would be back. I would go with him to the town clinic to see what could be done. We found Lina lying in the clinic crying out in pain. She obviously needed help desperately, so we hurried out to search for the young doctor. It turned out he had gone to an outlying *barrio*. It seemed an age before he finally appeared. He looked at Lina and immediately wrote out a prescription for Gregorio, who ran off, barefoot, to the little shop which sometimes kept medicines. In a few minutes he was back: they did not have the medicine. The doctor wrote out another prescription. Again Gregorio raced away, only to return once more breathless and empty-handed.

"We need dextrose intravenous fluid," said the doctor to me, "but so far as I know there's none here in the town." We fanned out through the neighborhood, asking people at random if they had any. Finally a woman produced a half bottle left over from when her husband had died. I brought it back to the doctor.

In the meantime, however, he had discovered that the clinic had no dextrose needle. He said we would have to take Lina down to Kabankalan.

"Doctor, you know she'll die on the way. Isn't there anything you can do?"

He then tried to use a large syringe, which was all the clinic had. But the veins in her hands and feet had closed up. He tried on the neck. That was no good either.

We all stood there helpless as Lina continued to scream with pain. Gregorio was blank with confusion. Their little child was wandering around the bed.

At last the doctor gave her the only medicine he had—some Coca-Cola— and insisted that she go to Kabankalan. There was still no sign of the parish jeep, so there was nothing to do but rent a jeepney. These were jeeps converted for passenger use that plied between Candoni and the surrounding *barrios*. It would be expensive and Gregorio had nothing, but we were in no position to bargain with a life at stake.

Gregorio laid Lina in the same baby's hammock in which he had carried her down the mountain, and we strung it up inside the jeepney. All the time Lina was crying out. We had no sedatives, of course. Nothing but that Coca-Cola. The doctor sat beside Gregorio. As the jeep pulled away I whispered to Lina: "Be brave. Hang on. You'll make it."

The jeepney took off, bouncing slowly along that terrible road to Kabankalan, while I stood watching it disappear, staring blankly down the empty road long after it had gone.

When Hilary returned the jeep to the *convento* the following afternoon, I poured out my story to him. As we talked, we heard steps coming slowly up the stairs. Through the door came Gregorio. He had walked the whole way back—more than twenty miles. His face told me what I had feared. Lina was dead.

Halfway down the mountain she had begged them to stop the jeepney: the pain was too much. They did stop, and there she died. And so also the child within her. Inexplicably, the driver and doctor insisted that maybe she was still alive; they would not heed Gregorio's pleas to return to Candoni, and the jeepney continued on and deposited Gregorio and his dead wife at a doctor's house-clinic in a large *barrio*.

The doctor was not there, and the doctor's wife naturally remonstrated with Gregorio for bringing in a dead patient. The jeepney driver would not carry Gregorio and Lina any further. "Against the law," he said. And of course it would be very bad luck too. The driver set off with the doctor, leaving Gregorio there.

The young doctor must have had no understanding of just how destitute Gregorio was—what he did next still amazes me. Passing through Kabankalan with the jeepney driver, he stopped at an expensive Western-style funeral home and ordered a hearse. For Gregorio, who would have to pay for it, that was as outlandish as sending for a helicopter.

Now Gregorio stood there exhausted before us. What could he do? The funeral home had taken Lina's body and would not return it until the bill (which included embalming and bringing the body back to Candoni) was paid; it came to eight hundred pesos—a little over a hundred dollars at that time. That is not exorbitant by Western standards, but it was more than Gregorio could ever expect to put together. In view of the fact that fifty pesos' worth of medicine would have saved Lina, I was exasperated and almost in despair. But not so Gregorio. He would borrow the money from us, he said, and sell his little piece of land.

I suggested we send down the Landrover for the body. But there was a problem because to carry a body in a private vehicle was indeed against the law. And also maybe Perfecto, our parish driver, would feel reluctant to carry a dead body. Also, as Hilary pointed out, the Landrover had a cracked chassis and might not survive the trip. If the chassis broke on the way back, it would cost a fortune to retrieve the jeep, and there would be the added problem of being stuck on the road with the body. But I was in no mood for prudential considerations. I felt it was one of those occasions in life when we should take a chance. Gregorio watched us arguing, voiceless. Finally we decided to consult Perfecto, the parish driver.

When Hilary went out of the room to get Perfecto, Gregorio broke his silence: "Father, don't leave Lina in Kabankalan." And he wept.

At that moment my feeling was "To hell with the jeep." While in the final analysis I was the parish priest, I was not going to ignore Hilary's opinion. I regarded him as co-pastor and felt we should make most decisions together. To overrule him would go against how I felt a parish should be run. But then he had not been through the terrible scene at the clinic. He had not met Lina. And now, just when it would have helped Hilary understand something of what I was feeling, Gregorio waited until he left the room to make this anguished plea.

Hilary came back with Perfecto. Perfecto was brief: "The Landrover can make it down the mountain, but not back. I'll get it welded in Kabankalan and drive it back. I'm not afraid to carry a dead body."

Then we plotted how to deal with the funeral home, which held the body in ransom. Because they had fetched the body and now had embalmed it, it would have to be "bought" back from them. I knew a little about the procedure. It was important not to mention that we were the ones paying, nor to show our jeep. Perfecto would go in with Gregorio and bargain for the body.

In this way Gregorio was finally able to bring Lina's body home for burial. At the funeral in Candoni Gregorio asked for the lid to be taken off the coffin so that he could be photographed with Lina—their last time together. I never saw Gregorio again, but I still have the photo.

My stay in Candoni was not long, but it showed me that the injustices of the lowlands had their counterpart in the mountains. The system was rotten through and through.

After eight months in Candoni I was appointed to be chaplain of the sugar mill of Dakong-Cogon and parish priest of the village of Tabugon in whose area the mill was located. It was about twenty miles away, still in the Kabankalan mountains.

I had now been thirteen years in the Philippines, and this was my first appointment as parish priest. I was delighted because Tabugon was close to the cooperative farm, the *kibbutz,* which I had set up. But as I set off for my new appointment, I no longer had a plan of action all ready as I had when I first arrived in Kabankalan long ago. I had found out some things about what I shouldn't be doing, such as anything that would strengthen the present structures of injustice. I knew the *direction* I should be going in. But how I would go there I knew not at all. I would have to learn that from the people.

Before I left Candoni news had arrived from Manila about our general chapter. The first documents were being released. It was probably the most dramatic chapter since our founding. We had taken the plunge. The chapter decided that our aim as a society was to minister to the poorest of the poor and work against all forms of injustice. The sorts of things I should be doing in Dakong-Cogon and Tabugon were coming into sharper focus.

Chapter 14

*T*HE WINDING valley of the Tablas River lies in the middle of the Kabankalan mountains. At the upper end of the valley and the source of the river is the town of Candoni. If you were to take a raft down that river you would pass many bamboo groves, corn and rice fields, and cogon grass and sugar, and after an hour you would come to the *barrio* of Magballo. And after another half hour you would come to Dakong-Cogon, "the place of the tall grass," the place I was going now.

Of course I did not go by raft. I went in the old Landrover, carrying with me all those books that had originally made the journey through the Suez Canal, then from Manila to Bacolod, to Kabankalan, to Sipalay, to Kabankalan again, to the plantation at San Ramon, up the mountain to Candoni, and now over to Dakong-Cogon. This would be their last trip. I also had two steel cabinets of papers collected throughout the years, including papers connected with all the translation work I had been doing.

My new assignment was as parish priest of Tabugon and chaplain to the sugar factory built beside the Tablas River about a kilometer from the *barrio* of Tabugon. I was to live at Dakong-Cogon. The *convento* at Dakong-Cogon was really a one-room building with galvanized iron roof and walls. It looked a mess from outside. But inside there were bright lights, running water, a refrigerator, and an air conditioner. Compared with Candoni, absolute luxury! There was even a wind-up telephone to the sugar mill nearby.

On my first night a group of parish leaders arrived bearing rum. These men were laborers in the sugar mill, all in the labor union and all engaged in giving seminars around the parish to bring to light the injustices they all witnessed. They were the trusted core group of the outgoing parish priest, Father Brendan O'Connell. Most had done the Sa-Maria retreat with me at one time or other, so they knew me well. They came to welcome me and to tell me about their work. They also brought with them a form, which they asked me to take to the management of the sugar mill to be signed. This form would allow them time off with pay to give the seminars and the loan of a factory truck to go to the places where the justice seminars would be held. I had a very special reason for demurring, but I said nothing at that time.

Next day, an invitation came from the management of the mill to come to supper. But before I go any further, I must tell you a few things about the sugar factory.

In Spanish times steam mills imported from Britain were used to crush the sugarcane. When the Americans came they introduced the centrifugal sugar mill. It was much more efficient and was able to crystallize the sugar, but a much bigger quantity of sugarcane was required to make it economical. The small steam mills on each plantation died out, and groups of plantations got together and pooled their sugar at one large mill, now called the *central*.

Dakong-Cogon was no ordinary mill. It was a third-hand property, having been originally set up in Puerto Rico in the 1920s; when it was no longer serviceable it was sold to planters in Negros; now in its extreme old age it had been transported to the mountains, through the intervention of the bishop, to serve as a cooperative mill. This allowed small family-owned farms to mill cane locally and therefore cheaply precisely because they had cultivated and harvested it themselves. Father Luis Jaladoni, while he was social action director, had helped to set the mill up. The bishop had been inspired by Paul VI's encyclical *Populorum progressio*. The top management were handpicked by the bishop and sympathetic to the work of the Church. Hence the loaning of trucks and granting of time off to do the seminars. It was the dream of the bishop that the mill would raise the standard of living of the poor people in the mountains. And it had already done this: the area was now visibly better off than Candoni, Magballo, or Oringao.

The next day the management threw a welcome party for me in their guest home and made it quite clear they wanted me not just as a chaplain but as a friend. Anything I needed I was to tell them and they would do what they could. I also had a subsidy of a thousand pesos a month. That was more than one hundred dollars and would make a big difference in running the parish. But in my mind I had a problem from the start. Looking back on it, I see that it surfaced on that very first night, because I introduced myself not as chaplain but as parish priest of Tabugon. For me that had carried a big meaning. I wanted to tell them that I saw as my first obligation the eighteen thousand people who lived in the surrounding area, and to whom I would serve as parish priest, and not primarily the mill and chaplaincy. My impression was that no one had heard my remark . . . in that I was naive.

I had discussed the matter carefully with the outgoing parish priest who told me the mill people were well-off by Filipino standards. Even the workers in the mill, who suffered their own grievances vis-à-vis the management, were rich compared with most of the surrounding population. I was determined to give priority to the poorest of the poor, who in this case would not be the mill workers.

I was also determined not to make the same mistakes I had made with the Blanco mill. First, I must keep my independence, and that meant keeping some distance from management and accepting no gifts. Second, I could not be close friends with the management while I had the labor union leaders as my parish council (as they now effectively were) and was privy to their side of the struggle against management. In fact that was a role—that of reconciler between the two sides—the bishop had hoped the chaplain would play. But I was for some reason unable to accept this role. The memory of the hurt I had experienced at the Blanco mill was very present. I still felt the pain of that remark about lacking courage. I could still recall the silence of friends, a silence which hurt and said: "We don't understand." I had found myself caught between labor and management, and vowed it would never happen again. This was why I postponed the decision on that first night, when the parish leaders asked me to sign the request to management for the loan of the truck and time off with pay to give the seminars. I felt this sort of favor would tie my hands eventually.

Within the first week management organized a party in my house. They all arrived bringing food and drink, sweeping me off my feet, so to speak. They brought a cassette player and music, and everyone danced and everyone felt at home. And from the way they moved about the house and settled in it was clear they regarded the house as theirs. I liked that. That's the way the priest's house should be—everybody's! But out on the balcony, in the shadows, sat some of the parish leaders and some visitors from the *kibbutz*. They never came in to the music and the laughter.

The very first thing I did was to ask a group of Filipino priests to come up to Dakong-Cogon to sit down with me and other parish leaders to discuss what we should be doing. I had resisted all the invitations from Sa-Maria and *maharlika* groups since I arrived back, much to the dismay of Dondoy and Meding and Baby. They were wondering what had come over me, but I was determined not to get involved again without first hearing what the Filipino priests had to say.

When Father Peter Hiponia and Father Gerson Balitor and their companions arrived in answer to my invitation, I did not know what to expect. I had all our parish leaders present. They asked for a blackboard and chalk, and when we had convened and prayed a little, Gerson first asked us what our aspirations were. What were the things most dear to us that we wanted for the people? What did the people themselves want? What were their aspirations? He wrote all our answers down on the board. When all the bits and pieces of our answers were added together, eliminating the overlapping ones and clarifying the confused ones, we came up with a picture like this: what our answers said we wanted was a community in which people cared for one another, served one another, shared with one another, and from which oppression and violence were absent.

Peter took over from Gerson. He went to the board and drew a five-pointed star. He turned around and said to me: "I don't mean to criticize you, Niall. When you started all those *panimbahons* in the mountains and all over Negros, it was a good thing. It gave people a chance to worship which they did not have before. . . . But in a way, don't feel hurt now, it might have done more harm than good, because implicit in that movement was the idea that if the people worship, then that's it. Oh, I know that's furthest from your mind, but that's the way our people take it. Prayer is cake. Once they have the cake they are no longer interested in more mundane foods. What you were establishing was worship services, not Christian communities. But it's communities of love and sharing which we are all about. Look at the early Christians." And he flipped open the Acts of the Apostles, reading aloud as he wrote on the blackboard: "And all who believe were together and had all things in common; and they sold their possessions and goods and distributed them to all, as any had need. There was not a needy person among them."

Then Peter returned to the star: "Christian community is like this five-pointed star." Opposite each point he wrote some words: (1) Sharing: time, treasure, talent; (2) Group decision-making; (3) No injustice; (4) Reconciliation; (5) Prayer together.

"Don't be shocked that I wrote prayer last. For too long we have put it so strongly first that the other essential parts of being a disciple have been lost. It must be there, but as a culmination, a celebration, a part of the whole, not itself the whole. I put sharing first because if we are sisters and brothers then we share. That is our 'good news,' our 'evangelion': we are brothers and sisters."

He paused for a moment and added: "If we are not sisters and brothers then there is no God and we have nothing to say."

He went on to explain the other points. Group decision: the people must share in decisions that affect them, not just the priest or the village captain or the local big man must be involved, but everyone. . . . But by this time I was no longer listening because the first point had already gone home so deeply that everything was falling together for me in advance of his words.

There is something in the human mind which wants to simplify, to reduce a sentence, a book, a philosophy, a religion, to one word. As you go on in life you keep realizing that one word is inadequate because things are complex and there are depths within depths. Yet nothing can take away the power of that moment when you glimpse through the complexity and see the underlying unity, the simplicity: like a person looking into a very deep well who sees first the insects playing on top of the water; further down he sees some moss or jutting rocks in the growing darkness; but then there is a moment when the light is right and he catches sight of a shining object way down at the bottom of the well. I seemed to catch sight of that object: being a disciple of Jesus means sharing, means community. There is no Christianity without community, and conversely atheism is in the last analysis the refusal to share—and that holds no matter what religion I profess and even if I am a priest.

Back at the blackboard star Peter was saying: "By 'no injustice' I mean that we cannot have community between two groups, one of which has its foot on the other's neck. There must be an attempt not only at charity but at changing the very structures which almost force people to oppress each other. But then again, we are not only after cold justice, some sort of mathematical equality. We want to work *toward* reconciliation . . . a warmth, an intimacy, affection, love! And then we can pray together without it being a mockery. If this star represents a basic Christian community, then our immediate aim is to start basic Christian communities."

But how?

In the next session we discussed the "how." It was clear that we would first need leaders. Where would we get them? Gerson took over. We listed on the board the various categories of people in the area:

1. Large landowners
2. High government/private company officials/mill management
3. Large business owners
4. Medium-sized landowners
5. Public school teachers
6. Small landowners (the ten-hectare group)
6a. Sugar mill workers
7. *Agsadors* (that is, sharecroppers: they worked someone else's land for them and got a share of the crop)
8. Part sharecropper, part laborer
9. Landless peasants, agricultural laborers
10. *Sacadas*

From our list it was clear that the parish was stratified socially like a pyramid, with the large landowners on top and the landless peasant at the bottom. We decided to pick our leaders from categories 6 and 6a—the small independent landholders and the mill employees—and maybe some from the layers immediately above and below. But we decided to omit the medium and large landholders because of the temptation for them, if they got a leadership position, to use their new "spiritual" power to consolidate their control of those over whom they already had economic power. However, I insisted that we must leave room for a Nicodemus or even a Zacchaeus. Nicodemus was the rich man who came to Jesus secretly during the night, afraid someone would see him; eventually, he went public when he confronted Pilate for Jesus' body, thus becoming a "witness." Zacchaeus was a publican—a collector of taxes for the Romans—but he changed when he met Jesus; he did not just start saying, "Praise the Lord," but gave back what he had stolen from the people and started afresh.

We also excluded the destitute because their lives were taken up, we felt, with the search for the next meal; they had therefore very little independence of action and could easily be "got at."

We needed to analyze the social strata of the society we worked in, to anticipate how people would be inclined to react to our suggestions for a change in that structure. We called this "structural analysis." I was aware that this could be a two-edged sword, but for me the Nicodemus clause saved our tool of analysis from becoming too rigid and ideological, thus dominating us rather than serving us. The danger was ever present that categories would depersonalize the categorized and dehumanize us, the categorizers.

We finished the seminar by deciding several things—our overall goal, the means we would use to achieve it, and the immediate task ahead. The overall goal would be "total human development." We borrowed the concept from *Populorum progressio,* Paul VI's letter on justice. We used this phrase so often that we shortened it to THD. In biblical terms you could call it the reign or the kingdom of God.

We would achieve our goal through small Christian communities. The immediate tasks were to recruit and train parish leaders who would visit the *barrios* and try to start these communities. My specific task was to get to know the parish, and I should plan to shift my living quarters quietly from the sugar factory out to the village of Tabugon. Pete felt that the right thing to do was to start by saying Mass in Tabugon every Sunday, and if the reaction of the people was positive, then I should gradually shift over without ruffling too many feathers in the mill.

By the time Pete and Gerson and the others left, the word "community" had a new meaning for me. For years I had heard it praised both in the old theology and the new. Since the Council everything had pointed toward community. I knew the word and the theory, but the penny had never dropped. In fact there was a time when I had found the idea of community a bit suffocating. I had been brought up on a religion and a personal philosophy that were individualistic—a sort of spiritual capitalism. Each one of us is out there in the spiritual marketplace fighting on our own, masters of our own soul. We needed courage, stick-at-it-ness, fortitude, to the end. Community seemed to take the edge off personal effort. Community was a special vocation, not for everyone.

The result was that those who would have been the natural builders of community among Christians often left "the world" and joined religious orders—perhaps to find the community that parish life just did not have. The only door to community then in the Church was a door that led out of the world. But this had not always been so. In the early Church people had community; witness the Acts of the Apostles! Ordinary people could have community again through these small Christian communities. And, come to think of it, that was what was wrong with some huge amorphous parishes in which everyone was anonymous, the kiss of peace was an embarrassment, the priest was a functionary dealing out grace. No wonder young people were attracted to the sects. No wonder the parish priests were always inviting me back to revive the Sa-Maritanos. The parish life offered them sacraments but did not demand true and radical sharing, or offer true community. No wonder just being a Christian was no longer enough; one had to join other organizations to get one's teeth into Christian living. But the very fact of being a Christian *should* be enough, because being a Christian means being one of those people who believe that we are sisters and brothers and that sharing our time, our treasure, our talent is our life's breath.

Sometimes we should be grateful for confusion. It can mean we are aware of conflicting evidence and it intimates to us that something is awry; it is the first step toward clarification and makes that clarification all the sweeter when it eventually comes. The mist of confusion was beginning to lift, and the outline of where we should be going was beginning to appear.

Chapter 15

THE VISIT of the Filipino priests marked a special moment for me. It was as if I had been benighted on a long journey and continued plodding on through the night and dawn had caught me on a hill from which I could gradually see all the ground I had covered. I could see how so many of the paths I had traveled in the twenty years since I had left home came together in one place and led away into the distance to a fine highway—a highway I knew I and my companions would be now following.

With these thoughts in mind, I went to sit beside the River Tablas, which ran beside the sugar factory, and brought with me a small battery tape recorder. I wanted to gather my thoughts, to try and put into words what had finally dawned on me. I wanted to talk to my mother and father and share with them the new vista that was opening up before me and, in so doing, maybe clarify it for myself, look at it . . . and maybe also a sixth sense was telling me that this road would eventually be dangerous, so unconsciously I was preparing them.

Hello Mom and Dad . . . I am sitting here on a rock above a bend in the River Tablas which flows not far from my *convento*. As I sit here the swifts are diving and kissing the water as they swoop for insects. It's quiet and I am alone. I thought I would take this chance to tell you how things are going . . . and about some plans I have.

There's something special I suppose about being parish priest for the first time. Unusual that it's so late in my case because here in Negros we usually take over a parish a few years after arriving. But I have been here thirteen years already. I'm not complaining . . . it's because I was involved in the Sa-Maria work, and that was worth it. If I was at home in Ireland I would be getting a parish just when I would be about to retire here. Anyway, that's not the point. The point is that now I am able to make plans and, of course, those plans will be based on all that I have learned and unlearned during the past thirteen years.

We seem to have tried everything in those years—schools, liturgy, retreats, organizations of every type. The place has been spiritually "blitzed" . . . and you can see results—a great increase in Mass attendance and you no longer see that sea of veils at Mass. There are nearly as many men as women at the communion rail now.

But in another way there has been no change. In fact there has been a deterioration: the poor have been getting steadily poorer and the rich richer. You can see the quality of life going down for the poor. In Tabugon most of the people buy secondhand clothes; the things for sale in the market are tinny and shoddy like the things we used to get in Woolworth's from Japan just after the war. In fact it's like wartime. Bob Burke's brother was visiting from Chicago and asked someone to buy him cigarettes. "One or two," he was asked. "Two," said Bob's brother, thinking it was packets the fellow was referring to. The lad came back with two cigarettes! People buy cigarettes and aspirins one or two at a time; children buy single sheets of paper for class and bring their own seats to school; school fees are paid by the month. The school is supposed to be free but that's gone by the board a long time ago. People cannot even afford the kerosene for a light at night. The dead batteries from their transistor radios are lying out in the sun in the hope of getting a bit of life back into them. And here things are much better than in Brian Gore's parish or Donie Hogan's, where there is no mill to give work. I suppose the worst thing is that they cannot afford medicines that could save a life and they have to watch their loved ones die of what are now curable diseases, like T.B.

But I have only been talking about poverty; I have not even touched on oppression, which is something else. Poverty can be borne with patience because the source is not visible. People can be made to believe that it's the will of God or fate or bad luck, but oppression has the added sting of injustice . . . people feel it deep within their souls when their little bit of land is taken from them by a man from the city who has done the paperwork. They came up here in the first place to escape the semi-feudal life of the lowlands, looking for freedom, but they are pursued even here.

And then it's well known that the military are becoming more abusive. Marcos is increasing their number every day. He says he needs them to keep the New People's Army in check, but the New People's Army has been born out of the injustice created by the regime. It's like a boiling pot . . . the lid is jumping up and down because the flame is too high. The military solution is to pile more weight on the lid. Someday the whole cauldron will explode. Why can't they just lower the flame? Why can't they just give the people a little justice?

What kills me is that so many middle-class people who are well educated and devout remain totally without outrage at what is happening. You explain it to them and hardly get a flicker. As for the public school teachers, well, many of them have sold their souls. They are the ones who have been changing the names on the ballots for all these referendums and elections which Marcos calls.

The question now is where do we go from here? For me it has at last become clear. . . . The raison d'être of the church is to serve the poor: without that the other things don't make sense. The only way to do that effectively is to set up small Christian communities. Instead of the monolithic parish, we want small communities in which people share what they have, no one is lonely, no one is hungry, no one is oppressed, no one sick without being attended to. In the old system the priest or specific parish organizations did all this.

Recently in the village an old man collapsed from exhaustion and hunger. He had walked all the way from the lowlands. When I heard about it I brought him over to the *convento* and we gave him food. He began to recover after a few days, though he was still very weak. Then I had to go to Manila and wondered how I would get his meals to him. Suddenly I said to myself, "This is ridiculous and arrogant. I am acting as if I were the only person who cared and as if I had the right to monopolize the problem." So I went to the place where the man had collapsed and the people came out of their houses. I explained to them that I was going to Manila and would they be able to look after the old man's food. "Of course we will. Don't worry, Padre, we'll look after him," they said. "We'll organize it. You go off to Manila." I realized that this is what I have been doing for so long and what some parish organizations are doing—substituting for the people and taking away their right to look after each other. Even when it comes to teaching religion, they should be the ones to teach their children themselves. Each community should be able to look after itself and have something left over for others outside. Anyway, that's the dream.

How to do all this? Well, I like Dorothy Day's dictum—build the new within the shell of the old! So I plan to stir as few hornet's nests as possible, but I know all the time where we are going even if I rest along the way here and there.

One other thing. I plan to change my house from the factory out to the *barrio* of Tabugon, which is the true center of the parish and will help me in setting up the communities. Dad, if you come for a visit next year, I may already have moved to Tabugon.

From where I am sitting I can see Mount Kanla-on, the island's only active volcano. Bishop Fortich says the whole island is a volcano—a social volcano—and it's about to explode. To the south I can see Mount Kan-asa.

That's where the N.P.A. go home. They grow in number every day. From what is going on around us they are clearly justified, but I cannot convince myself that it's the only answer.

It's almost dark now. You know evening falls very suddenly here—there is no twilight. Give my love to Niamh, Frank, and the children; to Terry, Janine, and the children; to Fergus and especially to Auntie D. The low noise you hear in the background is the sound of the mill grinding the sugarcane.

Chapter 16

DAKONG-COGON had originally been a wild rocky district of the village of Tabugon, but because it was nicely situated beside the river, it was chosen as the place for the cooperative sugar mill. Stores and houses soon grew up around the mill, which supported more than six hundred laborers and some forty persons in management. The mill was the only place in the mountains with electricity and that drew people there. If I left Dakong-Cogon it would mean leaving that electricity behind. You only know how much depends on it when you don't have it. Even water stops, because the pump will not work without electricity. All roads led into Dakong-Cogon because the sugar trucks had to get there. But Tabugon had its advantages too. Apart from being the geographical center of the parish, the weekly market took place there, and on that day people from every corner of the parish could be seen arriving on buses, jeepneys, horses. And one old man rode a brahmin cow. If I wanted to send messages out to the hamlets, all I needed to do was watch at the market to catch someone going home to that place.

On July 17, 1977, a few months after my arrival in Dakong-Cogon, the Rosano group struck in Magballo, the adjoining parish where Donie Hogan was parish priest. At dawn a Dakong-Cogon sugar truck pulled up outside the house of Vilma Riopay, one of Donie's catechists. They took Vilma away, despite the pleas of her father, Domingo Riopay. As soon as they were gone her sister Nilma ran to the *convento* to give the alarm. Donie searched in vain for Vilma. When he relayed the bad news to the rest of us, he found us at a seminar in Bacolod, where our new superior general, Tony O'Brien, had come personally to tell us about the new direction our recent chapter had taken: to move toward a solidarity with the oppressed.

Donie's bad news dramatically underlined the urgency of what we were discussing. Donie left the seminar to resume the search for Vilma. He tried prisons and detention camps all over the island, but could not find her. The military denied any knowledge of her whereabouts.

Eventually Vilma was discovered in the constabulary headquarters on the island of Cebu. Under pressure from Bishop Fortich they released her to a Cebu hospital, where the doctor diagnosed her as having "acute psychotic reaction." It turned out that she had been taken to a so-called safe house (read: "secret place for torture") in Bacolod City, where she was interrogated and tortured. She had been denied sleep, given electric shocks, beaten about the genitals, and given the "water cure." From time to time, pictures were flashed on the wall and she was asked to identify people. One of the pictures was of Father Hector Mauri, the Italian Jesuit who had written the book on land reform and started the National Federation of Sugar Workers Union. When Vilma was first released she was indeed half out of her mind, and only coherent enough to recall flashes of what had happened to her.

Vilma's experience was traumatic for all of us. The torture was more chilling in that it seemed so systematic; the torturers seemed to have been trained.

Though Vilma had been found in the constabulary headquarters, they blandly denied all knowledge of Sergeant Rosano, and no action was taken. It was a warning to us all.

I was shocked by the fact that a Dakong-Cogon truck had been used. As soon as I got back to Tabugon I confirmed the details with our own leaders. Then I went straight to the transportation manager at the Dakong-Cogon mill. I tried to conceal my trembling as I said that I had authority from the bishop and that I wanted the dockets whereby the truck had been loaned to Sergeant Rosano and gasoline supplied. He looked a bit alarmed, but he gave them to me. These dockets were documented proof of army involvement. I sent them immediately to Donie, who was trying to get the whole story to the media.

At Sunday Mass at the mill-site chapel many of the management were present. I made a decision to do something we had always been told not to do—and which in the Philippines you never do and which I agree you should rarely do and which now I was afraid to do. But keeping the picture of Vilma before me I began: "You have all heard of Adolf Hitler but you may not have heard of Auschwitz. Auschwitz was one of the death camps which he set up for the systematic extermination of the Jews. During the four years from 1941 to 1945 he killed around six million Jews: men, women, and little children. They were brought into shower rooms and gassed to death instead of washed, and when the gold or silver fillings had been wrenched out of their mouths and their hair taken for mattresses, then their bodies were burned in the furnaces. Their bones and ashes were used as fertilizer. One million little children died in this way. Look at your little child and think: it was not Hitler who did this; it was the whole German people, most of whom were baptized Christians. Some did it by actions: they designed and built the gas chambers and ovens, manufactured the Zyklon-B gas, and transported the people to the death camps. Most others cooperated by their silence, by never raising their voices. My dear people, there is nothing louder than silence. Without it, the murder of these people would not have been possible.

"Near one of these camps was a big beautiful cathedral. People were going to Mass to worship God only five kilometers away from the torture chambers. The smoke from the chimneys, like the chimneys of our sugar mill, must have been visible. I have seen a photograph of the priest of that church standing with the Nazi soldiers, posing with them before a statue of Our Lady. That priest, by mixing with the military who operated these death camps, was consenting. It was the same as saying: 'You're doing O.K.' So the blood of those children is on his hands. But I have been silent too. I have seen so many children here dying of hunger or for lack of medicine . . . and killings too. I am sometimes afraid to speak out. You don't want me to be like that priest, do you? What would I say to St. Peter at the end of my life? That is why today I want to talk about Sergeant Rosano.

"You know and I know that he has been going around the mountain here torturing and killing people. A week ago he got from the property department of this sugar mill the truck he used to abduct Vilma Riopay, whom some of you know, a catechist of Father Hogan in the parish of Magballo. '*Our*' truck was used to take her to a 'safe house,' where she was tortured with electrodes attached to her nipples and body. My dear people, I tell you these things because I don't want to be guilty of the sin of silence. If I don't speak, when you stand before St. Peter you could say: 'Father O'Brien never told us. He is to blame.'

"When Rosano comes here we mix with him, drink with him, laugh with him. What would he say if we were to put our arm on his shoulder and say: 'Brother, what you are doing is wrong'? But we are afraid. When we fail to do this we are consenting, we are supporting, we are encouraging him. If we are silent, some of the blood he spills is on our hands also. . . ."

As I spoke I had moved away from the altar to the head of the aisle so that I did not need a microphone. I could speak in my natural voice, as if I was speaking to each one of them. The store where Rosano drank with some of the mill officials was right next to the church, and the people were so silent when I spoke that I am sure my voice could be heard there too.

After that Mass word was passed to me that two of the sugar mill officials who had attended Mass said they would not go to Mass again as long as I was the priest. Both were from the second highest level of management, one had probably been involved in okaying the use of the truck by Rosano. Like many others they drank with him whenever he passed through Dakong-Cogon, in the store next to the church.

Now, on the *kibbutz* lived a young man called Renato. A few years before, his brother Perfecto had asked to come and work on the *kibbutz*. He was an orphan and with him he brought his younger brother Renato and their little brother Toto and little sister Nena. The four had had a very unhappy life. Their father had fought with the guerrillas and was regarded as a veteran of World War II. Both parents had died and the four had been taken in by an aunt. But their aunt committed suicide, leaving them orphaned again.

When they arrived at the *kibbutz* they had no possessions except an American flag given by the U.S. government on their father's death. It was large and strong and covered them all at night.

I insisted that Nato continue going to school in the local village until he was at least sixteen before he began working on the *kibbutz*. He was restless to start working and said that in school he was learning nothing. It was all about "the new society"—Marcos's name for martial law. Also teachers never prepared for class; they just gave tests in class, and went off and talked or did their shopping, or did not come in at all, in which case the students were told to go out and clean up the grounds. I relented, and Nato became a trainee member.

Nato would always come to visit me. Knowing I liked lettuce, he grew some successfully for me and would often arrive bringing some. He never called me Padre. He called me Bok. (Every now and again an albino carabao—water buffalo—pinkish-white in color, is born; these are called *bok-ay*. I assumed Bok was short for *bok-ay*.) When we were out somewhere far from home and girls would pass, Nato would immediately get into conversation and, giving me a wink, he would make a point of addressing me as Bok, so that they would not know I was a priest. He reckoned he was opening up options for me! Nato became very strong and was afraid of nothing. One day when he and I were crossing a stream together, a snake reared its head from the mud bottom. I fled but Nato ran after the snake and chased it away. Nato was also a great prankster. One time we were going on a long journey with Nato leading the way. Suddenly he stopped and said: "Let's call in here for a rest." And he launched into a description of the next half of the journey, which he assured me involved terrible hazards. But when I wearily got up to start again, he began to laugh and revealed that this was the house we were going to. He got a great kick out of seeing my relief. . . . Nato and I were friends.

One night Nato arrived at the *convento* in Dakong-Cogon. I remember it well. He asked to speak with me. I let him in and closed the door.

Nato's face was very serious. "I am going to leave the *kibbutz*."

"Did something happen?"

"No. I like it here."

"Then why are you leaving?"

"I am going to join the New People's Army."

"Why?"

"I'm going to kill Rosano."

Chapter 17

As NATO stood there waiting for my reaction to his announcement, I knew that I must finally declare my hand—a mixed hand of hearts and spades. In Spanish *espada* means sword. But I knew then that I could never choose the sword.

Most of my changes in thought have happened gradually, culminating in moments of consolidation in which the gradual changes are summed up in an insight, experience awakens the intellect, or the suspicions of the intellect are confirmed by experience. In many cases a book or a film, reflecting someone else's experience, laid the groundwork or served to put a name on a groping idea trying to be born in my own mind. Looking back, it is not too hard to mark some of the milestones on the road to the radical position on violence I now embraced.

* * *

When I was about thirteen, my parents sent me and my brother to see *All Quiet on the Western Front,* an American film made after World War I. We were used to seeing films in which the "Jerries" were the bad guys, but in this film there were no bad guys. The film was set on the German side and a young German soldier, Paul, was at the center of the story.

The last scene made an indelible impression. We are in the German trench. Paul is crouching there at the ready. Suddenly a butterfly lands within arm's reach. His thoughts go back to the fields at home; he is playing there with his sister and they are running after a butterfly just like this one. Letting his rifle slip a little, Paul very carefully raises his head and reaches out his hand. He leans forward and, as he does, his head comes into the sights of a rifle. We are now looking down the barrel of that rifle held by an Allied soldier—one of "our" guys. He is pressing his finger on the trigger. Now in the distance we see a German soldier reaching out of his trench. The trigger tightens; a shot rings out. The far-off soldier slumps forward . . . just another Jerry. The butterfly flies away.

When the film was over, another one followed immediately, but I could not watch it. Nor could I explain why. Getting up, I left my brother behind and went out into the sad afternoon.

A few months before my ordination I went to see a German film, *Die Brücke—The Bridge*. It was the story of seven young boys just turned sixteen. We see them playing at home in various idyllic scenes. One has a pet rabbit, another gives his new watch to his first girlfriend.

It is the last week of the war, but suddenly they are called up and put in charge of guarding a bridge. This bridge lies along the path of the oncoming victorious Allies, but it is strategically unimportant. The captain in charge is compassionate and human. He knows what the boys do not know: that the war is lost. He realizes that boys this age should not now be exposed to a useless death. He plans to blow up the bridge himself so that the boys will not have to defend it and can just go home to their mothers. But he himself is killed and the boys are left alone guarding the bridge. The war has only forty-eight hours to run. The Americans are coming. Fired by all the propaganda about the fatherland, the boys start to defend the bridge. The GIs see that they are only boys and try to head off a fight, but the boys open fire. They fight bitterly and bravely. As the smoke clears after the battle many GIs are dead, and all the boys are dead except one, who now at least is able to cry like the child he is for his lost companions. The screen then carries a short notice: "This event took place in the last week of the war, 1945."

Back in the seminary I discussed the film with one of the professors. He concluded by saying: "But that film was an *anti-war* film." I knew he felt that a film or novel that attempted to give a message was betraying its medium. In spite of my admiration for the professor, I went away from the discussion saying very clearly to myself: "If that's anti-war, then so am I."

In our moral theology studies in the seminary we had briefly touched on conscientious objection, and I wish my textbook had not been eaten away by termites because I was sure I wrote a lot of dissatisfied comments on the page where conscientious objection received its minuscule treatment, and I would love to see them now. The author of our text was Genicot, a Flemish moral theologian known at the turn of the century for his liberal views. (On seeing Genicot approach, Leo XIII supposedly said: "*Ecce qui tollit peccata mundi*"—"Behold him who takes away the sins of the world"!) Anyway, the most that the liberal Genicot could say for conscientious objection was that it was not a sin and that those who practiced it should be indulged if in good faith. I was outraged by this.

It must have been around 1966 that I met for the first time some Filipinos who were dead set against the U.S. presence in Vietnam and who even rejoiced when the Americans suffered a setback. I was taken aback. I took their attitude as sour grapes, but it set me thinking . . . the unthinkable. I suppose I had automatically accepted the popular belief that this was a quasi-religious war against communism. There was more news about it in the Philippines than in Ireland. The Philippines were closer, Americans were heavily utilizing their Philippine bases for the war effort, and the Philippines themselves had a force in Vietnam—an engineering battalion called "Philcag."

My earliest objection to the Vietnam War was simply the pointlessness of the deaths. I often mentioned *Die Brücke*, but maybe *All Quiet on the Western Front* was also there in my unconscious. I said to myself: "If it's for Christianity we are supposed to be fighting, can't one go on being a disciple under communism? It's harder, but it's possible."

The escalating Vietnam War, coupled with the growing conviction that the United States should not be there at all anyway, led me to think a lot about violence. Was it that inevitable? There had been a time when dueling was a normal way to solve differences in some societies, but that had been done away with. There had been a time when family feuds were carried on by vendetta, but the court system had gradually done away with that. There had been a time when city-states had solved their differences by going to war, but we had outgrown that. However, nation-states were still solving their differences by war: surely we could outgrow this too?

Ever since I had left the seminary I had been getting the *Catholic Worker,* a most unusual newspaper published by an unusual woman, Dorothy Day. Dorothy had been a communist in the twenties, and when she became a devout Christian she did not lose her passion for social justice but brought it with her. Not an easy thing in the days when an interest in social justice was suspect in her newfound Catholic Church. She also espoused nonviolence—equally suspect from both the Left and the Right. I liked Dorothy Day's spirituality and theology. She said it was the personalism of Emmanuel Mounier, a French Christian philosopher, that had inspired her—which did not mean too much to me at the time—but what was clear was her commitment to justice, her respect for tradition, her dedication to nonviolence. In a way a strange combination. The three positions were rarely found in one bed, but it was a bed I was comfortable in.

The *Worker* helped to form my attitudes. Through it also I got to know the Fellowship of Reconciliation, an international and ecumenical organization dedicated to active nonviolence. There I learned more on the nuclear threat, especially through articles by the pediatrician Dr. Helen Caldicott. Her writing on the effects of mining uranium on miners was deeply disturbing. If merely mining uranium could cause cancer, sterility, and birth defects, then what sort of an evil genie were we calling up by processing it, even for peaceful use? It struck me that all our struggle for justice would be utterly irrelevant in the event of a nuclear war. Further, the possibility of nuclear war made the rational and reasonable argument for armed self-defense in an internal revolutionary situation, such as the Philippines, irrational when applied to war between the superpowers.

My pull toward nonviolence did not arise from individual passages in the Scriptures like "If someone hits you on one cheek, offer them the other" or Christ telling Peter to put down the sword and saying, "He who lives by the sword shall die by the sword." For every individual passage "pro" you can find a passage "con," such as "I have come not to bring peace but a sword." That sort of proof-texting has always been a deadend. For me it was the heart of what Jesus did that mattered. Everything he said must be interpreted in the light of what he did: his walking up to the jaws of death, his struggle at the threshold with himself, his cry of anguish before it swallowed him . . . all spoke to me of nonviolence.

My convictions about nonviolence were disturbed and tempered by two things. First, the *Populorum progressio* justified, under certain circumstances, the right of people to defend themselves with arms as a last resort. And this was confirmed by what I was seeing around me. Vilma, Jimmy, Padot's boy. These were situations in which one could not tell people that they had not the right to defend themselves. Even so, in my heart I felt that even justified counter-violence was not the answer.

* * *

But what could I say to Nato?

I looked at him. "You want to kill Rosano?"

"I don't really want to kill anyone. I want to save lives. Removing Rosano will mean a lot more people will live. He has already killed about fifty, and that's why I want to join the New People's Army."

"In some ways," I said, "the N.P.A.'s objectives are the same as ours: a just society, a society where everyone will have enough. But we have chosen a different route. Imagine a mountain with two different paths up to the summit. Our path is different from theirs. We have chosen the path of the Christian community and we don't use arms."

Nato had obviously thought this over. By the look on his face he was determined. He had really come to tell me his decision.

I went over to the bookcase and took down the copy of *Populorum progressio*—the one I had helped translate. On its cover I had put Merida's Peruvian Christ, superimposing on it a starving child from Biafra. On the back cover we used a photo subtitled: "Sacada working on Christmas Day in Hacienda Sta. Barbara." I opened it at paragraph 31 and read: "We know, however, that a revolutionary uprising—save where there is manifest, long-standing tyranny which would do great damage to fundamental personal rights and dangerous harm to the common good of the country— produces new injustices." I closed it, saying, "The Church teaches that when there are circumstances such as ours today in the Philippines, *you can make a decision for armed revolution.* The N.P.A. have made this decision. I find it difficult to accept the Church's teaching here but understand your decision, Nato. You are always welcome here. We'll miss you, and if you change your mind there's a place in the *kibbutz.*"

"I won't change my mind," he said.

When he was gone I thought it all over. We were not offering any alternative to the gun. The Church was saying: "No violence. But when you can take it no longer, *as a last resort,* yes, counter-violence. But what of positive, active, assertive nonviolence? There was no mention of that. When would we come up with this vision? When I had mentioned Gandhi and Martin Luther King to Eugene he had said, "That's all right for the U.S., Niall, or in India under British rule. There you had a rule of law, but that couldn't work here." I had never heard my peer group of priests even mention the word nonviolence in a positive context; it was almost a dirty word, because it was more likely in the Philippines to be used by violent people as a screen for protecting the violent status quo. These people talked of nonviolence when they really meant, "I am against a radical change in the status quo." They did accept armies, guns, army chaplains, capital punishment, just wars . . . but not peasants rising up against their governments for social reasons. They did accept the English "Glorious Revolution," the American Revolution, the French Revolution . . . but they did not accept a Filipino Revolution because, as they endlessly repeated, "violence begets violence," and of course they are against violence. But when they say they are against violence, what they mean is, "We are against your violence, not ours." In the revolutionary climate of the Philippines, to say, without qualification, "I am against violence," meant when decoded: "I am for the status quo."

But what I wanted to say by nonviolence was: "I am for revolution. I am for a radical upturning and turning around of the present social system. I am for a redistribution of the nation's wealth, but by means other than counter-violence."

If asked at this stage what specifically these means were, I think I would have said, "What specifically we should do I don't know yet, but I know it can be done. It *is* possible. After all, we humans have got to the moon. We *can* learn to live together in equality without forever killing each other. But whatever means we come up with must be decided and implemented by the people themselves."

I do not know if at this stage I was beginning to see that the small Christian communities would be the natural locus for such awareness and such action, but it was not long before I did.

Chapter 18

*T*HERE'S a special thrill in going around your new parish for the first time. You don't know what you are going to discover. Usually you miss the most important social feature. In the case of the parish of Tabugon it would have been hard to miss the most important economic feature. It was the sugar mill introduced by the bishop about ten years before. All roads led to it; new roads were made everywhere to bring the cane to it. Its chimneys and their smoke were visible for miles around. Crowds of makeshift houses elbowed their way into the factory area to avail themselves of the electricity. On a bulldozed knoll above the factory were the guesthouse and the houses of the management staff, cement houses laid out neatly like a subdivision. Dakong-Cogon had its own church and of course that GI-walled, air-conditioned, one-roomed *convento*. The previous parish priest had made sure it was not in the management area.

The factory brought money to the surrounding mountain area. First, it milled the cane of the local people. Otherwise small farms would not have grown cane. Second, it gave permanent work to some six hundred mechanics, drivers, maintenance men and office workers, and temporary work to some three hundred others. The salaries were relatively high because, though the mill was uneconomic and did not make any money, it was bound by the same laws that governed mills making millions down in the lowlands. Any full-time job, even as a cleaner in the factory, was a prize much sought after.

In setting up the mill the bishop had borrowed the money from the Philippine National Bank. It was to be paid back gradually, by taking a percentage off the sugar milled by the planters. When all had been paid back, it would be theirs. But the bishop insisted on one thing, which was to make all the difference between disaster and modest success: he insisted that the planters' land not be used as collateral for the loan. In this way the government could never call in the loan and take the people's land. They had to keep coming across with more loans during difficult times, otherwise they would have lost everything. It was like paying the hospital bills of a sick person in the hope they'll get well and work again and pay off their debt to you.

Fortich made another smart move when he insisted on having one vote per holding, so a farmer with fifty hectares would have one vote at the election of the board of directors and a farmer with ten hectares would have one vote too.

However, he made one decision that was to cause him endless trouble. This was the decision to allow management to own land in the area and mill their own cane at the mill. He himself owned nothing, but almost every member of management did, and that gave rise to endless possibilities for abuse. In the beginning it was so hard to entice qualified people up to a barren mountain plateau, far from the amenities of the city, that he felt this extra attraction was necessary. He regretted it.

The parish of Tabugon was made up of four *barrios,* Tabugon at the center, and around the periphery Tagoc, Pinaguinpinan, and Inapoy. Each of these *barrios* had elementary schools and lots of outlying hamlets. Inapoy, like Tabugon, had a high school. I said Mass in each *barrio* and was surprised at the low attendance. People would come to have their children baptized. And a few adults and maybe some children from the school would come to Mass if there was a catechist. I think two adults came in Pinaguinpinan. Of course for a *fiesta* the church would be full. Part of the crush then was due to the sponsors, godparents for the children who were to be baptized.

One significant social phenomenon was hardly visible at first. In all the rocky outcroppings of the parish, where the land was hardly land at all, an immigrant population of Cebuanos made a living. These were not from Cebu, but Cebuano-speaking peasants from the other side of the island of Negros—Negros Oriental. They were landless and made their way over the central mountains in search of a little place to farm. They got the leftovers or became sharecroppers or day laborers on the land of Ilongos. It took me some time to realize they were there and that they were at the bottom of the social barrel. They looked thinner and more haggard and even more ragged than the others. They grew corn rather than rice, they chewed betel nut which made their teeth red, and they were more easygoing and less competitive than the Ilongos. They had less formal religious education. I rarely met one who had been to high school. But they were very faithful to two sacraments: baptism and marriage. They seemed not to have heard of the others. They usually spoke Cebuano among themselves. I determined someday to learn it. When there was heavy work to be done they, with their undernourished bodies, were the woodcutters and water bearers.

What made Tabugon a much easier place to live, compared to the other three mountain parishes of Magballo, Candoni, and Oringao, was the clinic. It was small and it had little equipment, but it had a doctor on weekdays, and that made a great difference. You were continually faced with the agonizing decision as to whether this or that sick person should take the rocky road down to the lowland hospital or whether they could be treated at the clinic—and that was often a life-and-death decision. With a doctor around it was easier.

One morning I was called over to the clinic. Was it the nurse who called me? I cannot remember. Maybe it was the father who had no money for medicine and the nurse directed him to try me. This was a frequent occurrence. A nurse, knowing that the particular medicine was available in the little *botica*—pharmacy—nearby but that the people had no money, would often direct them to the priest. Anyway, in the corridor of the clinic there lay a little girl. The mother and father were watching over her. Over the years I had become quite an expert at telling the degree of people's poverty. This time one look told me that they were not just poor, but destitute. The little girl was so thin that, though she was probably seven years old, she was the weight of a four-year-old. She was in great pain and struggling for life. Her eyelids were caked with dirt as if she had been crying for a long period. Her hair was lank and matted. Her eyes were full of pain. I helped with whatever medicine we could get in the *botica* and in the process of being there I was told that the child was not baptized. A discreet inquiry revealed that the parents were not Catholics: another Christian denomination, I did not ask. But the nurses approached me now to baptize the child, probably part of the reason for calling me in the first place. A slight pressure or even suggestion from me to the parents would have surely got permission. The child was obviously dying. I could not remember *not* having baptized a dying child before. At the moment of death you want to help in any way you can. As a priest I had the extra responsibility of the people's salvation. In Catholic theology you should have the permission of the parents to baptize, but they were so poor and were getting help from me, that psychologically they would have had no freedom to decide. I decided not to ask. There was nothing to stop them asking me. They had not, so for me to ask now would be to take advantage of their poverty.

But what of the child? I looked at the child, and when I saw those eyes with the marks of the tears—surely weeks and maybe months of suffering—I realized that to push baptism now was to imply that otherwise God would not take her to his heart . . . and that was an insult to God. I put my hand on her cheek and kissed her forehead gently, and took my leave.

Chapter 19

THINGS began to go wrong: encouraged by the early success of the *kibbutz* we borrowed some money from the British aid agency Oxfam and bought two new farms. This expansion was a disaster. First it was too soon. We did not have the leaders for the new positions. Second, the huge injection of money, though it was a loan, created the idea that there was loads more where that came from. So the two new farms were not making ends meet like the first one. The election system was probably too egalitarian. We had agreed to change the leaders each year. But two of the leaders could not accept being deposed so soon. They left as the first year came to an end, and it looked as if there was not sufficient food put by for the second year. Others left. There was too much equipment. Much time was spent just mending it or running around in it. The new farms were clearly neglected. I would be slogging my way through the mud to the farm on foot, while the large truck would pass me on a ten-mile journey to buy a box of cigarettes. Meanwhile the bottom was beginning to fall out of the sugar market. The price plummeted to a fifth of its previous high. Sugar was piling up in warehouses and in swimming pools all over Negros. Then the oil hike came, putting the price of fertilizer and everything else through the ceiling. The first *kibbutz* was doing fine, but the two new ones were on the brink of collapse.

Our first Christian community seminar was a flop. Very few people turned up. I had left it to the labor leaders who were the unofficial parish council, presuming they had the contacts. Their attempts at forming Christian communities in outlying places had not come to anything. They did not seem to be enthusiastic about it. They were more displeased with me than I realized. I had continually postponed borrowing the trucks from the factory and getting them time off. Any time now that they spent with the parish was docked from their pay packet, and I rarely spent a night over a bottle of rum with them, which could have helped smooth things. They announced that they would be taking a rest. This is the Philippine euphemism for resigning, and it is not a bad one because it gives everyone a chance to breathe and to change their minds. I accepted their announcement and asked them to make it for only six months and then we would have a chance to review things.

But behind the various smaller irritants there were basic differences between us that I was unaware of at the time. The seminars they gave had a strong ideological orientation, based on social analysis and a fiery anti-rich note. The orientation I was asking them to take was liturgical, strongly based on Scripture and the social teachings of the Church. I felt social analysis was essential but must have the Nicodemus clause and a vocabulary that was less rigid, less ideological. They found the new waters tame after what they had been used to.

Then there were the Christian communities. Because of certain seminars the labor leaders had taken, they had come to realize just how much religion had been used to domesticate people, and these small Christian communities seemed to them like more opium, whereas to me the small Christian communities were potentially dynamite.

At this stage our differences were not surfacing in that form. Neither of us pushed our opinions too strongly, so our positions could have gradually merged. But working in a factory as they were, with rigid shifts, time off on company time was essential to them and I was not prepared to ask for that privilege from management. I knew I was right, but it did not soften the blow of their unanimous resignation.

I brought my troubles to Eugene, the parish priest of nearby Candoni.

Eugene had one extraordinary characteristic which I do not think I have seen in any other Western priest. I was going to say "ability," but rejected the word because it implies effort, and this thing was no effort for him. It was his special identification with, his compassion for, the people without ever compromising his own personality. The scene that comes to mind is Gene sitting in the *sala* lost in conversation with an old man. They both have a beer in hand. The sounds of hammering are coming from downstairs; someone is making a coffin. Meanwhile next to Gene the door of one of the sleeping rooms opens. A young man comes out and announces that his wife has given birth to a baby girl. Twenty people emerge from different rooms to look at the baby. The church bell begins to ring. A sacristan comes up quietly, holding a white soutane and a gold stole: "The bride has arrived, Padre. They had to wait till the river went down." As Gene makes his way to the church, he steps over several sleeping figures wrapped in blankets, which happen to be the *convento* curtains—the ones his sister Mary donated when she made a visit from Ireland. He passes some people cooking outdoors on stones. They don't want to smoke up the *convento* . . . their *convento*.

Well, I went to Eugene with my problem. I told him everything, including what I felt were my own faults in the matter. He had heard them anyway. So what should I do?

"Relax," Eugene said. "I've been through this myself. Several times. We are talking about a core group, the inner circle who help you run the whole thing . . . or rather you help them run it. More will come. They will emerge from those working around you. Don't force it. Don't spoil them. Just wait. And when they come, listen to them. You don't listen. By the way, that lad Junior who you've had working with you for the last seven years, I don't think you appreciate him half enough. You don't realize who you have there."

We spent the night drinking beer and swapping stories, although I had nothing to match Gene's stories of characters around his own village in County Kildare. My conversation tended toward analyzing situations and trying to understand them. Gene always moved back to people.

The plans for me to move out of the factory compound were very delicate. I first got the bishop's permission for a second house. He accepted the idea because he himself wanted the workers in the mill to move into *barrio* Tabugon eventually. He thought it was healthier and more normal than living in a factory compound. He wanted them to be able to have gardens. So he was trying to get loans from the bank for them to build their houses. But he wanted me not to neglect the management. He knew I was not close to them. So I planned a retreat for management immediately. But I also got down to planning the house.

It is amazing how the geography of a house can affect the relations of the people who live in it. The upstairs-downstairs, Spanish style of the *convento* meant that theoretically the priest was upstairs and the people down. But in fact some people were always allowed up. And the "some" tended to be the powerful ones. The "little" people stayed down. On the other hand, the few one-storied *conventos* I had seen allowed no privacy for the priest. The people were right on top of you. Philippine society is not particularly obsessed with privacy. I wanted a house in which people, all the people, would feel welcome, but in which I would have privacy when I wanted it. The house also had to be inexpensive. After all, it was a second house. And it would have to be naturally cool, as there would be no electricity with which to run a fan. So that meant it must be made of native materials.

I devised an octagonal shaped building with a balcony all around so that you could be away from the sun at any time of the day. Inside would be one big room divided in two by a bamboo wall. Looked at from above it was like a cake. I had three slices, the other five were for the people. My three sections had a bedroom, toilet, and study, with a door to my own balcony. By that balcony I could enter and leave privately if I wanted to at any time. Meetings or whatever could be going on in the main *sala* and I would be undisturbed. I would dine with the people, and the public balcony would allow casual visitors and delegations or groups to relax in the shade. Anyone who had more personal matters to talk about need only come right in.

Chapter 20

E_{VERY} now and again, a book comes along which puts a name to something important which for a long time you have been feeling or sensing but have not been able to articulate. This happened to me about this time. The book was a slim volume called *Power and Struggle*. It was Part I of a three-volume work: *The Politics of Nonviolent Action* by Gene Sharp.

Quite apart from my "religious" feelings about nonviolence I had an instinct that nonviolence worked. It made sense. When I got into Sharp's book I knew it was what I had been looking for. It was the confirmation and proof of what I had been suspecting all along. It is worthwhile taking a few minutes to look at his central thesis.

Sharp's theory of nonviolence emerges from his understanding of power. Theories of power can be boiled down to two theories really. In theory 1, power is monolithic; it comes from above; the people depend on the goodwill of the ruler; to overcome this power you must confront it and vanquish it with greater power. In theory 2, power is not intrinsic to the power-holder; it comes from below; the ruler gets power from the people, so if the people withdraw their consent, the ruler can no longer rule. It is to this second theory of power that Sharp holds. The only reason the first survives is because people believe it. It is very important, then, for those in power to keep those under them believing it. In a word, if Sharp's theory, that power comes from below, is right, then as soon as the people withdraw consent the government, no matter how strong militarily, will fall. I had no doubt that Sharp's view was right. Marcos did not depend on his three hundred thousand troops and one hundred thousand militia; even more he needed our consent, and the consent of each interlocking sector in the social pyramid, if the commands were to come down effectively to the lower levels. The whole world was to see this illustrated a short time later when the Shah fell, leaving his great armies intact behind him.

In Volumes II and III, Sharp explores the ways of getting people to withdraw consent—the art, the science, of nonviolence. He moves nonviolence out of the sphere of religion and says simply that it is a science which has been utterly neglected and which we must work at if we want to sharpen its tools and make them more effective. The three volumes look dry, but to me they were meat and drink. But I had no one to share them with.

When we Columbans met every couple of weeks at our central house in Batang, everyone had gruesome stories from their parishes of the latest atrocities against the people. I said little about nonviolence because I feared that it would sound unrealistic—another foreign theory being applied to the Philippine culture, even a ploy to distract us from the task at hand. One might expect to be asked: "Why only now are you talking about nonviolence? Have you spoken about nonviolence to the military?" Some would have been sympathetic to it for the wrong reason. They would grasp at the word since it expressed their opposition to the New People's Army. I do not think anyone understood it as a potentially all-powerful weapon against violence. In fact, I never found even one other person who understood it as I did, so I knew I must wait. Inside I was deeply happy because my own mind was content that the basis for nonviolence was not just a religious ideology but a historically demonstrable fact–when people withdraw consent, the powers fall. But I knew too that, in the history of violent weapons, we had come from using the jaw bone of an ass to nuclear warheads that could destroy the whole of the earth; in the history of nonviolent weapons we were still in the stone age.

Just about this time someone brought news of Elias. Elias and his family had come to live on the *kibbutz* from Sipalay. There he had shown extraordinary bravery when abducted by the military. He was a very gentle man and his parish priest, Terry Bennett, hoped to get him a chance for a livelihood away from danger. The members of the *kibbutz* agreed to accept Elias. He was a great worker and things went well for a while. But his wife was garrulous and did not get on well with the other women, who also greatly objected to the rowdiness of Elias's many children. They wanted Elias to punish his children. Elias said that this was out of the question. At a meeting they decided that Elias should punish the children, and Elias became depressed and disappeared. It was discovered that he was in a shack somewhere further up the mountain. I was asked to go to him. I did, and found Elias in this tiny shack sitting on the floor. "Elias, everyone wants you to come back. They miss you." Elias was silent. He just smiled shyly. "At least will you come and visit me tonight and we'll talk it over?"

That night Elias came and we spoke. I gave the other members' point of view: "Look, Elias, no one can stand children who are rowdy. They have to be told." Elias was silent. "A gentle tap on the back of the leg would not even hurt, but it would let them know that you disapprove of what they are doing."

"I couldn't."

"You couldn't give a little slap to the child?"

"I have never laid a hand on them. I couldn't. I could never lay a hand on a child." He was weeping.

I was now silent.

Eventually Elias told me about his life and how he had never laid a hand on *anyone,* how he had said to the people who had abducted him: "Do what you want to me, but I won't hit you back." They had obviously been confused by him. But he meant it. And so his life had always been. I extracted many of the stories from him.

When he had left that night I took out my diary and I wrote: "Just as I was despairing of ever meeting anyone who believed in nonviolence, from the most unexpected place one came. Elias, a man on the *kibbutz* who has never been to school, shared with me his life and how he would rather be killed than lay a hand on anyone. I now believe that I was wrong in thinking nonviolence is not known. The people have a vast treasure of it but we must know how to recognize it, to learn it from them, to develop it, and to hone it."

Finally, after all these years, my father was coming. He was stopping at Manila, part of a United Nations consultation team, and after that was going to come down to Negros. I was excited and planned to meet him in Manila. The night before leaving for Manila I stayed with the Redemptorist Fathers in Bacolod. Patrick Sugrue, one of the Redemptorists, was there, and he was the one who told me there was going to be an attack on me on television that night on a program called *Feedbacks,* sponsored by the Negros Planters Association. *Feedbacks* had been going for some time. It attacked any attempt at Church involvement in social matters and ridiculed or denigrated it. When the La Salle Brothers had started to teach social justice in their school, the program had organized a boycott of the school. It accused the Social Action director of the diocese, Toto Suplido, of stealing the funds. It was insulting to the bishop. And there were many attacks on the Columbans. Oddly enough we almost enjoyed them, they were, to us, so ridiculous. But I did not realize how many people who did not know us were beginning to be affected by this continual barrage of propaganda. Anyway, when I heard it was going to be against me, I was uneasy and wondered what the attack was going to center on. The style of the program was that the compère had guests or sometimes a sidekick who told him things about certain priests or religious orders. The compère always questioned such accusations with incredulity, whereupon the sidekick brought forward the proof. The compère was then reluctantly convinced.

The actual program opened with the sidekick saying something like: "Did you see the Columban Fathers are getting into the sugar industry?"

"No?"

"Yes. Father O'Brien has started a sugar farm. They plan to run it more justly than the planters do."

They then took the figures of our production and income for 1975 for the farm that was doing well and talked about them as if they were the figures for 1978. Of course the three years had seen drastic changes in sugar prices and in peso/dollar ratios so that they gave a completely false picture. Then they began to point out all sorts of contradictions, saying sarcastically that maybe the Columbans ought to take over the whole sugar industry. However, where were the profits going? That was the question. The implication was clearly that they were going to the New People's Army. And then came the personal attacks. The compère said: "I used to know Father O'Brien. He used to be a nice guy." And he shook his head sadly. The program seemed to go on and on. It was strange to be sitting there listening to a whole program exclusively given over to attacking you and a project which had been much criticized by others for being the opposite of radical—reformist and cosmetic. But so powerful are symbols and myths, even the shadow of a "socialist" experiment was considered a threat. And maybe they were right to consider it so. Its very acceptableness made it unacceptable. Sometimes reform preempts revolution. But they feared it would precipitate it.

The attack would have got me down if my father had not been arriving the next day. That was something so special that as soon as I was on the plane the next morning I put it all behind me.

Two things shocked Dad. One was a visit to a squatter area in Manila where a Columban priest, Colin McLean, was living in a tiny shack beside the others. The second was a trip we made over the mountains through the last of the logging concession of a lumber company, a U.S. company, which had been cutting the rain forests of Negros since the 1920s and now had reached the last stage of its noble work. On the way we had asked directions from a man. After getting the directions I asked him where he was going. He said he was just leaving his house at that moment to start on the long journey to Bacolod to attend a court case.

"A lawyer from the lowlands has claimed my land," he told us. And he pointed toward the piece of land around his house.

"How long has the case been going on?"

"Two years. Every time I go the hundred and twenty miles to Bacolod the case is postponed."

Dad was incensed that this poor peasant, living on a pathetic piece of land at the top of a mountain, would be the object of the greed of well-off lowlanders. And what was more it was clear that the courts were working against the poor man. This firsthand encounter did more than all I had said.

Many people have described how a relationship is transformed when a parent visits them for the first time on their homeground. In my case the transformation seemed to be from parent–child to father–son. Dad and I found ourselves able to talk about things we could never have talked about before, and Dad told me about some of the difficulties in his own life. When the holiday was over I said to myself that I would never have known him if he had not visited me.

Dad left a couple of weeks before Easter, and it was then that Nato reappeared. He had been rejected by the New People's Army and had a fever. In fact he had typhoid. We got the medicines, and he wrapped himself up in a sheet and lay on the floor. The tablets would help him to sweat it out.

Nato recovered from the fever and stayed with me for a holiday. When he was about to leave I gave him a letter recommending him to a Filipino priest as someone who could help with the parish work. Off he went, and the next news I had was that he was supporting himself by selling fish door to door; at the end of the day's work, he would help the Filipino priest, Father Rodelo, with his seminars on justice.

The rejection of Nato by the New People's Army was a mystery. The most likely reason was that he was a security risk. They were not sure of him. But his background was me. Was it that they were not sure of me? Had my position on nonviolence been interpreted that way? The thought disturbed me.

Chapter 21

O*N THE* road south from Bacolod to Kabankalan, at the town of Bago, you pass the white statue of a man on a prancing horse. It honors General Gregorio Araneta, a military gentleman who is credited with having helped defeat the Spaniards in 1898. That revolution did a lot for the *mestizo* élite and little for the peasants. The Aranetas still own the local sugar factory and a vast amount of the local land. The spot is called Crossing Araneta, but the people call it Crossing Cabayo ("The Crossing of the Horse").

Eighty years after that revolution another little revolt took place in Bago. On the five-hundred-hectare farm of Anghel Araneta, hungry laborers planted rice and vegetables on twenty-four acres of idle land. It looked as if there would be a major confrontation. To head this off, a dialogue was arranged between all the interested parties in which there would be a reasoned discussion of what had happened. The planters were anxious to avoid a precedent of land reform being set. Present at the meeting in the Bago City Hall, apart from the owner and the workers, were the city mayor, the city police chief, and Colonel Luzada of the constabulary. Father Edgar Saguinsin was there on the side of the workers. The bishop was invited to act as mediator. His presence assured the workers that they would be safe.

Halfway through the meeting, as the workers began to make their point with fearlessness since the bishop was there, the military appeared from nowhere and arrested Father Edgar Saguinsin and all the workers, including women and their babies.

The military made a mistake in doing this in the presence of the bishop. For years the bishop had heard it all secondhand from us. He believed us, but when he would confront the military, they would always either deny it absolutely or say that they had no control over the particular military unit.

Since we were always reporting on events that had taken place way up in the mountains or in the deep south, it was hard to contradict the military unless we had photographs; we were only gradually learning the value of the camera. This time, however, the bishop himself was present and he saw with his own eyes and shared the anguish when the thirty women and children were herded away with the others. He was incensed. And he resigned from the Church/military liaison committee and issued a pastoral letter. He wrote: "It is a sad commentary on the present situation that workers have to resort to means clearly high-handed in themselves in order to stave off hunger. What is clearly deserving of condemnation is the conduct of the military, which I denounce in no uncertain terms. The suspicion is very hard to shake that this meeting was arranged so that the people could be gathered together and picked up. . . . I have formally informed the provincial commander that I have resigned from the committee and withdrawn the Church representative."

Under this sting the military soon released the people, but a turning point had come in Church/State relations in Negros. It was clear that the military were not there to defend the rights of the people but to defend the rights of property against the people. This event marked a watershed in the life of the bishop. He had tried to be even-handed. We thought sometimes that he was too even-handed. But the attacks on his Social Action director, the personal attacks on himself, and the Bago "incident" raised his awareness.

Around this time a strange rumor had been going around Negros. It was clearly untrue, and even impossible, but the majority of the peasants and laborers, and most of the middle class, gave it a lot of credence. I think the only ones who did not believe it were the priests, who are after all trained in skepticism. The story was that children had been disappearing. What happened to them? *"Guinkidnap sila!"*—they had been kidnapped by Imelda Marcos. Everywhere you went people had stories to back it up. Two nuns I knew were sure they heard a cry from a suitcase in a bus. A doctor I knew said he did not believe it . . . except for two cases which he was sure of! All over the parish of Tabugon, school stopped because a great number of parents would not let their children out for fear of kidnapping. The supposed reason for the kidnappings was that Imelda was growing scales on her body like a fish, and the only way this could be stopped was for her to offer up sacrifices of children on the San Juanico Bridge—the huge multi-million-dollar bridge built as a prestige project between her own native island of Leyte and the island of Samar.

The kidnap story was believed by a huge number of people. It conveyed more of their feelings about the regime than their lips were capable of uttering. A myth can sometimes tell the truth more accurately than a historically correct narration of the "facts."

And in a sense, the tens of thousands of children who died from malnutrition were indeed offered up on the altar of San Juanico Bridge, of the Bata-an nuclear plant, of the Folk Arts Theater, and the other extravagant prestige projects which have left the country bankrupt and the poor starving, while money that should have been going for food goes to pay the interest on the debts of the regime.

Chapter 22

IN THAT first meeting with the Filipino priests we had fixed our order of priorities, and the first thing on the agenda was to recruit and train leaders for starting small Christian communities. After the attempts by the labor leaders had collapsed, I, two Sisters, and a seminarian called Ciano started to go out to the hamlets to try and start the communities. We got them started all right, but they soon died out. It became clear that it could not be done by leaders from the mills, or outsiders like ourselves. It would have to be leaders from the *barrios* and hamlets themselves who would start the communities.

So we fixed a date—in August of 1978—for a seminar to which we would invite all the potential leaders from the *barrios* and their surroundings. During this seminar we would try to discover those who would make suitable initiators of the Christian communities. All preparations in the parish led up to this seminar and, in my mind, it began to take on very great importance. I had been in the parish for nearly eighteen months and was just now about to shift my operations to Tabugon from Dakong-Cogon and the factory. It was really important that the seminar go well and that I start in Tabugon with reliable contacts from each area of the parish. So in my round of Masses and funerals and visits to the villages I kept my eyes peeled for possible candidates for the leadership seminar.

We held several meetings with the labor leaders (they had remained on friendly terms) and others who had joined the parish council since I came, and planned the seminar carefully. There would be five people from each of eight areas. Our method would be evocative—instead of trying to tell them what was important, we would evoke ideas from them. They were to teach us. We would ask them to try to define the problems of their area, and get them in groups to identify possible resources and come up with solutions to the problems. The story of the Philippines and the origin of the present land-holding system would give a rational basis to the discussions. A résumé of the social teachings of the Church would add direction. Songs carrying a justice theme would touch the heart. And Mass said in the intimate style of the Last Supper would give a taste in ritual and prayer—to experience the sort of caring communities we hoped to build. The seminar would last three days, so the living together would in itself be an exercise in community and a chance for people to get to know one another. But for me the most important thing would be to have a chance to observe and determine who was basically pro change and who was status quo.

By being aware of the role the different social classes played in the running of the system, we knew who *not* to make into leaders, but on the other hand the fact that you did not belong to a certain land-owning class said nothing positive about your qualifications *for* leadership. Social analysis did not tell us who would make good leaders. We had still to come up with some other "tool" to help us do that. Meantime, observing them at the seminar was the best we could do.

It must have been a week or more before the seminar that Perfecto, Nato's brother, arrived with bad news. Nato had been working very well in Bacolod with Father Rodelo, helping in his seminars while he supported himself selling fish. In Nato's *barrio* the son of the *barrio* captain had been accused in court of beating up a young man. Nato had testified in court against the captain's son. And the captain had responded by fabricating a case against Nato, something about throwing stones at the captain's house. Oddly enough, this case was thrown out of court.

Nato used to wash his fish at the faucet in front of the captain's house. The captain's wife now told Nato not to. He answered by saying that it was a public faucet and he had the right to use it. He continued to wash his fish there. His involvement in the seminars on injustice was provocation enough without all this. One evening Nato was set upon by the Barangay Brigade, a *barrio* militia—young thugs authorized under martial law to police the *barrio*. Some poor women of the *barrio* found Nato in a ditch, bleeding from eleven knife wounds. He had been in the hospital now for several days but his condition seemed stable. Perfecto had come to tell me this and was also collecting bottles which he was reselling to help pay for Nato's expenses. Father Rodelo and the women's group were making collections too. I didn't let Perfecto leave until I was sure of Nato's condition. I was relieved to hear that though he was serious he would pull through. I would visit him next time I was in Bacolod.

I went on with preparing for the seminar: food, sleeping arrangements, speakers, blackboards, song sheets, last-minute reminders to the candidates. Then on Friday afternoon a telegram came from Father Frankie

Connon: "NATO SERIOUS STOP HE WANTS TO SEE YOU." I read the telegram many times. The seminar was just about to begin. I told myself that I had no jeep, and that if I went the hundred-and-thirty-mile journey by public transport, I'd be gone for at least a day. I also knew that Nato was as strong as a horse. The long and short of it is that I convinced myself that the most sensible thing to do would be to go down on Monday on the public jeepney, change into the Columban van leaving Batang at eight, and get to Nato by 10:00 A.M. on Monday morning. I plunged into the seminar.

A great crowd came, unlike the first seminar. I soon got to know who was who. They divided naturally into three groups. The first were those who clearly saw the poverty of the people as the will of God and something that was of no great relevance to being a Christian—the poor were to be the objects of charity, thus increasing the merits of those who helped them. The second group could see that we should struggle to change the things that made people poor, and that this struggle was part of the struggle to be a Christian (this group was very small). The third group did not really know what the issue was.

We were supposed to be using the "evocative method," finding out from the participants what they felt their needs were, not telling them what we thought their needs were. Eventually, through open discussion by all, we hoped that the group would come to see that not every *felt* need was a *real* need, or at least not every felt need was a priority and that there were other needs. So *barrio* X would say they felt they needed a new church and *barrio* Y would say they felt they needed a nurse, or a lawyer to defend them, and as they gave their reasons we hoped that *barrio* X would say: "Oh yes, we too need a nurse, now that you mention it." Such was the planned process.

However, what happened was that almost all the groups—in spite of the talks which spoke again and again in favor of justice—took us by surprise when they met to list their needs. Most of them put the need of a chapel first. Sister Maria, who was helping as a facilitator, finally got so exasperated with one group that she spoke out: "You don't need a chapel. You need to demand the minimum wage for the menfolk working on the farms round about." And at this point, as I watched her obvious steamrollering, the scales fell from my eyes. What Sister had done openly we had all been doing unconsciously right through the seminar: putting words into the mouths of the people and trying to get them to give us back the answers we wanted to hear. If we went on this way we would end up with a parish plan that came from us and not from them, and that would be doomed to failure.

I called an emergency meeting with the staff when we had a break and pointed out what we had fallen into doing. We changed our approach in midstream. If they, after careful discussion, said they needed a chapel, then we must accept that.

In the last part of the seminar each group made up a plan of action for their *barrio* based on the needs and resources they had identified. Most had planned to build or renovate their chapels.

Though tired, we met that night to evaluate the seminar. It had been a success. We had identified several possible good leaders. We had identified a couple of people who must be avoided at all costs. And we had learned a lot about the parish. One thing was clear: for the majority of people in the parish being a Christian basically amounted to ritual and its needs. It was good to have no illusions and to know that one of our major tasks would be "relating religion to life."

We now had contacts in every corner of the parish and they had each prepared their plans—in most cases, to build a chapel. By this stage I was realizing that that was a good thing—the working together at something they all believed in, the teamwork, the sense of something achieved when it was done. And they had chosen something that was specific, attainable—and yet it held a challenge. I saw too that precisely in working for this community project the natural leaders would emerge. This would be the "tool" I had been looking for. Listening to them had paid off. I was happy with the outcome and prepared my overnight bag to travel north the following morning.

A jeepney took me the thirty miles down the mountain to Kabankalan, where I changed to a bus for Batang and where we had our resthouse. There I caught up with our own Highace van which used to go north every Monday morning with any Columbans who wished to go to Bacolod. It was still the old road, as bad as when I first arrived. Though millions of pesos had been appropriated by the Negros provincial government to do a new road, the money had disappeared without a trace, leaving the roads in an even worse condition, because the company supposedly hired to do the job folded after it had broken up the good parts of the old road. The journey was tortuous, and as Rolando painstakingly steered around the potholes, we lapsed into silence. Suddenly Paul Richardson said to me: "That was sad about your friend Nato. He was your friend, wasn't he?"

"What was sad?"

"About him dying."

"No. I think he is recovering."

"No. He died on Saturday."

I was frightened. I did not believe him and I did not want to believe him. How would he know, anyway? I began to quiz him up and down, picking holes in each of his answers as to how he had heard.

As soon as we reached the city outskirts I asked Rolando to stop the van and I got out and hailed a taxi and got the driver to rush across the city to the parish of Father Rodelo where Nato had been helping. I paid the taximan and hurried to the door of the church. There was no one around.

Inside the empty church, standing on trestles in the middle of the aisle, was a coffin. A solitary figure stood bent over the coffin, gazing into the little window which had been made in the lid. It was Nato's younger sister, Nena.

Nena looked up and, seeing me, threw herself into my arms, her whole body shaking with sobs of grief and despair. Mine were of compassion and loss and guilt.

Father Rodelo had been away when Nato died. In the following days, as we waited for him to return, the stories began to come out: all the work Nato had done in the parish, his bravery, how his days in hospital had galvanized the women of the parish to get together and make collections for his medicine, how when he would be selling his fish if it was an old woman who was buying he would go into the shack and gut the fish for her as well, the way in the hospital he would insist to visitors, with a wink at a comely nurse, that he was going to get better. And then, when he knew he was dying, his words that he was happy that his suffering had united the people of the parish. His last words had been: "I can't take it any more." And with those words he died instantly. He must have hung on by sheer willpower long beyond the time he should have gone. Had he been waiting for somebody? Only I knew.

The rain streamed down on the kilometer-long funeral procession. Nobody cared, certainly not I. We were silent as we walked, but the banners and leaflets made it a protest for all the victims of the regime. When we got inside the Bacolod cemetery, we assembled in front of the ten-foot-thick wall in which a hole stood ready to receive the coffin. The coffin was opened for the last time, so that Nena and Perfecto and little Toto could have a last look. I noticed a young man, all serious, slip something into the coffin. I craned to see what it was. It was a bottle, a bottle of one-year-old rum. The young man saw my look and whispered: "It was Nato's wish." I smiled through my tears and the rain, thinking that in years to come someone would discover it and never know what it meant or whose bones these were.

They began slowly to push the coffin into the deep cavity in the wall. Suddenly there was a blood-curdling shout, and Perfecto threw himself on his brother's coffin. I cannot forget that terrible cry of rage and desolation.

On the way home I remembered many things Nato had told me: the death of their mother and father, the desolation when their adopted mother committed suicide. One image in particular stayed in my mind. Nato and Perfecto are orphans, still only eight and eleven years of age. They are looking in a canefield for spiders to play with. Suddenly the owner of the field appears, draws a gun, and terrorizes the children by firing at their feet. I remembered too Nato's arrival on the *kibbutz* and his excitement at being put in charge of the horse Diablo. He would charge up at breakneck speed and stop within an inch of you; I remembered the time when we had gone on that long trek together and he had pretended we were a long way off when we were already there; the time he walked thirty kilometers to get a parrot for Betty, my visitor from Ireland. I thought of Perfecto selling bottles to try and pay for Nato's medicine. And the urgent telegram: "NATO SERIOUS STOP HE WANTS TO SEE YOU."

And I thought about myself. Nato had wanted to say goodbye to me because he was an orphan and I had become his father and yet I had not come; I was too busy. I was struggling so hard to help the people that I could no longer see the person. I was so intent on being a Christian that I had failed to be even human. I looked back over the years and all I could see was the same pattern. And I was filled with fear that somehow I was only a shell.

Chapter 23

SOON after Nato's death I moved to Tabugon. I was the first priest ever to live there, and the *barrio* people appreciated that I had left the much more comfortable surroundings of the factory. There would be no electricity, therefore no running water, no lights, no fan. There were a few kerosene refrigerators in the *barrio* and one automobile-battery-run television. Roads were nonexistent.

The wooden church was crowded for my first Sunday. I told the people why I had moved, and I chose as my text the passage from the Gospel of St. Luke in which Jesus gives his first sermon in Nazareth, his hometown: "The Spirit of the Lord is upon me, because he has anointed me to bring good news to the poor. He has sent me to proclaim release to the captives and recovering of sight to the blind and to set at liberty those who are oppressed, to proclaim the acceptable year of the Lord.

"Sisters and brothers, you are dear to me, and that is why I have come to live among you. I have chosen this Gospel specially because it describes the first time Jesus spoke in his hometown just as he was beginning his life's work. This occasion was for Jesus like a priest's first Mass: a very important moment. It was also the time he spelled out just what he planned to do and why he had come. He said: 'I was sent to bring good news for the poor, . . . to set the captives free, . . . to liberate the oppressed.' That was to be his life's work: working for the liberation of the oppressed. If I want to be faithful to my obligation as a disciple of Jesus, then I must do the same, and with your help I would like to do that here. That means taking the side of the poor; and this is not easy, because we priests are always tempted to be silent, to keep quiet, then some people will donate to the church and leave sacks of rice at the *convento*. My problem is that among my many weaknesses I have one special one: when I get to know someone I find it hard to oppose them; and yet it's something I must do if they are land-grabbing, using the military against the people, taking poor people to court in order to scare them, acting as informers for the military. So if you are doing these things, please don't make friends with me. It will only make it so difficult for all of us when we have to oppose each other and maybe break the friendship. Why do I say all this? Because as your priest you want me to lead you into the presence of God, and I want you to lead me there. But it cannot be done unless we are struggling for justice. That is why at his very first sermon Jesus said that this was the number one reason why he had come into the world."

It would be a long time before the church was so full again on an ordinary Sunday, and when that happened the makeup of the congregation would be distinctly different.

In the Catholic tradition sacraments have been a very important part of religious life ever since the earliest times. There is a sacrament for every stage of life: baptism at birth, confirmation at puberty, marriage and ordination for settling down, confession and Communion all the way through, and anointing for sickness, viaticum at death. They are meant to bring the reality of Jesus risen into daily life, but they keep getting out of hand. They easily decline into superstition and become an escape from life instead of a challenge to live boldly. They can be used to bless an unjust system and deodorize it instead of critiquing it. They can become a fearful obligation instead of a joyful gift. And most obviously they can become a part of religious commerce—the sort of commerce Jesus banned from the Temple.

Most people felt that the way sacraments were done when they were a child was the way they were always done, whereas in fact the sacraments had changed radically again and again throughout the centuries.

Being on the liturgical commission, I had been involved a bit in the translation of the sacraments. As soon as we had them translated, we knew they had to be "inculturated," the symbols adapted to the culture of the Philippines. The commission had done a good job on this, bringing Philippine customs into the marriage ceremony and the Easter liturgy. Now two more things needed to be done. The sacraments must be separated from money and they must challenge the unjust system under which we lived. It must be clear to someone receiving a sacrament that the Christian life to which the sacrament summoned them was a life that worked against injustice. For example, in baptism there was the dialogue between the priest and the people:

"Do you believe in God the Father?"

"We do believe."

"Do you believe in God the Son?"

"We do believe."

"Do you believe in God the Holy Spirit?"

"We do believe."

Now we had it read:

"Do you believe in God the Father who created the earth for all men and women to have enough to live?"

"Do you believe in God the Son who came into the world to bring good news to the poor and to liberate the oppressed?"

"Do you believe in God the Holy Spirit who makes us all sisters and brothers?"

Then there were the renunciations. The traditional formula read:

"Do you renounce Satan?"

"We do."

"And all his works?"

"We do."

"And all his pomp?"

"We do."

Now it read:

"Do you renounce land-grabbing?"

"Do you renounce militarization?"

"Do you renounce usury?"

"Do you renounce the use of torture?"

It was necessary to separate the sacraments from money because when people saw, for example, that they had to do a seminar before baptism some of them just took their babies to a parish where no seminar was required. The fact that they were paying for it seemed to justify "shopping around." Baptism was reduced to a commodity, whereas we were trying to say that it was a challenging encounter with Jesus—challenging us to confront the unjust system which would not let us be the sisters and brothers baptism proclaimed us to be.

It was easy for a foreign priest to talk about dropping payment at the time of sacraments, but some sort of acceptable system of funding had to be found, or how could the Filipino priests take over? As it was, they lived very frugally compared to me. They had not invented the system; they inherited it from us. An obvious way to change would be to emphasize the voluntary offering at Mass, but the collection at that first Mass brought in only about ten pesos (equivalent to about a dollar). It was clear that the Sunday Mass offering had never developed. Why should it? People felt they were paying already when they got the sacraments. It was a vicious circle.

Until now I had had no right to introduce anything, as I had not been a parish priest. Now I was beginning anew in a remote parish where what I did would not embarrass others, so I decided to make a start. If I could not do all, I would do some, and I would try gradually to wean the sacraments away from being a *quid pro quo*. I felt they could never have their full spiritual and human meaning as long as they were caught up in commerce.

The first thing I did was to refuse all payment for funerals and services for the dead. I felt death was no time to be talking money. No one could prepare for it and they had enough on their minds without that. True, there were those who could afford it, but the majority were so poor. So give the services to the poor free. No, that stigmatizes them. Let all be the same: free. So, no payment for funerals.

Now that had an interesting result. While I was in Dakong-Cogon the poor just did not bring their dead to be blessed. I thought the distance might be the problem. The Cebuanos I had seen walking barefoot along the road carrying a coffin and a bar to dig a hole looked wretchedly poor and exhausted. At first in Tabugon it was the same. They walked straight past the *convento* carrying the coffin to the graveyard and did not stop to ask for a blessing. But as they realized that it would not create a financial embarrassment, that changed. After a while no one passed by, and I would often come home to find twenty people sitting silently on whatever side of the balcony was away from the sun, and the coffin waiting there with them.

Baptism and marriage were more complicated. The offering at baptism was paid by sponsors, as was part of the wedding offerings. To interfere here, Paul pointed out, would be to disturb an intricate web of social relationships. I decided that I would freeze these fees at the present rate and let inflation gradually reduce them to a nominal amount. Meantime I was trying to discuss with the other priests in the mountains some sort of common policy.

Mass offerings posed a special problem. It is an old Catholic custom to have Masses offered for the dead or for a special intention or in thanksgiving for some grace you have received. For this people give a gift of money to the priest. In countries where there are many priests there is a set sum designated and everyone can afford it. But in a country like the Philippines, where the gap between rich and poor is so great, the poor could not really afford it. So once again the sacrament was confirming the gap instead of challenging it. I solved this for myself by announcing: "If you wish to have Mass offered for your personal intentions, for thanksgiving, for the dead, write the name or the intention on a piece of paper and leave it on the altar. I will read out the intentions and offer the Mass for them. And if you wish to make an offering, drop it anonymously into the collection box when it is going round."

That left blessings. Philippine religious custom is full of blessings: boats and buses, tricycles and houses, just about everything. It is a way of saying,

"The things of the earth are good." Well, I just let the offering for these drop, but I made sure that in my blessing just wages for the driver of the truck were mentioned, as well as the safety of those who travel the roads.

Sometimes the thing to be blessed occasioned special difficulties. The previous parish priest had refused to bless the house of a planter who was not treating his laborers properly, and I hoped the man would not ask me, because I would have had to refuse him too under the circumstances. On one occasion I was inveigled into blessing a boat of a wealthy man. I had reason to refuse, but also reason to say "Yes." His fishermen looked really wretched. So out we went into the sea up to our thighs, the crew of the boat and the owner and me, the book of blessings in one hand, the holy water in the other. After the opening prayers and a reading from the storm on the Sea of Galilee, before I blessed the boat, I introduced some catechesis after the manner of the baptism ceremony.

"Do you promise to pay these men a fair wage? . . . Do you promise to look after their social welfare cards? . . . Do you promise to look after their families if anything should happen to them at sea?"

If I surprised the fishermen who were witnesses, the owner surprised me by saying a fervent "Yes" to each request. And somehow I felt he meant it. At that moment anyway.

Chapter 24

S*MALL* Christian communities in the *barrios* and hamlets began to take root. Our three first approaches had failed. Approach one was when the original labor leaders had gone out to the villages and tried to start the communities; that had come to nothing. Approach two was when I and Ciano, a seminarian, had gone to the villages; we were received with open arms, the communities were initiated, but soon after we were gone they died out, and we heard no more. Approach three was when two Sisters volunteered to concentrate in one *barrio*. They spent months, most of a year, and when they were finished all they had was a very obedient *barrio*, with lots of songs at worship but no community, because the people were not making their own decisions. The Sisters had made the mistake of allowing themselves to be continually supported by the local landowner, who knew just what he was doing. His foreman was elected worship leader. He made all the decisions and now controlled the community even more completely than before. The Sisters succeeded in getting the landowner to raise the wages, but he did it because they requested it, not because the peasants got together and asked. So the people had a little more money until the next bout of inflation wiped it out, but no community emerged in the process.

The approach which finally worked was startlingly simple. At a marriage interview or at a funeral, I would meet a group from a certain hamlet the name of which I had hardly heard before. I would say: "Do you want to start a small Christian community?"

"Will you come and say Mass for us?"

"No, not yet. Why don't you start your own worship service yourselves?" And I would give them a *panimbahon* book with all the steps for a worship service made out simply. "Now you see the Gospel's here. . . . There are questions after them in which you can apply the Gospel to the problems of your own community. The next step is to list all the sick, the old, and the lonely in your village and start to attend to them. And then of course you can start building a chapel. When everything is going, then call me."

Months would go by and maybe I would never hear from them again. But sometimes someone would arrive to say that they had started the community, their chapel was built, things were going, and they wanted Mass. The seed had fallen on fertile ground.

Then I would say: "Well, first I would like you to have a small seminar on what a Christian community really is."

And out our little team would go to give what amounted to a simple explanation of the five-pointed star, the five essential points of a small Christian community. Then there would be a group discussion of the passage from Luke's Gospel: "I was sent to bring good news to the poor." And sometime later they would have their first Mass.

By the time I arrived for the Mass they were ready. I made sure I did not leave there without making it clear that being a disciple meant sharing in community. The Mass became the celebration of that community. We finished with a community meal for the whole hamlet.

I had gone back to worship as an entry point. People wanted to worship. They made it clear that worship was very important to them. The answer had been to concede it as an entry point, but not a finishing point, to insist from the beginning that worship unaccompanied by community sharing would be a counter-sign—a backward step on the road to discipleship.

The next step was that people in the next hamlet would witness the results and come in to the *convento* and say: "We want to start a Christian community."

Now I was in a position to be more demanding because they were asking me.

"So you want to start a Christian community. Well, it's like this. . . ." And I would tell them the following story: "The man who cut the grass for this thatch"—pointing to the roof of the *convento*—"lives out in Na-Salayan. A few weeks ago he walked in all the way from that place, which is about ten kilometers away, carrying his wife on his back. As he walked his little child of three ran along beside him clinging to his trouser leg. And another child of eight carried the baby. His wife was so far gone with T.B. that she was only bones. He told me that for a year she has not been able to sleep well. They have no pillow, so at night when they lay down he would stretch out his arm and she would lie on it the whole night. If Na-Salayan had had a Christian community, that man would not have walked in alone. The men of the hamlet would have carried his wife in a baby's hammock, the women would have looked after the children, and the community health committee would have looked for medicines for the sick woman and told us about her condition months ago. Now it is certainly too late. You have a Christian community when you can lie down at night knowing that in your village no one is sick who is not being attended to, no one is persecuted who is not being helped, no one is lonely who is not being visited."

I knew in my heart that I was asking from the people a degree of sharing which I was not doing myself and which I was not capable of; but it was now quite some time since I had come to the belief that I should not prevent others from reaching something I could not reach. Nor did I regard it as hypocrisy to encourage them to aim for something which I was not able to do. I was not their model; they were mine and each other's.

As time went by, we came to the conclusion that about thirty families was just about right for a community, a face-to-face community. Any more would dilute the experience of personal caring. There seems to be a human and psychological limit to the number of people to whom you can relate closely, so we multiplied communities rather than having big ones. In the village of Tabugon alone we had seven or eight communities.

Living in the *barrio* of Tabugon, close to these communities, I got to know their leaders very well. They formed a natural group and felt at home coming to the *convento*. Together we planned two one-day seminars to be given to the new communities. The first was the "five-pointed star" seminar, which we called phase one, and then we had a phase-two seminar in which the details, the nitty gritty, of justice were spelled out. Going back to Paul Hitz's study of the early Church, our phase-one seminar could be called evangelization, announcing the good news, while our phase-two seminar was like catechesis, spelling out the consequences for daily living of the good news. The consequences were mostly social, but not exclusively so. In practice, phase one acted as a mechanism for "screening out" those who were only prepared to accept religion as a "consolation." They did not come back to phase two. The type of people associating themselves with the Church throughout the parish began to change.

The *kibbutzim* got back on their feet, and their leaders too were able to give a seminar on human rights, traveling around the new communities.

Finally, to round out our educational plan we gave two other seminars: a pre-baptism seminar and a pre-marriage seminar. The first emphasized the idea that being a Christian meant challenging the unjust status quo. The second was on family life. People who were free on Sundays gave these seminars.

All the seminar-givers would meet in the *convento* each week, and we would plan the schedule for the next seminars, especially the monthly meeting of all the Christian community leaders. That monthly meeting became the most important day of the month for us. It took place every last

Saturday, and on the Thursday before the meeting I would stand around the market and remind new communities about the meeting.

The meeting started with a reflection on a Scripture passage. Then reports from all the communities on how they were doing and their problems. The other leaders offered advice. Then some sort of "in-service training"—for example, how to run a group dialogue. Then news from the diocese, and schedules for the coming month.

Some leaders came twenty kilometers, others only ten, but from inaccessible places. Without realizing it we had developed a powerful communications network, which would be invaluable when the military began to threaten us later on.

Jimmy Martin and Eugene McGeough constantly reminded me of the necessity of picking two or three from these leaders who would be very close to me and would monitor the decisions I made, and better still make them with me. It would be a core group. It was the job of the core to keep in touch with what was going on in the diocese and to help chart the direction we were going in by planning the weekly and the monthly meetings. Except for Junior, who was working with me since the Sa-Maria days, I still had no core group. Things were beginning to get very busy and I noted that basically they all depended on me. Meetings would not begin without me. Decisions would not be finalized in my absence. I was the only one who was in on everything, and as a result I was the only one with a grasp of the overall picture. I was also full of ideas and suggestions. I was the center of the wheel, and that was not a good thing. It could lead to paralysis or disaster. I must plan to broaden the center and lessen the dependence on one person. And I had another special reason for this.

Up to this time no scholarly history of Negros had been written. Recently, however, there had appeared a *Historia de la Isla de Negros,* the dissertation of a Spanish Recollect priest, Angel Martinez Cuesta. It was a faithful chronicle of Church events between the coming of the Spaniards and the eve of their expulsion. As I read it, one recurring pattern leaped out at me. The Spaniards had come to the Philippines in 1565. They had come to Negros but never had enough people to make inroads. Their first attempt at evangelization when they arrived all but died out for lack of priests. Also, the Muslim pirate raids from the southern Philippines made it impossible to keep things prospering without having troops for self-defense. Such troops were not available. The Muslims, like the Vandals in Europe a millennium before, would burn everything, cut down trees, kill the old, and make slaves of the young—so the chronicle of Cuesta records. Once the friars left, the first Christian settlements died out. Then around 1630 the Jesuits threw themselves at the job. They took over Kabankalan, Ilog, and Isio. They were from Bohemia and their diaries are preserved in the Jesuit archives in Rome. They describe journeys down south from Kabankalan toward Sipalay. They could not go through the forests, but went by boat. Fowl, they recorded, had not been domesticated in that part of the island; an egg was a treat. Everything prospered with them because they worked as a team and had a clear idea of what they wanted.

The Jesuits in the Philippines were suppressed in 1767 by Charles III, and when they left Negros everything went to seed for a second time.

In the mid-nineteenth century, Negros breathed new life. The new steamships brought more Spaniards through the Suez Canal instead of around Africa and the Cape of Good Hope or all the way across from Mexico. And the same steamboats were able to outdistance the *moro vintas*—fast sailing boats—which had terrorized Negros for so long. The Recollect Friars arrived around 1850, building churches, *conventos*, roads, bridges, and a few schools. By the end of the century they had many thriving parishes. However, after the Philippine revolution the Recollects were expelled with the other Spanish officials, and the Church in Negros collapsed again.

Why had the Church all but disappeared three times? Why had the parishes evaporated when the priests were removed? It seemed to me that the answer lay in the fact that religion to a great extent had been reduced to ritual. Since the priest was the sole guardian of the ritual, when you removed him everything else went too.

We were a fourth wave in four centuries, and the same would happen to our work unless the people themselves became the Church. With the present social unrest it was not inconceivable that there would follow a long period in this mountain area without priests. Now we too were priest-centered, even in this parish, because in fact everything came to depend on me. The priest had become the Church. Organizationally this was a bad idea; historically it had been fatal; theologically it was heretical. The Church is and always was the people, the community of *disciples* who loved each other and lived in the presence of the risen Lord and in service of "the world." Ritual had no meaning unless it sprang from such a community and gave expression to it and confirmed it. What became clear was that the Church in Negros had been so priest-centered that it almost vanished when the priests were taken away. Christians seemed to be always getting their energy from outside. It was being pumped in. They were not their own motors. There was nothing to stop a recurrence of the same phenomenon should the priests be taken away again, unless the people themselves were the generators of their own faith. They must become self-supporting, self-nourishing, self-propagating communities.

To the extent that faith did survive, you discovered that the people had preserved it often through their own popular religious devotions, the very devotions of which I had been so critical when I first arrived—their saints' days, their statues, their processions, their tattered novenas, their *fiestas*—and they had even incorporated pre-Christian symbols into these Christian rituals.

I was justifiably worried about the degree to which so much of the activity depended on me, and I felt I must be able to hand everything over to them more and more. I must translate into our organization what I had realized theologically.

Because the new leaders had emerged from the poorer classes, few of them had education beyond elementary school, so it was difficult for them to move to the level of general discussion and analysis of where we were going. There was also going to be a problem with the Scriptures.

The small Christian communities rely heavily on the Scriptures. It is necessary, however, to steer a course between the hazard of treating the Bible as a mere symbol and that of succumbing to a fundamentalist literalism. Christian scholars have come to considerable agreement on the basic or first-level meaning of the Scriptures in the last half-century; these developments were being accepted by the Church as far back as the time of Pius XII. Nevertheless, even educated Catholics were more or less unaware of this consensus and contented themselves with asking the priest if a question arose. Now the comparatively unschooled people of the mountains would be expected to interpret these Scriptures in their own communities. Did we not risk their falling into a combative fundamentalism on the one hand or being co-opted by a narrow dogmatic Marxism on the other, well capable of using the Scriptures for its purposes?

There were other areas—for example, group dynamics—in which our leaders needed training I was not capable of giving. We needed a method of teaching that took into account our belief that the people themselves had the answers to most of their problems, that the joys and hopes and yearnings of the people must be listened to and read by us as God speaking to us in our time. The traditional method of teaching, which Paolo Freire called the "banking" method, implied that we had all the answers and the people should just listen and be filled with our wisdom; we had it stored up, and all we needed to do was to transmit it to them. Since the Council we had rediscovered the "evocative" method. This method held many pitfalls. It was so easy to imagine you were evoking *their* ideas, imagine that you were listening to *them*, while all the time you were just getting back the echo of your own voice. The evocative method demands honesty, humility, skill, and a bit of common sense, because it does not cover all knowledge and, for a believing Christian, there is a core of enlightenment which is not reducible to experience. I knew I was not good at the evocative approach. My training had been in the banking system, in debate rather than in dialogue.

In the seminary we held debates, and the aim was not to give your opponent an inch. In philosophy class we learned the art of logic. The aim was often to pin your opponent into a corner with relentless premises and conclusions until you showed him that you were right and he was wrong. But dialogue is quite a different matter. It starts with the premise that both of you have something to contribute. Learning the truth is going to be a process by which you combine the knowledge and experience of all into a coherent whole.

Behind the two methods of teaching—the evocative and the banking, dialogue and debate—were two theological visions: one which saw revelation as ceasing with the death of the Apostles, or at least fixed at that point, and the other which saw revelation as ongoing in history. The Church had room for both insights, but Church people were uncomfortable with paradoxes and preferred to push for one or the other. I felt it had to be both, but I did not feel I had the ability to get across to our leaders this twofold skill of reading the "word" both in the Scriptures and in the lives of the people and then teaching others to do this as well. It's one thing to understand something yourself, another to teach it to others, and another still to teach it to others so that they too can teach it. But that was what I wanted.

So when I learned that Peter Leonard and Elizabeth Moran, both Columbans in Ozamis City on the island of Mindanao, were running a course in Christian community living and offering just those skills, I was delighted. The course was called "The Community Life Seminar." It differed radically from the Sa-Maria. The Sa-Maria looked to conversion; this presumed conversion and insisted that "community" was one of the unavoidable consequences of discipleship, something which had been missing from the Sa-Maria. This course taught community and the skills necessary for building communities. Back to Paul Hitz: If the Sa-Maria was the evangelion, the good news, then this was the catechesis—the true second stage.

The team in Ozamis agreed to accept four of our leaders to do a six-week course. As the group set off from Tabugon to the eastern side of the island of Negros to take the boat to Mindanao, I knew that we had passed another milestone.

Chapter 25

ONE DAY a young girl called Neneng came up to Tabugon from San Ramon. I had known her when I lived on the plantation. Our knowing each other came about by an unusual chain of events.

I had won first prize in a raffle, and this entitled me to a lot near the sea on which to build a house. One of the priests of San Ramon parish, seeing the plight of Neneng and her widowed mother and blind aunt, put them to live on the lot I had won . . . or what he thought was the lot I had won. The map they consulted was faulty, so that they were in fact put to live beside the lot which I had won. No one was aware of this at the time. The widow and her sister collected the fronds which fell from the surrounding coconut trees. From their fronds they extracted the spines, and bunching them together they made brooms to sell.

Neneng's mother then came to me and said that now that she was living on *my* land I was her *amo* (master) and was bound to support her. She was not trying one on; she was simply articulating the feudal principle of land. In return she would doubtless defend me, and if I was going for election (which, before martial law, was the way of doing battle), she would carry my standard. Very thin and sickly, she looked pathetic, but she was in fact a formidable creature. Her only son had been killed in a brawl and she had received no satisfaction. She carried this wound of injustice all the time. She insisted it was my duty to put her daughter through school. Which I did. The daughter in return directed anyone in need to me! Among those she directed were an ailing old couple for whom I had arranged operations in the Bacolod provincial hospital. The doctors in that hospital did both the operations free. This couple also suffered subsequent illnesses, which I looked after as best I could.

Now, when Neneng appeared in Tabugon carrying a letter, I gave a sigh. The letter said that the old man was sick and would I visit him.

"Neneng, you've got to understand that living now in the mountains my circumstances are much more difficult. I'm short of money. The transportation is so expensive, and it's fifty miles from here . . . and you know we are training the people here to look after the sick themselves, so that the priest should not always be the one."

"Well, they just want to see you."

"I know, Neneng, but it always means one thing. And they have a parish priest down there much better off than I am. And why don't you start a Christian community?"

"Are you going to go to them?"

"Yes." But as I said it I thought: "I will not surrender easily. I am up to my eyes with the sick people here."

When I got to San Ramon I made my way to the coconut grove where the houselots had been designated. It was a commentary on the declining sugar industry that that particular housing project had run out of steam. The old people lived in a simple one-room shack. They were both lying on the floor. The old man said he would like to confess. I asked those who had come with me to leave the room for a moment, then I knelt down beside him. When he had done I sat down on the floor and we talked about this and that till we came to his illness. He was not feeling well at all.

"Maybe you need a visit back to the hospital," I said, going back on all my resolutions and capitulating before the first shot was fired.

"No, it would be a waste of money."

"No it wouldn't. Anyway, you know the doctors are very understanding. They don't charge me, except for the medicines."

"No, Padre. That's not why I called you."

"You have a special reason for calling me?"

"Yes, Padre. I called you to thank you for all you have done for me and my wife, and to say goodbye."

In the Philippines it is customary for a father or mother to "say goodbye" to their children before they die. These farewell words are called *panu-gubilin* in Ilongo. I realized then that that was why the old man had called me.

I prayed with him and, bending over him, I whispered in his ear. I told him that sometimes I found the going tough and I needed the help of his prayers. I took his hand and touched the back of it with my forehead in the *amen*—an ancient Filipino act of piety.

As I took my leave his wife pointed to four coconuts and two papayas waiting near the door. "Take those, Padre, they are our gift to you."

The problem of providing care for the sick was getting worse. When I was in Kabankalan I hardly noticed it, mainly because I did not consider it part of my business. In the Sa-Maria house on the plantation it was forced on me. But then there was Meding, who got the doctors to do most things *gratis,* and searched for free medical samples for my patients. Candoni was a nightmare without a permanent doctor, and with such a long, rocky road to Kabankalan. By the time I got to Dakong-Cogon I had realized that caring for the sick was as essential as announcing the word. In fact it *was* announcing the word. But by this time I had also realized that self-reliance was essential to people's dignity and growth, and however I helped it must be in a way which did not undermine this dignity. That created conflict and at times agony.

The root of the problem lay in the Philippine medical system. It was unabashedly a profit industry, modeled closely on its American counterpart. You could not even enter most hospitals without showing some proof of collateral. Many hospitals had guards at the door to stop patients escaping. The local drug industry was cornered by Marcos's cronies. You paid more for an aspirin in Tabugon than in Manila by the time all the middlemen had had their cut. Doctors were offered coupons by drug companies for prescribing their drugs; I knew of a doctor who purchased a jeepney with these coupons. Drugs forbidden in the United States were exported to the Philippines. The World Health Organization had been complaining of this and the fact that generic drugs were unavailable in the Third World countries; you could only get them in brand name form, which was much more expensive. They said that one hundred giant Western drug companies controlled most of the Third World drugs trade. To put it bleakly, the profit from sickness in the Third World was going back to the First World.

The medical schools were another industry. Even the Church-sponsored ones prepared doctors and nurses not to work in the Philippines but to work in the United States. The courses were geared toward taking the U.S. medical exams. The training was a carbon copy of the training in the U.S., and it was so expensive that even those doctors and nurses who would like to work at home had also to think in terms of paying off the debt that they had incurred during long years of training. At that time some ten thousand Filipino doctors—about forty percent of the total—were in the United States, and fifty thousand Filipino nurses abroad, at a time when most *barrios* and many towns like Candoni had no doctor. The distribution of each new graduating class of doctors was forty percent abroad, thirty-three percent to the cities, and twenty-six percent to the rural areas (where seventy percent of the people lived).

In one direction I saw hope. For a few years now a group of nuns from several orders had banded together to form the Rural Mission Sisters, and under the inspiration of a young Filipino doctor, Jimmy Tan, they pioneered what they called the Community-Based Health Program (the

C.B.H.P.), not unlike the barefoot doctors of North Vietnam. It seemed to be just what we needed.

Jimmy Tan had been a star student of medicine at the University of the Philippines. One summer he spent some time on an island helping out. Heavy seas made it impossible for him to get medicines and so he resorted to herbs and other native cures. When he got back to Manila he had some of the herbs tested, and discovered that the people had worked out the exact combination of herbs which would produce the correct antidote to a dangerous and little-known poison. Jimmy was converted and his approach to medicine became very similar to ours in Church matters. He said the people could do most of it themselves. He pushed self-reliance on all fronts: the use of herbs rather than drugs, home rather than hospital, and prevention rather than cure. Since malnutrition was a main cause of sickness, the trail led clearly back through lack of food to lack of land to land reform. So Jimmy felt that most of all we needed structural change—a government that would give genuine land reform, which would provide anti-T.B. facilities rather than the expensive prestige lung center, vaccines against communicable diseases rather than Imelda's huge heart center, four-year trained doctors who stayed in the Philippines rather than nine-year trained doctors who emigrated to the United States.

I got to know Jimmy and asked him to speak to the Columbans at Batang. The diocese decided to start the community-based health program which he advocated. For Tabugon it was timely. Our communities were beginning to develop and, without strong communities, this program would not work.

Since the community-based health program was very much for self-reliance in every area of life, it frowned on any handouts. Jimmy taught the people to make their own medicines, even to make tablets from a concoction of flour, to make tinctures using alcohol, and to make syrups using sugar. He advocated using the hollow stem of a papaya frond if you did not have a stethoscope, or you could just put your ear straight to a child's breast to listen for the breathing. Some of his colleagues even came up with the idea of using coconuts for intravenous fluid instead of the expensive dextrose. One St. Paul's nun had in her clinic in a mountain area a whole ward with coconuts hanging up instead of dextrose bottles. She told me that she had had the fluid tested and it was not only distilled but it even contained the necessary other ingredients to stop dehydration—a little sugar and salt. She attached the tubes directly to the eyes of the coconuts and added a strainer to make sure that no fiber passed through. Lina's life could have been saved by a village health aide who knew how to do that. In Jimmy's scheme ordinary village health aides could give injections and even do suturing and small operations. In every way Jimmy sought to demystify medicine and to give it back to the people. Nothing that Jimmy proposed appealed to the authorities, and especially not to the Minister of Health, Pacifico Marcos, the brother of President Ferdinand Marcos. Soon Jimmy had to go around incognito. Later, as things got worse, some of his companions in the program were gunned down.

I found that I just could not always stick to the self-reliance bit, no matter how hard I tried. What do you do if a man comes and says: "My wife is giving birth but the child is only halfway out. We have carried her down the mountain. Can you help?" You cannot just say: "Sorry, my son, we're working on a far-reaching program which will get to the root of this problem. Come back in a few years."

It was an agonizing dilemma because the very help we gave at times helped to perpetuate the system that caused so many people to get sick in the first place. But I could not always refuse. I had allowed myself to be dehumanized enough already. It was the borderline cases that caused the anguish. When I did reluctantly help directly, I knew that the only thing that justified it was the fact that we were working as hard as we could to strengthen the Christian communities and to get the barefoot doctor program going. In fact funds I had got for health I had used for sending the leaders to do the course in Mindanao, so convinced was I that education in self-reliance was ultimately the real answer.

Now those leaders were coming back.

Their arrival back from Mindanao caused great excitement. The wives and husbands were waiting in the *convento,* and soon after the leaders arrived I could see the change. Until then I had been used to making out the agenda and presiding over the meetings, but now they no longer waited for me to start things. After supper they divided up tasks among the group: prayer-leader, minute-taker, song-leader, discussion-moderator. They made an agenda and asked me whether I had anything to add. Then they set up a priority for the items to be discussed and allotted a cutoff time. Next came a reading from the Scriptures, followed by a short sharing of reflections and then into the first topic, which turned out to be nothing less than setting up a proper leadership course for our Christian community members. They were going to attempt the ambitious plan of echoing in the Christian communities of Tabugon the six-week course they had received in Ozamis City, but they would do it in a ten-day seminar! I realized immediately the logistics this would involve—communicating with all the communities, organizing them to collect the food from each community to support those members who would be going, and so on.

Until now I would never have gone off before a meeting was over. I couldn't—the meeting was me. I would stay on, hurrying them up impatiently, saying that they were taking too long to get to the point, and coming in too often with the solution. But this time I went off to bed and left them still planning. I felt a very rich man.

When the actual leadership seminar began some weeks later, I was delayed and arrived back from the lowlands when it was already in session. The doors of our little seminar house were closed. I walked over to the open window and listened. Inside, two of the returnees, Exor and Junior, were standing. Exor was guiding a discussion. The participants, about twenty in number, had broken into small groups of four. Each group had come to some conclusions which their secretaries were now presenting. Junior wrote the conclusions of each group on the board, while Exor asked them to say why they drew these conclusions, drawing out the members of other groups to say if they agreed or disagreed. The discussion was strong, and whenever the groups agreed, Junior wrote the agreed things in another column on the blackboard.

I could not help feeling that this was a far cry from flinging Bible texts and hunks of Church history at each other or monologues on the evils of capitalism, and I realized that the reason the returnees had progressed quite this fast was not just due to the course but because they had already been trying to give seminars before they went to the course; they had made all the mistakes, and those mistakes were valuable when they went to the course. They had not been fed the answers; they had worked hard for them. Now they themselves were asking the participants to identify the problems in their communities and they were evoking solutions for the various problems from the participants' own experience, not shoving answers down their throats. I knew now that we would soon be able to start the barefoot doctor program.

As soon as the leadership course was over we launched into the barefoot doctor program. Each community was to choose people to do the course. It would be three months long and would take place in Tabugon, so the participants, mainly young women, would need food to support them while in Tabugon, fares to come and go for those far away, and a pair of shoes and a dress. The communities were to collect the money for this. I was to find a nurse who would give the course.

I found Grace. She was quiet and very correct and insisted on calling the would-be barefoot doctors by the less flamboyant title of "nurse's aides." It did not sound as dramatic, but it was a wise move because it meant our nurse's aides did not raise eyebrows among the authorities. They cannot have gone unnoticed, of course, but they were not adding fuel to the fire by a provocative title. That was important, because as the months went by anything run by the Church was increasingly suspect and language was of the essence. "Barefoot doctor" had a revolutionary ring. The phrase "Christian community" was already "hot," but I would not compromise on that. I felt that only good could come from its being a bit dangerous to be Christian.

Grace turned out to be conscientious and thorough. She insisted that the last months of the training be in a hospital: more headaches for the Christian communities, because the distance increased the expense for their volunteers. But the chief nurse in Kabankalan Hospital, Mila Villavicencio, agreed to train the thirty students herself and even to have them receive lectures in the hospital from the doctors. Nothing was too much trouble for Mila. The nurse's aides would stay in the Sa-Maria house, which was just a mile outside Kabankalan. The struggle of the communities to provide the food was itself a sign of growth, and I resisted all the time the temptation to step in to help out the meager food ration because, if I did that, I would short-circuit the process. I too had come a long way.

Nurse Grace invited the *barrio* captain to the graduation, something I would not have done, but it was sensible because now the nurse's aides were both accredited by the hospital and approved by the *barrio*—a very important point in the political climate of the parish, which was deteriorating every day.

Chapter 26

THEY say that before the time of the Emperor Constantine in the fourth century it was a crime to be a Christian and after Constantine it was a crime not to be a Christian. Constantine changed the Church profoundly. He used it mercilessly for his own political purposes. The bishops he made into princes. The bishop's chair became a throne, his hat a miter, his staff a bronze crozier. The bishop now wore a royal ring and royal purple, his worship moved from the humble house-church to the basilica, and his house became a palace.

Soon after the early heroic days in the Philippines when the first friars defended the people against the military, the Church was co-opted into the system and became part of it—part of the Spanish government's ruling apparatus. Priests in the rural areas were as powerful as mayors, and the Archbishop of Manila could challenge the power of the governor of the islands. Church lands and power increased, and by the time of the revolution in 1896 the hierarchy was so identified with the colonial government that she fell with it.

The vestiges of that Church power were to be seen in the bishops' palaces sprinkled throughout the Philippines. Many of these, big and beautiful as they are, were not even built as a bishop's palace but as the parish *convento*. Such is the case of the bishop's house in Bacolod. It was originally the house of the Spanish parish priests of Bacolod. It was a symphony of cut coral-stone, baked red bricks, native hardwood, and Spanish wrought iron. Originally the roof was tiled, but the tiles had given way to galvanized iron—hot, and unsightly if it had not been painted. The last genuine Spanish house in Bacolod.

The day Bishop Fortich was inaugurated in 1967 he said: "This is no longer the bishop's palace. From today it is the people's house." And though it never lost its old title, under Fortich it did take on a new character and became the people's house. Visiting reporters could never get over the melée of ordinary people and even beggars who made their way right into the bishop's room. Traffic in there got so heavy that we, the priests, complained to the bishop formally that we could not have a private conversation with him because of the laypeople always swarming around.

When the nuncio gave the message to Monsignor Fortich that he was succeeding Bishop Yap, he said: "The Holy Father expects you to do something for the poor." *Populorum progressio* (*The Development of peoples*) had appeared a month after his consecration, and that encyclical must have been very much on the Pope's mind during the time the bishop's appointment was made. The new bishop threw himself headlong into development projects. First he created the office of social justice and put Luis Jaladoni, his best priest, just back from studying in Germany, in charge of it. Then came one project after another: garment-making as a cottage industry, a community farm in Candoni, a folk arts school; a plan to emancipate the *sacadas* drawn up in alliance with Bishop De Wit of Antique where most of the *sacadas* originate; the Dakong-Cogon sugar factory, with a rice, corn, and sugar cooperative; and a pastoral letter on the rights of labor. Father Saguinsin went full-time into labor union work, and the new office of social justice took up the cases of harassed laborers and tenants and provided free legal assistance.

Bishop Fortich was under pressure from two directions. There was pressure from us young priests to go faster. There was at first quiet and later hysterical pressure from many of the aristocracy to "control" the priests. He felt his job was to keep the lines of communication open between the two opposing factions. Often he ended by being criticized by both. One thing became gradually clearer and that was that, though there were striking exceptions, the planters as a group were not prepared to give up an inch. Moreover, the schemes which the "new society" government brought in ostensibly to help the people had always two things in common: they enriched those involved in them and they did not help the poor at all.

A typical example was the "Bliss" project. Huge sums were borrowed from international finance agencies to help the city poor to have housing. But first they must be removed from their wretched living quarters so that "Bliss" houses could be built there. Bulldozers were used to remove the ramshackle huts. But when the new houses had been built, rents were set that were far beyond the range of the poor people who had been put off the property. People employed in the government bureaucracy moved in.

The bishop, with his constant touring around the diocese, soon began to see through these schemes. Though he did not attack them publicly, he was not prepared to stop the priests from doing so. However, he continually cautioned two things: patience and common sense.

The planters began to see him as the mastermind behind the unrest, and he was attacked viciously in the same *Feedbacks* program that had attacked me.

One of the bishop's favorite escapes from all the fighting was to come up to Dakong-Cogon. He was proud of the little third-hand mill and how he had made it survive through crisis after crisis. He loved to point out a barefoot farmer coming into the bank in Dakong-Cogon to cash his sugar check. "O'Brien, if that man was back in the lowlands, do you think he'd even know what a check was?"

On his way to Dakong-Cogon he always called in to visit me. He would take out his pipe and sit down on the balcony off my room, and I would get him a cup of tea with *calamanse* (a native citrus) and brown sugar from the mill, and then he would give me the news in between puffs. What surprised me was how he knew each priest well and even the Sisters, who were not so permanent in the diocese, and how he cared about them, shaking his head with genuine empathy if they were in trouble. "What I tell the young men, O'Brien (but you never listen to your bishop, of course) is, don't give up your priesthood just for Marcos . . . for Marcos!" And he would shake his head again. He was of course referring to priests going to the mountains and joining the rebels.

I loved his visits and I loved Tabugon village. I was beginning to settle in. Ever since the first group of leaders had come back from Mindanao the pressure on me had eased, even though the number of different seminars going on around the parish had increased. I felt it was my duty to try and keep in touch with the other three parishes in the mountains, with the Columban meetings for rewriting our constitution, and with the diocesan meetings in Bacolod. They all took me away a lot, but I was always glad to be back and sit on my balcony and look out at the mountains around us. I would sit and pray the Psalms to the sound of the crickets, or take a stroll once the heat had gone out of the sun, down past the graveyard. I would always meet the little children playing outside the houses. A homemade toy truck was the most toys they would ever have and someone like me coming along was always an excitement. If there were no clouds, the top of Kanla-on would appear behind the graveyard in the evening sky. Sad but no longer serene, for in recent years it had begun to rumble and a dark streel of smoke to issue from its peak. After taking in the view I would invariably double back and land at the stores, where, as dark began to fall, I would have a beer and gossip with the people of the *barrio*.

In one store where I went to have my beer there was a small black-and-white television run on a car battery. There would be twenty or thirty children in rows sitting on the tables mesmerized by what was mainly advertisements. When the picture would disappear, the owner would send his son up on the roof to change the direction of the aerial.

Then I would stroll home for supper. We ate simply, in the sense that we took what was available locally, which was normally rice and fish and eggplant or some other vegetable. If I had said Mass that morning in one of the communities, there would often be something extra like some chicken or eggs given by the people. We were usually about seven in the household, plus any passing visitors from the communities, who had developed the habit of staying over with us if they had come to Tabugon for something. They would always bring some rice to add to the pot. If it was a quiet night with no meeting, the visitors would settle down on the bamboo part of the floor and chat, and someone would take one of the guitars down from the wall and strum away till they fell asleep.

I would retire to my balcony. I never lost the Irish habit of going to bed late (though I made it up with a *siesta*), so I would read for hours. There was always a pile of documents from the Columban Justice and Peace Office, which had the sensible habit of taking a good book, extracting the most relevant chapter from it, multiplying it, and sending it to us. There were letters from home and a weekly copy of the *Manchester Guardian, Le Monde,* and the *Washington Post* all in one issue sent to me by my father. Between that and the B.B.C. (the British Broadcasting Corporation) which I could get on my shortwave radio, I was probably as well informed on world affairs as any ordinary person in the U.S. or at home in Ireland.

Every couple of weeks I would make it down to Batang, our Columban house, and meet Paul and Mickey and the lads. The bright lights, a shower, a beer with the lads, the exchange of stories, letters waiting . . . it all added up to a little *fiesta* which I looked forward to intensely.

Our Christian communities were now about forty in number, and we began to think about organizing them into groups as Father Brian Gore had done in Oringao. If we did this, then each group of communities would be a mini-parish within the parish and maybe they could solve some of the justice and education problems at that level. With forty communities, each attempting to send in five representatives to the monthly meeting, there were too many people and no time to get through everything. But if each group met monthly and then sent the mini-parish representative to the *centro* or center, it would probably be more successful. It would also mean that we would be decentralizing and they would solve a lot of the problems on their own and only bring in the bigger ones to present before the whole parish. These mini-parishes could also take on the job of giving their own pre-baptism seminars. Gradually they would be assuming fuller responsibility for their own lives and becoming more self-reliant and developing their own inner dynamism.

Chapter 27

THE VILLAGE of Pinamulakan was made up of several hamlets set apart. It was a rocky area where the loggers found it difficult to go and the lowland Ilongos were not interested in going, so Cebuanos (not Cebuanos as such, but Cebuano-speaking Negrenses) from over the eastern side of the mountains had found their way there. It looked even poorer than the rest of the parish. People grew small amounts of corn where the rocks thinned out and planted papaya trees in the crevices. Any fertile area was planted to sugarcane, which the inhabitants tended for the real owners who always lived somewhere else.

When the people from Pinamulakan brought in a coffin to be blessed, it was usually a child or a teenager or some tragic death, rarely an old person who had reached the term of their natural life. Perhaps it was the fact that they had walked a long way and had been up the night before at the wake, but they always looked exhausted and listless. Before the blessing I would chat about the death of the child.

"What did the child die of?" It was usually a communicable disease like typhoid, measles, or cholera. If asked why the child had died, invariably they would answer: "It was the will of God."

Their Christian communities were weak. They had sent no one to our barefoot doctor course. Both the choosing and the supporting proved insurmountable obstacles for them.

As the rest of the parish progressed and communities began to start other communities, Pinamulakan and its surroundings remained moribund. I asked the Redemptorist Fathers, who had a special mission team for starting small Christian communities, to spend a few weeks there. They did, but an interesting thing happened: half the communities refused to attend.

They said it was "for reasons of security," and that was partly, but not completely, true.

There was a history behind this. A man called Wilfredo who had for a while worked with Magballo parish, then with the *kibbutz,* then with the nuns, then with the basic communities, had set himself up independently, using the skills he had picked up at the seminars he had done along the way, and became "leader" of half the communities in the Pinamulakan area. He had then taken up with the N.P.A. in an intermediary position, not actually joining them as a cadre but working closely with them as the controller of this half of Pinamulakan. My reluctant analysis was that he had used the people to give himself independent power. These people were now his; if the N.P.A. wanted to deal with them they must do so through him; if we wanted to deal with them we would have to deal with him. He seemed to fulfill the role of patron/protector that is so deeply a part of feudal society. When the communities of Pinamulakan now became a mini-parish, we at the center vetoed his membership in the new mini-parish's council. We were not inclined to hand over the other half of the communities to him as his personal fiefdom. Our veto was obviously the wrong thing to do if we had wanted cooperation. The nonattendance of half the area was his answer, and it raised the whole question of our relationship with the N.P.A.

We were groping to discover what that relationship should be. In the rest of the parish we were there first. They just had not been there when we started. But now the question was going to arise where the control of the Marcos government receded. As a rule of thumb for myself, I felt that if the N.P.A. were dominant in an area we should treat them as we would the government in an area where they were dominant. The strongest official endorsement the bishops of the Philippines had ever given to the Marcos regime was to say that it was the *de facto* government: it was in power whether they liked it or not, so they had to deal with it. On the same principle, if the N.P.A. fulfilled all the functions of government in a given area, which in fact they did in some areas, then they were the *de facto* government in those areas. The problem would obviously get more complicated when we got to an area where their writ did not run but neither did the government's. Pinamulakan was rapidly becoming just such an area.

One of the side effects of the general absence of government in what I will call the "in-between areas" was the proliferation of bandits, gangs, and private operators carrying any flag that served their purpose. These might be led by ex-army types, by ex-N.P.A. types, or by religious cult types. You had to keep a cool head as the rumors poured in, especially during the monthly meetings.

Late one night, long after we had all turned in, I was awakened by a man's voice calling from outside our front door. I was apprehensive. I remained still. Out in the *sala* Junior had woken up. He remained still.

The voice repeatedly said: "Padre, please help me. They are going to kill all my children."

Junior came into my room quietly and indicated he was going to slip out to my balcony and, looking from the side, see if there was more than one person, which was what we feared. He returned to whisper that it was safe, and I called back to the man to wait, I was getting up. We lit a kerosene lamp and opened up the door.

He was from Pinamulakan and his name was Luding. His story was that a robber had come during the night attempting to get the money he made from selling banana cakes at the crossing. The aggressor had fired shots at the house in the dark, and in his panic Luding had fled the house, leaving his wife and all his children behind. He was convinced now that all his children were in danger.

Who was it? Had he any idea?

Well, it was not the N.P.A., he was sure of that. That was not their style, certainly not in our area. He thought it was Trinio, a young land-owner who frequently terrorized the people in Pinamulakan and who Luding believed was in cahoots with the police. We could not ignore his request. How could we live with ourselves if anything happened to his children? But we could not trust the police, as they might be involved, so what to do?

Now there was an army battalion nearby called Philcag, which was mending the roads. They would be more likely to help to frighten away someone; and better still them if that someone was connected with the police.

It was about 2:00 A.M. I went over to the captain and asked him if he could send some men to help in case the children were in danger. He agreed.

When they got to as near as their vehicles could travel, they sent Luding himself (they were afraid to go) crawling on his belly toward his own house. There he found his wife and children alive and well. Later police investigated the place and found a holster which everyone said belonged to Trinio.

The next day Luding disappeared and everyone said he had gone to Mindanao, presumably afraid that Trinio would get him. We asked the police to confront Trinio about the holster. They said he denied that it was his.

After this episode the people of Pinamulakan, three out of the six Christian communities, held a meeting at the *convento* to discuss security. What could they do without necessarily forming alliances with the police, the N.P.A., the army, or private armed groups? Was there anything they could do?

The meeting went on and on. No one really had any hope. It was the same listlessness and despair one saw at their funerals. They had always led a feudal life in which they gave their work to someone who would feed them and their services to someone who would defend them.

"What is the problem?" I eventually interjected.

"The problem is Trinio. At night he comes around the place and terrifies us and sometimes robs the houses."

"Has anyone seen Trinio doing this?" I asked.

"No, because it's always at night. But we know it's him."

"What about having a *ronda*, a night watch," I suggested. "Just a team who would do the rounds of your village at night so that they would see anyone who came. They would not carry weapons, just flashlights."

"Trinio doesn't like us to carry flashlights, just small kerosene lamps."

"Why?"

"Because with the flashlight we can see him but with the kerosene lamp he can see us."

"If you know it's Trinio, why don't you go to his house and tell his mother? She would be anxious to stop him."

"He'd be angry at us for doing that."

"Well, his mother maybe might come to the *convento* sometime and ask me to say Mass and I could take the opportunity to tell her what her son is doing. How about that?"

"That's it. When she comes you could tell her."

"Like hell I will. It's you he's attacking, not me." And I strode out of the meeting and slammed the door. I was determined to provoke them to some creative action. Otherwise, under the influence of their neighbors, their hopelessness would push them to the simplest solution: a bullet.

An hour later I returned. The shock tactic had worked. They hardly noticed me come in. The air of fatalism was gone. They were busy making out the schedule of the men and women who would do the *ronda* of their area.

* * *

One of the weaknesses of the first course for barefoot doctors had been that we had no textbook in Ilongo. Some years before I had come across a wonderful book, *Donde No Hay Doctor* (*Where There Is No Doctor*), published in Mexico by David Werner. The book dealt with all the medical problems that the poor in rural Mexico would have to deal with, illustrated with drawings by Werner and his father. For a long time I had wanted to put it into Ilongo, so I consulted Doctor Jimmy Tan. His group met and liked the idea, but felt it was not a translation but a new creation which we wanted, inspired by and along the same lines as Werner's book. He put me in contact with a young woman doctor, Tessie Ludovice.

She knew exactly what she wanted. "The people will write the book," she said.

"I'm all for self-reliance, Tessie, but I don't think that's realistic."

"Of course it is. I did it before on the island of Samar and I can do the same again. I will get a representative group of the people together at a seminar and ask them to list the illnesses that most affect them. In that way we avoid studying maple-leaf disease and other illnesses that we learn about in Philippine medical schools but which we don't suffer from in the Philippines. This book was made for Mexico. We must make one for Negros.

"The people have been using herb remedies for a thousand years. When they put their knowledge together you'd be surprised how much they know. They know what they are talking about. It's life and death to them. I can add some modern techniques, but modern medicine deals with curing, and our emphasis is going to be on prevention."

Tessie got the seminar going. It took place in the Sa-Maria house. It took a couple of weeks, but by the time she had finished she had the bones of the book in notes.

The next stage was to hole up in my *convento* and start writing. She used conventional textbooks as a backup and to check things, but it astounded me that this young doctor could produce a whole book almost straight from her memory, so well did she know her medicine. I had often seen that the doctors who had made the choice to follow Jimmy Tan and serve the people were frequently from the top of their class.

While she was there I invited my old friend Lino Montebon, who had done the "Way of the Cross" for me in the Sa-Maria house in San Ramon, to come to stay, and as Tessie wrote he did the drawings. Lino was a perfectionist and, when it came time to draw the herb remedies, he would draw the leaf or fruit in its natural position on the tree, going out with the binoculars to draw the plant *in situ*.

Tessie's presence in the house had the added benefit of a doctor's opinion on hand for the cases that were referred to us from the communities. This was a real luxury. Her way of dealing with patients was in the true Jimmy Tan style: very careful listening, a complete explanation to the patient of why she came to her decision, and why she was recommending this particular herb. She always preferred herbs to drugs where possible and always made a reference to the community and how it might go about eradicating this condition from their midst if it was prevalent. A far cry from the doctor in Candoni scribbling down a prescription for Gregorio as if we were in a city.

*　*　*

The difference in the people of Pinamulakan since they started their simple *ronda* was visible. It meant organizing themselves and taking responsibility for each other, and it had at least an indirect effect on each member of the community.

Among Trinio's many abuses in Pinamulakan were his visits to the house of Rosa and her husband Bernardo. Since Trinio carried a gun, no one was about to stop him. Sometimes he arrived with a friend just to say hello, but everyone knew that Trinio had his eye on Rosa. Bernardo had advanced T.B. He was only twenty-five but he looked a skeleton-like forty. Tessie had told me she did not hold out much hope for him. We supplied him with the full range of anti-T.B. medicines, although Tessie said that without good food the medicines would come to nothing. It was precisely the sort of case in which you needed a strong Christian community who would offer to do his plot of land while he was sick and help out with food till the medicines took effect. But there was no guarantee of that in Pinamulakan. Rosa used to sell candies at *fiestas* to make a little money. Trinio would come up to her, buy some chocolate, and then give it back to her as a present. I told Rosa to be on her guard.

Anyway, one evening before dark, Trinio came along casually with a friend to Rosa's house. He was courteous enough, but he did not go home at all. He and his friend lay down on the porch. Trinio slept with his hands behind his head, his gun held in the right hand. Finally Bernardo, watching all night from his sick bed with growing anger, could endure it no longer. He took a machete, used for cutting sugarcane, and crept out to the porch and took three great slashes at the sleeping Trinio, two at his face and the other at his hands.

Next morning the news was brought to me that Trinio had been attacked and was on his way to the hospital in Bacolod and was probably dead.

"Don't you believe it," I said. "That man is the toughest fellow I have ever seen."

When I went to visit him in hospital a couple of weeks later, Trinio had a steel rod through his chin, but it looked all right except for the stitch marks. The tops of his bottom teeth had been neatly sliced off by another blow, but the blade had stopped short just as it reached his inner throat. He was missing a couple of fingers and could not yet talk, but otherwise was recovering rapidly. Bernardo had fled.

Chapter 28

THERE were limits to medical self-reliance. For some of the most serious cases we would go to Bacolod to Mommy Paz Torres. Mommy Paz was the chief nurse in Bacolod Provincial Hospital. Like Meding, she would approach the doctors and get them to do an operation free, and then she would personally see to the patients. We could not have survived without her.

When we discovered that Celia, the wife of one of our community leaders, had cancer, Mommy Paz got for me the name of a doctor on the island of Panay who was giving radium treatment. He agreed to do the treatment free of charge except for the materials involved. But Celia was expecting a baby, and both the doctor and Mommy Paz said that Celia should have her baby before beginning the treatment.

Celia already had ten children. After we got the diagnosis, her husband Roberto and I called them together and explained. I said solemnly: "While your mother has cancer and is with child she will need two things: food and rest. All extra food should go to her, and she must do no heavy work." All the family understood, as did the Christian community. It was agreed that when the time came Celia would have her baby in Bacolod Provincial Hospital under the special supervision of Mommy Paz. So that would mean another long trip to Bacolod.

The further up the mountains one lived, the more attractive Bacolod began to seem. But my visits to Bacolod too often involved hospitals, prisons, and meetings. I never seemed to get the time for a game of tennis or golf, which I would have liked, and rarely managed to stroll around the *plaza* with its royal palms and betel-nut trees, or just sit and watch the people go by.

Accommodation was never a problem. At first there was the Hotel Mallorca, owned by the Alonso family. They put by a special air-conditioned room in the hotel just for the Columbans. Not only the Alonso family but many other Bacolod families had open house for the Columbans and welcomed, too, our visiting relations and gave us the use of their cars . . . even though they did not always agree with our new pastoral approach. Later on, as the price of sugar declined, the Hotel Mallorca had to close, and we took to staying with the Redemptorist Fathers.

The Irish "Reds" had come to the Philippines long before us, as far back as 1910. The papal nuncio had wanted time to fill the gap left by the exile of the Spanish friars. In Bacolod they lived together in their monastery, going out to the parishes in teams to help in whatever way seemed best at the time. The monastery was most unmonastic in the sense that the house was overcrowded with poor people almost camping in the corridors. Many of these people were refugees from the various hamleting campaigns of the army; many others had suffered torture and were seeking a sort of sanctuary. The Reds refused no one. In fact, Father Frankie Connon, one of the Redemptorist Fathers, had built up a library of photographs and tapes documenting the atrocities committed by the army. When the situation became dangerous, these photographs were transferred to the United States.

It was normal for us on a trip to Bacolod to get in as many tasks as possible—all the more so when the price of gasoline had increased so much. There would be visits to the diocesan lawyers, Frankie Cruz and Johnny Hagad, visits to prisoners, shopping to be done, and of course visits to the bishop and the seminary, where we would have our monthly meeting of all the priests in the diocese. And of course visits to the hospital.

Soon the time came for Celia to give birth in the hospital. The prognosis was not good.

On the way to Bacolod I realized that it was a long time since I had been to visit my friends the Gonzales family. I liked going there. Their house looked over Bacolod Bay and they had a special room kept for me so that I could come any time and do any of my translation work while looking out at the sea. No one would ever disturb me. And it was air-conditioned. And most of all I knew I was sincerely welcome. I had got to know the children over the years, and they regarded me as an uncle.

Why had I not visited for so long? True, I was always too busy, but that was not the only reason. I seemed to be shying away from there as if there was something wrong about visiting them, as if my friendship with them was in some way not compatible with our solidarity with the poor. As the bus moved toward Bacolod I thought about it. There were cases where clergy lent themselves to the rich, becoming their instruments, not their friends. Wasn't I overreacting to this? After all, my friendship with Baby and Dodo, her husband, was of many years' standing. Baby had been so helpful in running the Sa-Maria. She had gone begging among her friends so that she could provide Mommy Paz with blood for our free patients when it was needed. She gave much of her spare time to looking after the disabled and retarded of Bacolod. And most of all she was a friend and had remained a friend although she must surely have disagreed with our forthright confrontation with the sugar industry. Where she would have exclusively preferred the Mother Teresa approach, we were going also for the Camara and Romero approach—whereas Mother Teresa ministered to the poor and hungry, the two Latin American prelates focused on the causes of poverty and hunger. And when I began to think up arguments again on the other side, I finally settled it by saying to myself: "Nonsense. Baby's a good friend and I am going to visit her."

But first I called in to the hospital. Celia had had the baby. The birth had been without event, but the baby was seriously sick. Celia wanted it baptized and she wanted me to be the godfather. So I baptized the baby— whom they insisted on calling Niall.

That night, when I had done my other task, I went to the Gonzales', by the sea. One of the household help showed me to my room, and after a while there was a knock on the door. It was Baby, inviting me to join her and Dodo out on the balcony. I was surprised, because they were usually in bed by this hour.

We spent a pleasant time chatting while we could hear the sea lapping away below our feet. The conversation came around to our work in the south. They had heard stories about Father Brian Gore—detailed stories portraying Brian as a rabble-rouser—and they wanted to check them out. The stories were not correct, and they were glad to have their minds put at rest. They did not tell me where the stories came from and I did not ask. All through the conversation I felt that Baby and Dodo were specially concerned for me. We turned in much later than usual.

Next morning off I went to a priests' meeting. We would hear reports from all over the diocese and problems would be discussed openly and hotly. The bishop sat quietly through it all, just listening. He reckoned the priests could decide the issues themselves. At the end he would have a few words of news or guidance. If it was of any guidance it would be in the direction of reconciling opposing opinions. He was not the son of a politician for nothing.

At the end of the meeting I was approached by a friend, a Filipino priest: "Niall, do you know the Gonzales family?"

"Yes."

"Well, you know my sister is very friendly with Baby, they work together for the disabled?"

"Yes."

"Well, you may not know that the Gonzales family have been approached by an army colonel about you."

"About me?"

"Yes. They were warned that it was not in their interests to have you visiting them."

"What did they say?"

"Well, they said: 'As long as he is a friend of ours, he is welcome in our house.'"

At lunch after the meeting, Frankie Connon asked if I wanted a lift over to their place.

I told him that I had to go to the hospital to see a patient first. "You know, Frankie," I confessed, "I hate going to the hospital. I hate walking through the wards. So many people desperately sick, lying in the corridor without proper beds, it looks more like a scene from the Crimean War than a government-run hospital. I keep my head down. I am afraid to look up in case I see someone pleading for help . . . they need plasma or blood or medicine."

"You're all wrong," Frankie replied. "The hospital is the most beautiful place in Bacolod. Don't keep your head down. Look. What you see in the corridors are patients without beds, true, but always in the arms of someone else, patiently holding them and attending to their needs. I think it's very touching and it lifts my spirits and renews my belief in human beings. The only analogy with the Crimean War is Mommy Paz Torres—she's another Florence Nightingale. Do you know that the other day I asked her how things were going. 'Oh, the same as usual,' she said. 'We had a scuffle in the operating theater.' 'What happened?' I said. 'Well, there were too many patients. A relation of one of them drew a knife and tried to force the doctor to do his patient first.' 'Did he?' 'No, the doctor just drew his gun and put him back in line.' She spoke as if it was a regular occurrence!"

The return journey from Bacolod usually involved a call at Batang, our community house, and sometimes a visit with Juan Jo and Paloma. Juan Jo's home was just outside Kabankalan, a last stopping place for us on the way to the deep south or a trip up to the mountains. His family had been farming there since the 1860s and the ruins of the old family house was nearby. Juan Jo himself ran his farm with the precision of a factory. He believed in the old Spanish proverb that the best fertilizer is the footprints of the farmer himself. The people who worked with him not only had more than the required social benefits, but if their children showed promise, they could go on to college. And many did. It was a model farm, a symbol of what the old system might have been at its best. Paloma, his Andalusian wife, ran the household with panache, introducing us to a pleasant blend of the best of Spanish and Filipino culture. It was a pleasure to come in off the dusty road to an immediate welcome, a cool drink, a well-stocked library, freshly cut flowers on the table, and accurate information on world events. Juan Jo was an aficionado of the B.B.C. But a guest who merely saw the well-run household and the generosity would have missed the real Juan Jo and Paloma—their warm personal care if an old retainer was sick, their patience with the newcomer's sometimes uninformed criticism, their deep social concern. On one occasion I was constrained to stay the night. Leaving before dawn, I was surprised to find Paloma already up: "Is something wrong, Paloma?" "No, I'm always up at this time." I showed surprise, because we had all retired very late. "Well, you know, I don't like to disturb the porter, so I open the gate myself for Juan Jo. He gets his first round of the fields done before breakfast."

What with my delays on the way, Roberto and Celia reached Tabugon before me, and an invitation awaited me in the *convento* to go to their home where there would be a celebration for the safe arrival of Toto Niall.

When I got to the house, which was in a far-out village, I found that all the children were there. I was the only guest. They were all proud of their new brother and the part they had played in working for a safe arrival. There was a special bottle of one-year-old. Roberto said that no one else was to touch it: it was just for me!

Suddenly there was a commotion in the other room. The eldest girl, who was about seventeen years of age and married, and had just been serving us, had gone into labor. Someone sent for the village midwife, a man in this case, but in ten minutes, before he could arrive, the new baby was born. Immediately a piece of bamboo was cut down and a sharp "knife" made from it to sever the umbilical cord. I suggested washing the bamboo knife in some of the one-year-old, since otherwise tetanus could come from it. So we did. And by the time the midwife arrived the most important part was over. Then there was a double celebration, and everyone said that I had been blessed to be in the house when a baby was born. And I knew it was so.

Celia now could have the radium treatment, and she began the trips to Panay. All had been going well for a few months when Celia suddenly took ill. After one night in the clinic she died. She had looked quite healthy. Now she was dead. What a journey to set out on, knowing you leave eleven children behind!

Cancer was very rare in the parish of Tabugon. Most often one could "blame" the system for a death, since so many of the deaths were caused by the misuse of human resources. But in this case there was no person or system to blame. I seemed to find it harder to accept than the people around me, and having spent much energy in knocking the spurious "will of God" philosophy so prevalent, I was now forced back to the awe, the silence, the submission, before the words: "Thy will be done."

A few days after Celia's funeral, Roberto arrived at the *convento*. I can still see him, holding his little bundle: "Padre, we have spoken much about Toto Niall. We love him dearly, but we feel that you should take him. He would not be alive but for you. And that is what we want, for him and for you."

I took up the bundle and looked in at the little face. All babies are beautiful, I thought, and I kissed him and said: "Roberto, I don't know what to say." And I cradled the baby in my arms, rocking him gently.

I really did not know what to do next. I called for Rachel, the teenaged girl who lived in the house next door, but she was away that day.

That day is now a blur. First I was called out on some important request. Roberto stayed on till I came back. I was not long back when the *convento* was filled with various people—a funeral to be blessed, a marriage couple to be interviewed. Roberto stayed on still. It must have been market day because people never stopped coming. All day I was looking out for some woman whom I could ask to come and help because Toto was being bottle-fed and I wanted to do it properly, but for some reason that day no such suitable woman darkened the door of the *convento*. Evening was coming and Roberto was still with us. In the Philippines a baby is never left alone, never tucked away quietly till its next feeding time. The baby is always being carried or else is under the watchful eye of someone as it rocks in a swinging hammock. Gradually it was dawning on Roberto that, no matter how willing, I would be under these conditions an unsuitable father. I can never forget that moment in the evening time when we looked at one another, both of us realizing that it could not be.

I often think back on that day. Why could I find no one, I who can be so resourceful and imaginative? Was I backing off, not wanting a little person to interfere in my work? Was it the old tension between the journey and the destination?

Chapter 29

DRAMATIC events were happening meantime across the river in Father Brian Gore's parish of Oringao. That parish differed a lot from the rest of the Tablas Valley in that the people were much poorer, and a large number of the people were illiterate, which was unusual in the Philippines, which has one of the highest literacy rates in the world. That area had something else unusual: a tradition of millennialism which went back to Spanish times. Every now and again a leader would arise among the peasants offering miraculous solutions to their problems of drought, floods, and illness, and protection against their enemies. At present there was a man called Alfredo Salvatore who had come from Mindanao where he believed he had received a message from God. He now performed miracles for the sick and, by wearing the amulets he distributed, one would be protected against bullets. He was not unlike the *ba-bylan,* the ancient pagan priest who existed before the Spanish times and for a long time after in remote areas. But as Salvatore's sect grew, they became more aggressive. They began killing people who did not go along with them, though in their own eyes they saw themselves as something akin to Robin Hood.

Alfredo Salvatore was eventually captured, but his followers then broke up into marauding groups. Soon after Lolito Olympus, a Christian community member, was killed by a group of *salvatores.* The people were so terrorized by this killing that no one would go near the body. Brian and his communities responded by mobilizing thousands of community members and trekking the five-hour journey into the inner mountains to bury Lolito. It was not the first time Brian's communities had mobilized nonviolently like this. Another time they had confronted Rosano himself, who had been sent by a landlord to make sure a piece of land grabbed from a peasant would not be planted by that peasant. Brian, Father Vincente Dangan, a

Filipino priest who was an assistant in Kabankalan, and hundreds of community members had gone into the flooded rice paddy, and with trousers rolled up had planted the seedlings, defying the watching Rosano and his armed companions. Rosano made no move to stop them and did not come back to Oringao.

The Christian communities, encouraged by these successes, began to nonviolently oppose the *salvatores*. They overwhelmed them with numbers and arrested them on behalf of the police, or forced truces on them. They then began to take on cases of land-grabbing, illegal gambling, corrupt local tax collectors and municipal officials. For example, in one case a local landowner had moved his fence and appropriated some of the land of a poor widow. When she complained to him he said: "Take out a case in court against me if you think I have done something illegal." She appealed to the Christian community, they appealed to the other Christian communities, and another large unarmed contingent of them arrived, pulled up the fence, and returned it to its original position. The man complained that the fence now encroached on his land. They replied: "Then take out a case against us."

Two things were happening. First, Brian's communities were discovering the power of courageously doing something in spite of threats by using large numbers, but without guns. In a way they were discovering something of active nonviolence as a technique, though as yet Brian felt that nonviolence as a principle for life was probably unrealistic. Another thing that was happening was that Brian's successful dealing with the *salvatores* where the town authorities had failed was offering a challenge to their authority.

In the month of March 1980, Brian and his Christian communities arranged a massive meeting to complain about the terror tactics of the Long Range Patrol, an army task force which operated in the area, and the abuses of the government officials in their parish. The mayor was invited to attend and was to be a speaker.

The format of the meeting was to give the people a chance to air minor complaints first, and then to work up gradually to the serious complaints. The minor complaints would naturally concern the running of the municipality of Kabankalan. This was to be merely a lead-in. The second part— the important and truly grim part—was to name and denounce military atrocities.

To the chagrin of the Long Range Patrol and other military personnel who were there in force, some ten thousand people attended. A gathering of ten thousand people or even a tenth of that number on a mountainside like Oringao for a protest is indicative of a strong infrastructure of organization, education, and awareness. The mayor was taken aback; the army was stunned.

As luck would have it, the minor complaints session about the officials and the indirect criticism of the mayor's administration were all there was time for before the heavens opened and the gathering was dispersed by rain.

The mayor left the meeting believing that the whole thing had been a political exercise aimed against himself. Self-appointed advisers found that it suited their purpose to encourage him in this belief. These advisers have a lot to answer for in the events that followed.

The Long Range Patrol did not wait long to react to this demonstration of people power. Three days later seven peasants from a nearby mountain area disappeared. But we didn't hear about this for a long time, because these peasants did not belong to any Christian community—if they had, it would have been known much sooner. So it was to be a long time before their fate was learned. Strangely enough, repercussions of the event would reach far beyond the Philippines.

Chapter 30

*E*ASTER was the most important religious holiday in the Philippines. In our parish it would now have an added importance because I had agreed that the small Christian communities, coming together in groups as mini-parishes, would run their own Easter services instead of gathering in the center at Tabugon.

Easter had meant more to me ever since I had understood and accepted Hitz's message that true evangelization was the spreading of the good news, now so often lost in the accretions of the ages that the Christian message came across as bad news—a list of do's and don'ts, of proofs, anathemas, and distinctions, a mere ethics for wise living. There was a need to recapture the simplicity and daring of that moment when Paul said: "I am in prison because I have maintained that *Jesus is alive.*" Easter was the time to rediscover this moment.

Holy Week involved three days of ceremonies. The first was Holy Thursday, on which we celebrated the Last Supper and the washing of feet. In the Philippines we followed the Spanish tradition; twelve people dressed as the Apostles ate a "Last Supper." Then the priest, taking the part of Christ, washed the feet of the twelve. On Good Friday there was the procession of the dead Christ. Nobody missed that procession, and when it was over, all the people came to the church to "visit" him as they would at a wake; they gave the "Besa" to his hand and kissed his feet.

At dawn on Easter Day came the Mass of the Resurrection with the baptism of new Christians. After that Mass was the enactment of the *sugat*, the meeting: A statue of Our Lady, veiled in black, would leave the church accompanied by the women. Suddenly she meets her Son traveling along the road with a group of men. They stop exactly under a high covered tripod. As they stand there facing each other a little angel, complete with white dress and wings, descends from the scaffolding on a rope. Greeting the Virgin with the words: "Be sad no more, gentle mother," the angel lifts off the black veil and replaces it with a white one, saying:

> Be glad and rejoice, O Virgin Mary,
>> Alleluia,
> For he whom thou didst merit to bear
>> Alleluia
> Has risen as he said
>> Alleluia.

Then the two statues return together to the church to begin yet another Mass.

This year—1980—was going to be very special because the communities were doing all the ceremonies themselves. They were very excited, and I had promised that each of them could have the Sacred Host taken out to their own mini-parishes from our church. Afterward I would come to each area and give them Benediction—a special blessing with the Sacred Host. This would involve quite some traveling for me because in addition to Dakong-Cogon and Tabugon there would be ceremonies at five other centers. But I knew that they would want me to see all the work they had put into decorating their chapels and, anyway, I was proud of them and wanted to encourage them.

There was an unusual man in the village of Tabugon—unusual because he was not a believer and made no pretense to be. Lorenzo was not indifferent or lazy; he just did not believe. I liked him particularly because when he talked I knew he was not trying to please me. He was exceptionally well-read. In addition to a treasured copy of *The Golden Bough,* he had some books which basically were an answer to Christianity, and he would lend me these. In return I lent him novels and very frequently he would come over to the *convento* for a cup of tea, a cigarette, and a chat. We could talk about the politics of the town and his views were always refreshingly free from prejudice. I found it a relief to be able to talk to someone without being too guarded. He was a veteran of World War II and I did not know he had a couple of old guns locked away in his trunk (he actually had a license for these). Lorenzo and I became good friends, each respecting the other's beliefs. His wife was a teacher in the school, and though I did not ask, I reckoned she and he were of one mind. They were a close couple.

It was Holy Thursday. Coming back from the washing of the feet in Dakong-Cogon, Junior (who had now been working with me for ten years and with whom I shared most of the parish decisions) came to me looking very anxious. It happened that a friend of his was in one of the stores of Tabugon where they served beer and there he overheard a group discussing how they would rob Lorenzo. To my shock, among the group were three men who were among our leaders and helped out with our seminars. According to the overheard conversation, Lorenzo had a whole cache of guns. Their plan was to wait until the Good Friday procession—tomorrow—when Lorenzo would be out of his house at the procession, and then break in and get the guns. Sandro, it appeared, was the leading spirit behind the venture.

Now for some time, as the situation deteriorated, a strange syndrome seemed to be manifesting itself throughout the parish: a gun syndrome. Young men wanted guns desperately. Rumors have always been part of Negros life where daily newspapers were not part of the culture and the radio was heavily censored. In the mountains people relied on rumors even more. A raid by a marauding gang, for example, even though it took place far away, brought panic to a very wide area and people would not sleep at home at night but out in the long cogon grass for days afterward. A gun gave psychological security (at least in my opinion it was only psychological—in fact you were in more danger with a gun, as the case of Lorenzo was now showing), but young men did not see it that way. It also gave power to its owner and put a young man in the noble shadow of the N.P.A. In our area that shadow was regarded as noble because they had not been guilty of abuses and they were clearly on the side of the people. Their image was that of freedom fighters.

Sandro had a brother-in-law who was a ranking officer in the N.P.A. Sandro lived in the aura of this connection and used it for personal capital. He was an opportunist who borrowed their vocabulary and used their name. He had probably been rejected by them, but now he had got a gun somewhere and in my opinion he was planning to get more guns and set up his own independent group. The fact that he had managed to involve three of our leaders showed how powerful the name of N.P.A. was and how rapidly the climate was changing.

It was a hare-brained scheme, planned almost in public, based on false information, and led by a punk who was stupidly unaware that Lorenzo was the only one in the parish who would not be at the Good Friday procession. It could result in a fatal shooting. For all sorts of reasons I could not tell Lorenzo: I had been told in confidence; the person who first told Junior might be shot himself if he was found out; Lorenzo would not be unjustified in bringing the military into it for protection, but the military were irresponsible and could easily bring about a shoot-out. The fact that they could connect the arms to the *convento* and the Christian communities because of the three men who had been working with me did not bear thinking about.

I met one of the leaders who had joined the conspirators. I broached the topic indirectly, giving him a clue that I knew more. He looked at me gravely and said, "I'm sorry, Padre, I can't discuss it and we can't change now," and he walked away, afraid that I would influence him if he stayed to discuss it. There were still two others, Exor and Raul, but it was my busiest day of the year. I would not get back from the mini-parishes till the early hours of the morning. Only then would I be able to talk to them. I sent them an urgent message asking them to come to the *convento* and wait for me there, and I set off for the five mini-parishes.

All through the ceremonies my mind was distracted by thoughts of the upcoming meeting with the two leaders and what I would say. My position on arms was known mostly by what I had not said up to this point; now I would have to be more explicit. If that meant losing some leaders, so be it. But I would attempt to put my point of view in a way that would respect the fact that mine was at this stage a minority opinion, not held by Church or State or revolutionaries, all of whom agreed that there are occasions when violence, or counter-violence as the case may be, is necessary. They differed only on the "when." The State said they could use violence when the State was threatened, although in fact they used it not when the State but when the privileges of the few were threatened. The Church said you could use it as a last resort when all other means had failed and when to allow the oppression to go on would result in irreparable evil. The revolutionaries said we had reached that situation right now.

I got back from the last Benediction in Inapoy at about 1:00 A.M. The two leaders were fast asleep on the bamboo floor. I went straight to my private balcony and set the chairs in a circle. By now they were awake and I invited them to come in and sit down. They had never been in there before. Junior joined us, and with us was a visiting Filipina, Sister Marie. We decided to start with prayer and, since it was Holy Thursday night, Sister read from the Gospel of Matthew—the Agony in the Garden:

> Then Jesus went with them to a place called Gethsemane and he said to his disciples: "Sit here while I go yonder and pray." And taking with him Peter and the two sons of Zebedee, he began to be sorrowful and troubled. Then he said to them: "My soul is sorrowful even to death; remain here and watch with me." And going a little farther he fell on his face and prayed: "My father, if it be possible, let this cup pass from me; nevertheless, not as I will, but as thou wilt." And he came to his disciples and found them sleeping, and he said to Peter: "So, could you not watch with me one hour? Watch and pray that you enter not into temptation. The spirit indeed is willing but the flesh is weak." . . . While he was still speaking, Judas came, one of the twelve, and with him a great crowd with swords and clubs, from the chief priests and the elders of the people. Now the betrayer had given them a sign, saying: "The one I shall kiss is the man. Seize him." And he came up to Jesus at once and said: "Hail, Master!" and he kissed him. Jesus said to him: "Friend, why are you here?" Then they came up and laid hands on Jesus and seized him. And

behold, one of those who were with Jesus stretched out his hand and drew his sword, and struck the slave of the high priest, and cut off his ear. Then Jesus said to him: "Put your sword back into its place, for all who take the sword will perish by the sword. Do you think that I cannot appeal to my Father and he will at once send me more than twelve legions of angels? But how then should the scriptures be fulfilled that it must be so?"

We sat in silence for a few minutes after the reading. Then, as was our custom, each of us shared what part of the story touched us. Sister and Junior shared their feelings without trying to preach, and then it came to Exor and Raul. I was apprehensive because up to this moment I had never put anyone working with me on the spot. The circumstances had forced me to declare my hand. In turn they spoke, telling us what their feelings were. Though I do not remember their precise words, they were more moved than I had expected. It was as if they had waked from a dream and suddenly realized where they had been going. To my surprise they saw the question not so much in philosophical terms but in terms of faithfulness to me!

I spoke last. In a way nothing needed to be said but I shared: "What struck me about the reading was the anguish Jesus felt in trying to know whether or not he was doing the right thing. It seems to me that in life the struggle to know what to do is often more severe than the sacrifice in actually doing it. Nothing has torn me apart so much as the struggle to know whether we should oppose the oppression with power or with weakness. I have chosen the path of weakness, but so often a doubt overshadows my mind. But in listening to the reading tonight I felt that, in spite of everything, when Jesus walked from that garden he had decided that weakness was stronger than strength, and part of his agony must have been that he knew that so few of his disciples would follow him in this path while others would recommend it to their opponents but never use it themselves."

It was maybe three in the morning when we finished. Both men had sincerely promised to make a fresh start, but they could make no promises for Sandro or his group.

When I lay down I was filled with a sense of gratitude but I was too tired to realize the special significance of that sacred night. Only when writing it now has it struck me.

Next day the Good Friday procession passed near Lorenzo's house and I was not attending to the hymns and prayers at all: my eyes were constantly in that direction and at one point I left the procession and made a short detour to let any observers see that the house was being watched.

Nothing happened. In the event, the plot must have fizzled out. However, Sandro was reported to be angry with me. I let him know that I was going to report him to the N.P.A. in whose name he was purporting to act.

The rest of Easter went off as planned in Tabugon, but not in all of Kabankalan. In the *barrio* of Tan-Awan on Easter Monday morning two of the Christian community leaders disappeared—Alex Garsales and Herman Muleta. Both had been leaders in the Christian community, both had had conflicts with the municipal authorities, and both had taken part in the just-finished Easter ceremonies. In fact Alex had played the part of Christ in the Passion play on Good Friday, and he had used the occasion to make a personal statement of faith. We still have it:

> My brothers: I, Alexander Garsales, of *barrio* Tan-Awan, do promise to be faithful, to continue teaching the people. I offer myself to defend the poor and oppressed, to stand for my brothers and sisters who are falsely condemned. I offer my life so that peace will prevail in this place of Tan-Awan. . . . And I will bear all sufferings so that you, leaders, will not be cowed by threats. I have experienced many sufferings, yet I was not shaken nor discouraged. You made me Christ whom we are now celebrating and all should stand for the truth, as Christ did in the past, so that everyone will have faith.

Looking at this last testament of Alex Garsales I realize how the theology we had grown into over the years had penetrated all through our communities. We were preaching it, but they were doing it with their lives.

Chapter 31

THE BISHOP was coming to Tabugon for confirmation, and with all the preparations I was unable to go down to Batang, our community house, after Easter to relax and hear the news from my colleagues as I normally would have done. If I had, I might have heard rumors of the disappearance of Herman and Alex. As it was, I and the rest of Tabugon were unaware.

This visit was to be the bishop's first "pastoral visitation" in the three years since I came. He would go around to all the areas of the parish to administer confirmation, and at the same time his secretary would check our baptismal, marriage, and burial books, and make sure that the parish priest had not sold off the statues or candlesticks—not an inconceivable possibility in these days of "liturgical reform." But the real importance of this visit was that the bishop was going to see a parish which was completely run on the Christian community model, and I was anxious that it appear at its best.

The Church had long been divided over confirmation. Some wanted it at birth, some at an age when the person could take part in the ceremonies. In a way, the controversy reflected different ways of looking at the sacraments. Those who promoted confirmation of infants tended to see the sacraments as mysterious powers that worked independent of the recipient. Those who wanted it at a later age put more emphasis on the personal involvement of the recipient.

Generally in the diocese of Bacolod the parishes had been moving away from infant confirmation but had got stuck halfway in "child" confirmation, which was neither flesh nor fish. Brian was one of the first to make the change. He liked to repeat the quote: "Jesus taught the adults and patted the children on the head. We teach the children and pat the adults on the head." So he put the age up to sixteen in his parish and abolished sponsorships. The Christian community would sponsor those to be confirmed and would make a collective gift to the bishop, which of course would be much less than came in under the old system, under which individual sponsors paid a fee on behalf of each confirmand, but Fortich had no problem with that.

Now in Tabugon we borrowed Brian's idea. We put the age up even further to eighteen and presented confirmation as the moment when the young Christian accepted the full responsibility of the promises made for her or him at baptism—to oppose the structural injustice of the society surrounding us, and to make her or his own personal formal, public commitment to serving the poor and oppressed. The change would mean a lot of hard work on our part, giving seminars around the communities and preparing people—far more than in the old days when it had been simply a matter of rounding up babies and making out receipts.

The bishop arrived in mid-week and toured the farthest parts of the parish. Everywhere he went the growth of the communities was evident: large crowds in attendance carrying the banners of their different communities, and a surprisingly large number of confirmations considering the new age limit. Seeing the full churches the bishop remarked: "O'Brien, I can't get over the number of adults. You haven't rounded up the children and brought them in to fill the gaps?" (A reference to the ploy of filling a half-empty church with school children to give the right impression when the bishop came around.) Each confirmation session finished with a communal meal with the people.

The last day of the bishop's visitation was to be spent in the *barrio* of Tabugon proper. The night before, we invited all the leaders in to dine with the bishop at the *convento* and then to have a session with Toto Suplido, the Social Action Director of the diocese. At this session Toto would brief the leaders on how to avail themselves of the free legal aid office of the diocese and give some elementary hints on how to defend their pieces of land.

As we were relaxing before supper on that last evening, a jeep pulled up at the door. In it were two Filipino priests, Dodo Dejilla and Peter Hiponia. They had bad news. They said that Alex Garsales and Herman Muleta, the Christian community leaders of Tan-Awan, were definitely missing, and that someone claimed to have seen them being tortured by members of the Long Range Patrol. The Long Range Patrol denied knowing anything about them, and there was no way the witness would come forward. Fortich knew Alex and Herman; he had met them at the confirmations in Oringao and remembered them. This action seemed to him to be the Long Range Patrol's answer to the peaceful protest in Oringao. The news cast a shadow over the last night of the bishop's visit and he left straight after the last confirmations in the morning, hurrying back to Bacolod to see what he could do.

A few days later we all came together in Kabankalan Church for a requiem mass for Father John Brazil, who had died suddenly in Ireland. He had been the co-initiator with Brian Gore of the whole Christian community approach in the Kabankalan area, and the bishop spoke strongly in praise of John and of what the little communities he had helped to pioneer were doing for the Church.

It was after this Mass that a group of seven women from the *barrio* of Tan-Awan came to the bishop in great distress because their husbands had disappeared. When? Three days after the great protest meeting in Oringao when the peasants had stood up and named the abuses they were suffering. Neither the bishop nor the women could know that this was going to lead to a life-and-death confrontation in the diocese between Church and State.

I felt John's death as a personal loss. He was very different from me in temperament, and often confronted me when he did not agree with me, but the two of us knew without ever a word being said that he had taken on the role of being my protector. I knew I would miss him. I was also worried by the stories concerning Alex and Herman. And now came this disappearance of seven peasants. It was with some foreboding that I returned to Tabugon from the funeral to prepare to take my leave and go to Ireland for my furlough.

Chapter 32

FOR SOME time now, all of our leaders had been meeting out on the *kibbutz* once every three months for what we called our "three-month target." The ostensible purpose was to do things in an orderly fashion by planning three months ahead, but for me there was another reason. This was to prepare them to take over. In running a parish the less you plan ahead the more the priest controls everything himself, because people must keep asking what comes next and asking permission. In this way one can keep a tight rein on things if that is what one wants to do. But if things are planned well in advance by all, then they can go on without you. That is what I wanted, because I had to be absent frequently in order to attend meetings and seminars, but also because I was convinced that for growth they had to do it on their own. And I had a conviction that in the long run the people would be on their own and they must learn how to do things themselves.

But my reason for giving them this scope ran even deeper—to the ever-present tension between the theology of St. John's Gospel and that of the Synoptics, Matthew, Mark, and Luke. John emphasizes the primacy of the Paraclete, of the Holy Spirit, in guiding and vivifying the community. The Synoptics emphasize authority, without which the idealistic community of love envisioned by John cannot survive. By putting both in the canon of Scripture the Church had accepted the two theological stances. They complemented each other: without John, the Synoptic communities would become legalistic and strangled with structure, and without the Synoptics the Johannine communities would become anarchic.

Just now our communities needed a little of John. So when we met for the last time before my furlough we planned for a full year ahead. . . . They and the Spirit would run the parish in my absence.

My last day was coming up. It was going to be May 1st, the Feast of St. Joseph the Worker, who was the patron of Dakong-Cogon workers. The mill had invited me over for Mass in the morning and a goodbye meal in the evening. I planned to have a special goodbye with the leaders in the *convento* in Tabugon at about 8:00 P.M. It turned out to be an eventful day.

In the morning before I left for Dakong-Cogon the leader of a community close to Pinamulakan arrived with a worried look on his face. He took me aside and told me that Trinio was back, alive and well, and out to get me.

"What do you mean by that?"

"He said it. I myself overheard him saying: 'Three bullets will be enough for him.'"

"What does that mean?"

"It means he's going to try to kill you."

"But why?"

"He says that if it wasn't for the Christian communities he would not have been attacked."

I determined to be careful; not to would be foolish. But I was also determined not to let it become known in the parish, because then Trinio would have gained something by creating tension. Rumors were weapons. I tried never to pass them on. So I asked my informant to keep the story to himself.

At the Mass at Dakong-Cogon, which most knew was to be my last for some time, who should appear but the gentleman who had said he would not go to Mass as long as I was parish priest. At the kiss of peace he came over awkwardly and embraced me. I was taken by surprise, only realizing the significance of it as I returned to the altar. I was happy that this little event had taken place. I knew it was not a real reconciliation—neither of us had changed his basic position—but I think that true reconciliations are not normally possible out of the blue. If you cannot even look at one another for anger, then how are you going to leap straight into a real meeting of minds? There has to be a first step, so I never belittled the so-called empty gesture: some day it could be filled! I think I learned this in the Philippines. Filipinos put great store by public gestures. Foreigners regard this as empty and hypocritical at times, but the Filipino tradition contains a profound wisdom. It is one way of keeping the communication lines open, and the people themselves do not regard it as betrayal. As a result this man and I came to be on speaking terms, and subsequently I was able to lend him a few books, including a very beautiful one on prayer. Later he was shot dead by the N.P.A.

On my way back to Tabugon the buggy broke down, and who should come to my aid but the local police chief. My relations with him had not been too good ever since I had accused him of backing the landlord in a land dispute. He took me on the back of his motorbike, and as he left me off he asked me if he could talk with me for a while. We sat on one of the balconies where we could be alone.

"Padre, you know I have a family. I am afraid that the N.P.A. are going to get me."

"Why?"

"Someone told me."

"Well, you know how many people are going around using the name of the N.P.A. to threaten each other. . . . But you know you police have the same temptation as we priests."

"What's that?"

"To accept privileges from the powerful and then favor them when we have to adjudicate in some way in cases between the rich and the poor."

"I am always very fair, Padre."

"I understand. But the way to be safe in the mountains as a policeman is to do the work of a policeman and not be used by another group to be a spy or an informer, because you know if they think you are doing that then you really are in danger."

"I know, Padre. That's why I never do that."

"I have a little present for you." And I produced one of my little Gospels. "Why don't we pray a little bit of it together?"

And we did this, and then he left. I felt happy that that little incident had happened on my last day. It seemed like a sign, maybe only another half-empty gesture, but a gesture which someday might be filled.

I spent the day preparing my bags for going home but kept my eye out all the time in case Trinio should appear. I was uneasy and tense without really knowing it. I went to the guest-house of the sugar *central* for supper as scheduled and then came back to our group, who had come to spend the last night with me. They had eaten and were sitting around in the *sala* playing the guitar and waiting for my arrival.

Arsenio was there from the *kibbutz* to close some accounts. This marked my final extrication from them. In the past two years our relationship had not been very good as I pushed them to do things completely on their own and not to be relying on me. I suppose unconsciously I was comparing them unfavorably with the Christian communities, which were far more self-reliant than the new *kibbutzim*. Junior was there, and the three of us were in my room going through the accounts. We made several attempts to straighten things out, but each time we got bogged down because Arsenio, on behalf of the *kibbutz*, was trying to bargain. That basically meant wanting me to pay a bill which they should pay themselves. Without my awareness, my irritation was mounting. Suddenly I exploded and began to shout. Not just shout, I was yelling at Arsenio and Junior as if I had gone out of my mind. The music and the conversation in the *sala* went quiet.

I stopped and then walked slowly over to my own balcony and slumped limply into a chair. I did not move. The whole house had become very silent. I sat there numbed by my own outburst, and gradually as I realized what I had done I began to think about how I had lasted right up till the eleventh hour and always been so patient and then my real nature had come out, right in front of all the leaders—those to whom I was father and guide and who looked to me for calmness in the many storms we had been through together. Anger is taboo in Philippine society. I had now broken this taboo in a solo exhibition before the whole parish. I had hurt Junior—I could see the dismay on his face. And there was something else: I had always been the one who had been unperturbed, especially during the dangers from armed groups and in confrontations and amid rumors. I felt that was one of my obligations to them—not to show my weakness. And now . . .

After what seemed a long time I felt a hand on my arm and a voice spoke. I did not look up. "I was the one who wrote those hurtful things about you on the blackboard"—it was Arsenio's voice. "Thank you, Arsenio," I said weakly. But I knew that in some strange way he had searched out a hurt of many months previously which I had completely forgotten about . . . and healed it. I struggled to my feet and the three of us returned to the *sala*, which was still silent.

I took a chair in the circle and sat there awkwardly. "I'm sorry for the outburst," I said to the group.

They pretended not to take too much notice of me but rather struck up a few songs.

Then Jaime, Arsenio's friend, said: "Why don't we take the blackboard and evaluate Padre's time in this parish? On the right we can write the positive things and on the left we can write the negative things."

But he was interrupted by Grisalda, a mother of seven, who said: "No, let's not talk about negative and positive. This is not the time for that. Why don't we go around the circle and each one say how he or she feels"—she emphasized the word "feels"—"now that Padre is going home."

They agreed, and she started herself. She had not got very far when she started to cry.

It went on around the group, with each of them saying how they would miss me.

It came to Jaime. He told the group that he had given me a lot of trouble (which was true) and how he regretted it.

It came to Junior. He said that the the last time I had gone home five years ago he had come with me to the airport and had said to himself: "'Now that Padre is gone, I'll get some rest from all the work.' But when the plane took off—" He did not get any further because he began to cry like a child.

Finally it came to me. I told them simply how ashamed I was of losing my temper in front of them, how broken, but they had put me together again.

What I did not say, because I could not put words to it, was that in my mind I saw more clearly than ever that the more I put myself above the people the more I locked myself out of the way of grace, and the more I melded into the community as another human being, notwithstanding my special task as priest, the more I became a disciple. And I thought of a priest friend of mine who, when his inner group of leaders were gathered around him during Mass told them how, in spite of his best efforts, he had been breaking his vows, and he wept bitterly as he spoke. They all wept too, but not bitterly; theirs were tears of compassion and care, and the community grew greatly in grace that day.

Next morning I left early. Junior drove, and I kept my head down completely out of sight when we passed the place where Trinio was likely to be.

Chapter 33

IN BATANG, a letter was waiting for me. Gearóid O'Broin, an erstwhile classmate in the seminary who had left to join the diplomatic service, was acting ambassador in Peking; he was inviting me to pass that way on my way home.

En route to Peking, properly called Beijing, our plane stopped at Canton, where the plane was boarded by Chinese domestic passengers, dressed in factory-work clothes. They swarmed onto the plane, looking very poor beside the well-dressed tourists and diplomats. It was a strange sight. I had never realized before that in the Philippines plane travel was basically a middle- and upper-class occupation. It gave me a jolt seeing these laborers piling in, unconscious at first of their workplace clothes. We were really in the People's Republic of China.

Gearóid was there at the airport to greet me and take me home to meet his Italian wife Roberta and their four children at the compound where the Irish Embassy was. I had stayed with him in New Delhi when I had gone to visit the tomb of Gandhi on an earlier furlough. A linguist, he was already reveling in learning Chinese. His family seemed to have no trouble in switching between Gaelic, Italian, and English.

Gearóid quickly introduced me to things Chinese and took me to all the sights. I hired a bike and began to go around the city and try out the restaurants. What struck me immediately was that no matter where I went the restaurants seemed to be the same, filled with workers in workers' clothes, eating their fill of rice or noodles. So different from other cities, where class distinction is so visible in the range of eating places and the dress of the people who patronize them. To me, coming from Tabugon where I had witnessed so much hunger, and aware of the miles and miles of squatter land in Manila where people live off dumps like "Smokey Mountain," this simple proletarian fare was adequate and wholesome. The Westerners I met were shocked at its drabness and monotony, however. To them it seemed like wartime fare or the fulfillment of the socialist nightmare in which everyone is reduced to the same colorless penury.

One little incident remains with me. I had looked assiduously for beggars in the streets and back alleys and found practically none, but one evening while eating in one of these self-service restaurants I noticed that after people had left their places at the table some young boys would slip in and sit in their chairs and eat the leftover food. Since the Chinese eat from a common dish, picking out with their chopsticks what they want, the food left at the table was, as it were, untouched and not leavings. It was clear that people turned a blind eye to these obviously hungry lads, but also that they were not encouraged. Otherwise, why did the boys look around furtively all the time? Where did the boys come from? Someone told me that they appear near the big railroad stations. They have "escaped" from the countryside and come to the city without a permit and are thus not eligible for assistance of any kind.

Beijing was a city for cyclists. They thronged the wide roads and among them, every now and again, would be a disabled person keeping up with the others in a wheelchair operated by two handles—to the right and left— which when pushed forward and backward, like vertical oars, propelled the large wheels of the chair.

There were two Masses at the cathedral on a Sunday, the first for the Chinese and the second for the tourists and embassy staffs. I cycled off to the Chinese one and was taken by surprise. It was a *Missa de Tres,* a Tridentine High Mass with three priests. I had not seen that ceremony for nearly twenty years. People prayed devoutly during it, fingering their rosaries, and went into confession boxes at the sides of the church. At the end of the Mass there was Benediction, the priest taking the Sacred Host, now placed in a monstrance like a gold sunburst, and blessing the whole congregation as they knelt and bowed their heads. After the divine praises which all said together in Chinese, all sang lustily in Latin the "Adoro Te Devote Latens Deitas" ("I Adore You, Hidden God"), a hymn written by Saint Thomas Aquinas five hundred years ago and at one time known all over the Catholic world. I joined in with the people around me and felt for a moment a deep nostalgia for that sense of universality the old Tridentine Mass used to give us. And I could understand why some people had fought so hard to keep it.

After the Mass people did not move from their benches for some time. They went on kneeling as they prayed their beads with old worn rosaries which looked as if they had been treasured for years—years when they had had to be hidden. Now there was a brief spring, but no one knew how long it would last and Gearóid had plenty of information on the suffering of the underground Church even to this time. I would have liked to have met them, but it was too dangerous for them.

Instead, something else happened. I was approached by some Lutherans from the Finnish Embassy and asked if I would lead their Sunday services. So that Sunday I said Mass in Gearóid's house where the embassy staff and other Catholics attended and, in the evening, I led the Protestant services in another house.

Finally I got the chance I had been waiting for to visit a Chinese family. A young Chinese-American girl said I could come with her to visit her relatives. Off we both went on our bicycles and arrived at a long one-story building. The family had two sons and one daughter. All lived in one room with their parents and grandmother. Everything in the room was spotlessly clean, though crowded. I hope my question was not too indiscreet when I asked about an ivory picture frame and a clock. Yes, they had been in the family for generations. So this was a family which had been well-off and now had to live in these conditions. The bathroom and kitchen were communal and shared with some of the other dwellings—how many I did not know. Mentally I was comparing everything with the conditions I had known in the Philippines, because it was to China that many Filipinos were looking for a model to imitate. This family had obviously come down in the world, though the children all had an education. The boys were carpenters. The girl had finished college but had then been banished to the country during the Cultural Revolution, the excesses of which were only then beginning to be revealed to the world.

In the Christian communities we had continually asked the people to list their needs. They were food, clothing, medicine, security. As for housing, any old house seemed to do in a tropical country, provided these other things were there. Compared with the people in my parish this family was well-off and the common telephone in the front of the house added that security against a sudden attack of illness. But then how were things in rural China? There seemed no question that Beijing was much better off than the rest of the country.

When the Chinese were challenged about the lack of freedoms cherished by the Western world—freedom of speech, freedom of the press, freedom of religion, freedom to move around and to emigrate, all of which were clearly lacking in China—their answer was that they put the "real" freedoms first: freedom to eat, freedom to avail themselves of medical treatment when sick, freedom to work. To most Westerners this seemed a glib stock answer, but I had lived for ten years in places where, although people technically had the first freedoms, one wondered what use they were to them as they lay dying on the floor of a hut sometimes for years for lack of elementary medical care and their children were forced into prostitution in an effort to stay alive. *Sacadas* were theoretically free to go to New York, but in actual fact they were not able to go to Bacolod. They were debt-slaves locked into the cutting and loading of sugarcane until they died.

Gearóid wrote out for me in Chinese ideograms anything I would need to ask. Although I had become quite good at sign language, asking for a public toilet, for example, presented a particular difficulty. It is not the sort of thing you can use sign language for without being misunderstood. So into my notebook we wrote such things as "How much is this?" Underneath, in Pinyin, Roman script, he wrote how it would sound. So all I had to do was go into a store and point at something and read out my little bit. One day I had gone to the Peking Zoo to see the pandas and had put in my notebook the Chinese equivalent of "Peking Zoological Gardens." Subsequently, while in a store trying to buy some things, I unwittingly got the two phrases mixed up. I bought all the things I needed and did not realize until I was finishing up that something was wrong. Maybe it was the understanding smiles on the faces of the attendants that gave it away. Meaning to say "How much is this?" I had all along been holding up items and saying with an engaging smile "Peking Zoological Gardens?" This had in no way impeded communication . . . which surely proves something.

When we had arrived we were issued special tourist money. That meant you could only enter those places where this tourist money was accepted— an effective way of keeping visitors from nosing around. When I presented too large a bill at the Temple of Heaven, however, I was given back Chinese currency in change. With this money I made my way into a popular cinema. The film opened with a scene on the quays in some Western port with weeping families looking on as their press-ganged sons left on a naval vessel. The decadent American captain spent most of the time in his cabin shouting orders, drinking from a bottle of gin in large gulps, while behind him on the wall hung pictures of equally decadent females dressed for a bath.

Meantime a Chinese vessel is coming into the sights of the big U.S. vessel. Life on board among the sailors on the small Chinese ship is straight from the Acts of the Apostles: harmony, brotherly love, sharing.

Finally the dreadful encounter takes place and guns open up on all sides. Immediately the U.S. crew mutiny and with glad cries rush for the rail and freedom. The U.S. captain has no life-belt and he shoots one of his men and takes the life-belt off him. Meanwhile on the Chinese boat the captain sees one of his men without a life-belt, takes his own off, and gives it to him. All is now lost, the boat is sinking, the men cling to the flag and sing the national anthem as the water rises around them.

I felt I ought to see another film. I went to another cinema. This time I was in time for two educational shorts before the main feature. The first was on how flashlight batteries are made. The second one seemed to be on how to butcher a sheep. Then the main feature. I sat back in anticipation. The first scene opened: the quays, the weeping mothers, the press-ganged sons. . . . I could not take it a second time.

The women seemed to be dressed the same as men, in blue suits and caps. They drove the buses and hosed them down when they got to the terminals. I also saw women doing light acetylene welding on public works. Gearóid told me they kept their own names after marriage. They seemed to have come a long way from the days of bound feet. At evening in the public parks you saw young women dressed in pleated skirts and white ankle socks sitting beside young men, shyly holding hands.

The airfare from Beijing to London was exorbitant compared with other comparable distances, so I decided to go by train. A train for Europe left twice a week, on Saturdays and Wednesdays. This was the Trans-Siberian train. One train was Chinese to the Chinese-Russian border and then became Russian; the other stayed Chinese all the way. Everyone warned me not to take the Russian one. I thought I detected a bit of prejudice and decided to take the Russian one anyway. As announced, it was Chinese till the border; we had a meal served with the usual Chinese quiet efficiency which lacked servility of any kind. I had noticed this right through my month's stay: the quiet unconscious dignity of a people who had "stood up."

When we got to the border we were taken by surprise with what happened next. We alighted and the whole train was lifted by winches into the air and the wheels were removed and replaced by the wider gauge Russian wheels. It was only then that I had a good chance to look at the magnificent steam engine, painted in red and green with glowing brass fittings.

The Chinese staff disappeared and a Russian staff appeared. After a visit to a Russian "bank" (where the tellers used an abacus) to purchase rubles, off we chuffed. Evening came and with it time for supper. I and some newfound Swedish friends made our way to the dining carriage. It was locked. We approached the Russian attendant. We made the sign for food, pointing to the dining carriage. He just put up both his hands in a blocking gesture and said, "Niet, niet." The response was the same to any other question we had. By the time the dining car finally opened it was twenty-six hours since our last meal. I had brought no food and was ravenous by that time. Some people had got into my carriage and eaten sandwiches they had brought. In the West it is quite normal to eat in front of others this way, but not so in the Philippines. The words "food" and "share" are as close as the words "man" and "wife." I missed the Philippines.

At last we sat down to eat. Caviar was on the table. A Swedish companion suggested we ask for the menu and do our own choosing, but I said, "There's no way I'm going to question this. They might take it back and give us nothing." And it was strange, but after six days on that train we had all become docile and accepting. We approached the attendants with diffidence, knowing that the chances of a civil answer were only one in ten and any sign of insubordination on our part would trigger a "Niet" and an immediate end to the conversation. We soon learned in the restaurant that if you did not leave a tip they took one for themselves.

Gradually I realized that we had traveled six thousand kilometers and passed through many towns without seeing one nice bungalow which had flowers in the garden, a couple of bicycles outside the door, and a sense of humble comfort. The only things to attract the eye were those parts of the railway stations built before the revolution. The rest was drab and second-class. The bricks were all crumbly and chipped like rejects. I wondered if the train was beginning to get to me and causing me to see it all with prejudice. But Ingergeerd, one of the Swedish women, reassured me.

"No, I've been on this trip twice, and you've said it exactly as it is. Of course, it is Siberia!"

However, rural Siberia was beautiful. Possibly it was exceptionally hot for May, but when the train left those drab built-up areas, it passed for thousands of kilometers through grassy land scattered with what seemed to me like silver birch trees and sometimes we passed a river and saw people fishing, their shirts off. You could see where their milk-white skin had been scalded lobster red by the sun.

We passed Lake Baikal, almost two kilometers deep—the deepest inland water in the world. And on one occasion the train stopped right in the middle of the steppe, with not a building around that we could see. One of the young men from the kitchen got down, picked some flowers, and came back with a bunch of them for the dining car. His action seemed out of keeping with the hostile way we were being treated by the train staff, but it gave strength to my inner conviction that their behavior could not be in any way representative of the Russian people. And I thought to myself, "If we could only speak Russian things might be different. Then we could talk to each other like humans."

Along the railroad line near the towns we saw groups of stocky women in shorts and halters carrying pickaxes and buckets. They seemed to be mending the railroad line. Once while the train was in a station I saw a man mending the line; he was the first I had seen. I raised my camera to take a shot. He caught my eye, and raised his pickaxe menacingly at me. I put down the camera. When I mentioned this to the others, someone said: "Maybe he was embarrassed to be seen doing women's work!"

On one occasion we went into the station at a stop, always with a sense of fear that the train might take off because Mr. Niet and his companions would never give us a civil answer as to how long it was stopping. We were hoping to buy some bread or some buttermilk. They had bottled buttermilk at many of the stations. We walked into a place which had what looked like food-dispensing machines. We were tugging at the various handles, trying to make them work, making wisecracks to one another and thinking we were alone, when suddenly we became aware that in fact we were at the front of a large hall and sitting behind us on rows of benches in eerie silence all the time were some hundreds of young men, their heads shaven, their faces expressionless. There was not a smile or a snigger from them at the antics of these odd foreigners who had entered unknowingly on stage. We fled. Later we wondered who they were. Were they military? Maybe. But they had no uniform that we noticed. Were they students? Hardly. When were students so silent? And why the shaved heads and the dead faces? Going where?

Military were in evidence whenever we alighted. They walked in pairs along the station with epaulets and peaked army caps, leather boots and leather leggings, and heels clicking. They were a far cry from the boy-scout-like soldiers who swarmed around the streets of Peking in happy groups, doing their shopping on a day off.

Toward the end of the journey food began to become scarce in the dining carriage. We had seen people buying food from the kitchen area of the train at the stations along the way, and we reckoned there was a connection between the two circumstances.

In spite of everything, I slept well and enjoyed the six-day rest on the train. I felt very refreshed by the time we pulled into Moscow.

Chapter 34

I SAID goodbye to my Swedish friends and got off the train at Moscow. I stayed for a day with the Philippine ambassador to Russia who was an Ilongo and an acquaintance. His sister was a St. Paul's Sister in Kabankalan. He was not a Marcos appointee but a career diplomat and one of the most distinguished in the service of the Philippine diplomatic corps. It was just after dawn when I arrived and a good time to have a look at the Kremlin and the Cathedral of St. Basil. The ambassador's driver, who met me at the train, told me that the Czar, Ivan the Terrible, had liked the onion-domed church so much that he had the eyes of the architects put out to prevent them from building one like it for someone else. We watched the sun rise on the red brick of the Kremlin fortress and the changing of the goose-stepping guard before the mausoleum of Lenin. We were alone in the great square in the cold dawn.

Nobody was up when we got to the embassy—it was still not 6:00 A.M.—so I went out for a stroll and a look in the shop windows. There was not much to see, so when I spotted a queue forming in front of a newspaper kiosk I decided to join. The woman in charge took her time and no one tried to hurry her, although she seemed to be arranging and folding every paper individually. She seemed to be making the point that she was in charge. When she was quite ready—or maybe when it was the official time to open—the line began to move. People moved along briskly and I got the feeling, maybe because of the way I was conditioned on the train, that I should have my money and order ready pat or I might be sent all the way back to the end of the line. I got a copy of *L'Humanité* and the *Morning Star*, and walked home.

The ambassador was up when I got back, and he and his wife gave me a

Filipino welcome and a great Filipino breakfast. He was amazed that I had got the papers.

"Where did you manage to get those? I have never been able to get them."

"It's probably just a matter of getting up earlier," I joked.

"But it's hard to get things here," his wife complained. "We can't get any vegetables at all. We always take a net bag when we go out, in case we see a queue forming so that we can line up and buy something."

"But there are dollar shops," said the ambassador, "and we'll take you there this morning in case you want to buy something. I have also arranged for us to see Lenin's tomb."

Out of respect for the national monument I thought I should be more formal than my jeans and polo shirts in which I had been traveling. When they were ready to go I appeared in Roman collar.

However, the ambassador said: "It would be better not to wear that. Take one of my shirts and a tie. It's the recognized way of visiting the mausoleum."

There were two queues of hushed visitors. One of them stretched away out of sight, but our official guide brought us to the shorter one. As we shuffled along we passed the busts of various military notables. In the midst of them in a humble position was one of Marshal Stalin. The ambassador remarked to me in Tagalog that even that was a promotion for Stalin because the bust had not been there before. The guide interjected a slight correction in Tagalog. The ambassador stiffened. None of us had realized the guide understood the Philippine language. The ambassador had been using it deliberately for privacy, and worried that he might have said something indiscreet.

The ambassador and his wife took me to dinner at a Moscow restaurant. His visiting son and some of the embassy staff came too. It was a high-ceilinged, old-fashioned place, with faded plush like a movie palace of the thirties. Caviar and smoked salmon were on the table, but first there was vodka. The ambassador explained that the Russians begin their meal with vodka. They also continue it with vodka. So he poured me a vodka. After the last scanty days on the train everything looked just great. We raised our glasses and took a sip. Then out of the blue the ambassador's wife said in a voice of deep concern: "Father O'Brien, we hear all this talk about hunger in the Philippines. Surely it can't be so? If people are prepared to work, surely there's no need for anyone to go hungry. I mean, people don't actually die of hunger, do they?"

I took a deep breath and gave the salmon a baleful look. I was deeply tempted to agree politely, but I knew I could not.

Everyone had paused and was waiting for my reply.

I put down my glass and said: "I'm sure it is possible that some people could go hungry through their own fault. However, my experience in the mountains of Negros is that people go hungry because the little bit of land they have is taken away from them by people from the lowlands who have the right connections. And though they may only rarely die directly from hunger, prolonged malnutrition is probably the ultimate cause of a great number of deaths."

The ambassador's son changed the topic.

When I said goodbye, the ambassador sent me off to the train with a bottle of whiskey and a bottle of vodka.

Back on the train I found myself sharing a carriage with a young man from Pakistan called Mahomet. He told me he had a scholarship to study welding in Leningrad. After a while he asked diffidently if I minded if he spread his mat and said his prayers. I said no, that I prayed all the time myself and would take the opportunity to pray the Psalms. So we both opened our scriptures and prayed. After that he told me there was great pressure on him in Leningrad, but he had tried to be faithful to his religion, especially the dietary laws. I said I fully understood and showed him my little Muslim rosary beads which I had picked up on a visit to the Muslim area of the Philippines where the Columbans were working in the hope not of converting but of learning from the Muslims and bringing about some sort of healing between them and the Christian community. I had almost been kidnapped on that occasion by some Muslim brigands, but I felt this was not the time for telling that story.

On this leg of the train journey the attendants were all women. They were as aggressive and hostile as the men on the first leg had been. When some students looked into our carriage from the corridor, one of the attendants came out and shouted that if they did not return immediately to their own seats she would report them to the train police for the crime of "buying and selling on the train"—quite a retribution for the fault of talking animatedly in the corridor!

Russian tea is an acquired taste. I had been presented with it many times on the first leg of the journey and drank it out of courtesy. Then, lo and behold, I was presented with a hefty bill for it when leaving the train at Moscow. So when a knock came at the door and the same woman who had just bellowed at us appeared with a glass of tea and wreathed smiles, I declined. But she insisted. I declined. She insisted. I knew now it was not a present, but she was not taking no. I turned to Mahomet (who spoke Russian) and said, "Explain to her that I have a bad stomach. I don't think my doctor would approve." Mahomet explained. She hesitated and withdrew to the door, frustrated that the authority I had cited was not present to be interrogated. "And what does his doctor recommend him?" she asked, unconvinced. Mahomet passed the question on to me. "Tell her this," I said, pointing to the two bottles given me by the ambassador. But when she saw me gesturing, she stamped away before the dismayed Mahomet had time to explain to her.

We awoke in the early hours of the morning to find ourselves suspended in the air. We had stopped outside the Polish border and the wheels were being changed again, this time with the passengers still inside. Russia has always had a wider gauge than most countries; why change it if it will only facilitate invasion? Anyway, while the train was in the air Mahomet heard someone walking along the roof. He said they were checking that no one was hiding in between the carriages. A few minutes later a soldier with a long gun appeared at the door. He ordered us out of the carriage and closed the door, leaving us outside. Mahomet said: "He's just checking that no one is hiding under the bed." The soldier came out and motioned with his gun for us to open our bags. He asked me something in Russian. "He's asking you if you have any rubles." I fished in my pocket and produced a small amount, my unspent rubles. The soldier spoke angrily. "He says you should have turned those in before. You're not supposed to have rubles." At that the soldier ordered me off the train with his gun. Mahomet jumped down with me from the still dangling train and said: "We're to go to the nearest station and change the rubles."

We ran off along the tracks in the dawn cold, wondering where this station was, because it seemed that we were out in the countryside. We had been ordered out so peremptorily that we had left our bags wide open and our money and passports unattended in the open carriage. As we ran I could not believe it was happening.

Soon the station, a large group of buildings, came in sight. When we got there we ran from building to building trying to find where we might change my rubles. All the notices were in Cyrillic script so I could not even make a stab at what they said. At last, almost panicked lest the train would be gone with our bags and passports and money, we found what looked like a bank. They told Mahomet they were just closed. Mahomet explained our predicament, but they pointed to a clock. Just then I spied a notice in Roman script: "Intourist." I ran up the stairs and into a room where several people were seated. I said, "I wonder if anyone here speaks English?" An exceptionally beautiful young woman with striking grey eyes stood up. "Can you help us? Our train is leaving and we are supposed to change this money, but the bank won't change it." "Follow me," she said.

The bank woman resisted her, but she eventually convinced her somehow. "I wonder how she did that," said Mahomet. "She probably knows her well," I said. She turned around with obvious annoyance and said: "I do not know her." Then she counted the money into my hand. When I realized how little was involved, I said: "Really, I would have willingly handed this money over rather than go through what we've been through." "You are that rich?" she said. "No," I stammered, "it's just that . . . ."

"Follow me," she said. And she led us into another room. We did not know where we were at this stage and both of us were thinking of our abandoned bags.

She disappeared for a minute and then came back and said: "Your train has gone."

"Wonderful!" I said, smiling happily.

She disappeared again. In a few moments she was back. "Your train is still here." And she pointed to another door, and left.

Once back on the train we rushed to our carriage. Our bags were still sprawled upon the carriage, but nothing had been touched. The soldier was gone and the train was pulling out. We collapsed and sat gasping for breath.

There was a great sense of relief as the train moved into Poland. We joined a group of African students in the corridor and discussed what we had all been through. "Let's get something to eat. There's a Polish dining car on now," said someone.

"What'll we use for money?" I asked.

In chorus they all answered: "Rubles," and waved the bills in the air. Everyone was laughing.

Mahomet persuaded me to get off the train at Warsaw for a couple of days. He wanted to buy some textbooks. These he could sell for a profit when he got back to Leningrad. We could stay at an Indian hostel. He could pass for an Indian, and if I remained out of sight maybe I could too. But that did not come off, so a student we met took us to a guest-house run by Sisters and meant for traveling priests. I reckoned that with all that praying, stretching a point, Mahomet was a sort of priest, and Sister accepted the two of us. When we got to our room Mahomet unrolled his mat and made up for lost time, and I went and said Mass.

Meat was scarce in Poland. It had all been shipped to Russia for the Olympic Games opening in a month, and the Poles were not amused. In fact, our student guide told us there would be trouble and that he had just seen a meat queue being guarded by troops. This was June 1980. The "trouble" erupted a few weeks later. Anyway, Sister managed to get a little sliced salami for us and produced it with pride the next morning at breakfast, telling us how difficult it had been to come by. Mahomet gave me a look, and I knew that this was against his dietary laws. I explained to Sister in sign language that his particular order did not permit him. . . . She was duly edified that at least some religious were keeping to the ancient disciplines.

I had not mentioned to Mahomet the nature of the place we were staying in, but by now with all the Sisters and priests around, many in religious garb, he had some questions.

"What is a priest?" he asked. He had heard the word a few times since we came.

I thought for a moment. "Well, it's like this. When Allah made the world he meant all of us to be brothers and sisters. Now everyone is fighting and killing each other like enemies. That is against the will of Allah. Well, a priest is supposed to work to bring the human family back together again so that they can be the brothers and sisters that Allah always wanted them to be."

"Are you a priest?"

"Well, I'm trying to be."

And we said no more.

In Warsaw we saw the sights, in particular the remains of the ghetto where the Warsaw uprising of the Jews took place and the prison where they were held and tortured. I had used the example of Christian silence during the Holocaust so often in Tabugon, and I found myself deeply moved when I saw those instruments of torture.

We were ready to board the Russian train again, standing opposite our designated carriage with our tickets in our hands, but the door was locked. A guard appeared and refused to open it. He sent us further down. The guard there sent us back. The first guard still refused to open the door, and then, raising his outstretched fingers twice to indicate twenty, he said: "Dollars!" I shook my head and walked off. In all my years in the Philippines no one had ever asked for money brazenly like that. But the train was warming up. Back at the other door the guard was gone. Our visas ran out that night. I came back and raised two hands once: "Dollars," I said, indicating ten. He nodded. He opened the door and in the corridor we each paid him ten dollars and took our seats.

All along on our journey through Russia it was clear that American dollars were acceptable and indeed very much sought after. In the train through Siberia a lot of trading went on. One of the waiters in the dining car had wanted to buy my shortwave radio and was offering me dollars, which he had presumably picked up from passengers. Then there were the dollar shops in Moscow.

As we pulled out of East Berlin to cross the border into West Berlin, Mahomet told me to look out of the window and up into the iron scaffolding of the station ceiling. I did. There I saw uniformed marksmen with rifles, looking down on us. When I asked why they were there, he said: "Just in case anyone is trying to escape by clinging in between the carriages. They will shoot them dead on the spot."

I said goodbye to Mahomet and took a bus to Tegel Airport to get the plane to Brussels and to Ireland. The friendliness of the airport took me by surprise. It felt as if they were putting on a show for me.

I have often thought about that trip through Russia. If anything, I had gone there with an open mind, determined to see through the shallow and puerile anti-Russian propaganda we get so much of. I also was and am convinced that one cannot judge a whole nation by a simple journey like that. Nor have I had much corroboration from anyone who has gone to Russia in a more orthodox way. But I have related the experience as it was and have not exaggerated. The trip was like an article you might see in the *Reader's Digest* during a period of frigid relations between the United States and Russia. People in public service whom we dealt with seemed to have no incentive for caring. In fact they used their position, however small, to extort "respect." Not having the language I found no way to break through and I ended up, against my will, by seeing them as adversaries.

Another thing was how different it all was from China. In China the people had gained their equality, enhanced their dignity, and remained human. In Russia they seemed to have gained their equality at some cost to their humanity.

Chapter 35

NOT LONG after I arrived in Ireland, news from the Philippines caught up with me. The bodies of Alex and Herman had been found while I was traveling home and the story of what had happened was taking shape.

Herman Muleta was aged forty-four and had nine children. At 11:00 P.M. on Easter Sunday men's voices were heard outside his house, requesting that he come out. They said they must accompany him to the *barrio* captain's house. Herman's wife could not see the faces of the men in the dark, but she could make out their green uniforms and the guns they carried. Herman was taken to the house of Alex Garsales, where Alex was roused and ordered to come with them. Witnesses said they heard a truck starting up and heading toward *barrio* Saise. A resident of *barrio* Saise reported that he saw a weapons carrier parked there that night and the next morning. People saw military combat-boot prints on the ground at that place.

Five weeks later a farmer plowing his field came across the bodies not far from the place where the residents had seen the parked weapons carrier.

Nobody had any doubt that it was the military, but these things were always hard to prove. The peasants were so afraid that it took a long time to get them to reveal what they knew. And then they needed protection, and sometimes they would disappear or be shot down in cold blood.

At the funeral our bishop deepened his own involvement and linked their deaths to their membership in the Christian communities:

"The Christian community of which Alex and Herman were active members must go on. We Christians should stand up with a firm determination that we cannot, and should not, and must not, tolerate abuses of this nature. People of God from Tan-Awan continue building the Christian community, for this is the true foundation of your human rights. . . ."

If the Christian communities were under fire, the bishop was backing us all the way.

The next thing that happened was that a petition was circulated in the town of Kabankalan for the removal of Father Brian Gore because, it said, "he is suspected of communistic leanings and under the guise of his office as a priest he is sowing the seeds of discontent, confusion and chaos among our people." The petition was signed by very few people; in fact, some people signed their names more than once. The petition was sent to the "highest authorities," and the papal nuncio, Monsignor Bruno Torpiglianini, contacted Monsignor Fortich to express his concern. However, the bishop assured him that the problem could be dealt with at the local level.

What was significant was that the small Christian communities were emerging as the center of the controversy. But I was on vacation and determined to build myself up. I knew it was a healthy thing to put Negros out of my mind as far as possible for the duration.

Ever since the Second Vatican Council the Columban Society had tried to reeducate its members in the new teachings and, even more so, in the spirit of the Council. One of the ways of doing this was that each of us was invited to take a renewal seminar for three months. I had not yet taken it, so I enrolled. It was held at Dalgan Park, the seminary outside Dublin where I had done my priesthood studies.

Before we started the course, when we were filling in the application forms, we were each asked what we wanted to get out of this renewal course, which was called "Faith and Mission." I reckoned that as far as "updating" was concerned I had kept up with the theology as it had been developing since the Council, but there were two things I felt I needed: one was to understand more deeply the renewed emphasis on the Resurrection, and the second was not to have a dichotomy between my own spiritual life and the work we were doing for the poor.

The term "spiritual life" is a very important part of religious vocabulary in the Catholic Church and for us it meant our living relationship with Jesus. But it tended again and again to get reduced to certain prayers that had to be said and certain actions, like daily Mass, fasting, or denying yourself something. Very often it happened that while we developed these to a high degree they came to have less and less effect on our daily life. The spiritual life became so "spiritual" that it was separated from and had no effect on the ordinary "real" life. For some time now I had been trying to unite and integrate these two aspects of my life. I thought that during this three-month period I would make a point of trying to forward this a bit and I hoped the seminar would help me.

As for the "sense" of the Resurrection, I was not too sure what I wanted, but I knew it was closely related to the question about the spiritual life. We tended to confine the risen Jesus to the tabernacle, which was a very important devotion for us. There were even Sisters who spent their whole lives before the tabernacle in adoration, vicars as it were for the rest of the world. But once again, in keeping Jesus firmly in the tabernacle, there was the danger that he would also be kept out of the marketplace and out of our daily lives. Like the woman who ran the *hacienda* near San Ramon, worried to tears about not being able to go to Communion but unworried about the children who were dying on her farm. Or the priest who spent an hour daily in front of the tabernacle but then would get up and bawl the people out unjustifiably. And then there was myself, so careful about keeping that light burning before the tabernacle all these years but so judgmental of those who I felt had not accepted the Vatican Council. Jesus was in the tabernacle, but he was also in those dying children, the old woman coming to the *convento* at an awkward hour, and those who were closet followers of Lefebre. And Jesus was present in China and Russia or else the Resurrection meant nothing. But how was this so?

The highlight of the three-month course was its ten-day retreat. This of course would be in silence and each of us would have a director, a man or woman who would guide us through the ten days. Each evening we would have Mass together. I chose a Jesuit priest for my director and he directed me in prayer, giving me short passages from the Scriptures and letting me "stay" with them in prayer. He got me to list the people I wanted to help and suggested I pray for them, not just by saying prayers for them, but by standing with them in the presence of Jesus, presenting them to him, as it were. I liked that.

As the days went on, however, I could see that, while others seemed to be walking on air, I was plodding along finding it a great struggle to keep my mind on the prayer. The director was patient with me and I was patient with myself. I felt that I did not want any great light. I feared "enlightenment" because I feared disillusionment afterwards. Religion made sense to me and I did not want to be knocked off my horse. I did not want to be inflated lest I be deflated. I wanted no miracles. On the ninth day I reported to my director as usual: Well, I had gone through several hours of prayer that day; no, it had not brought any particular enlightenment or message or "moment"; but I had done it knowing that it was good; yes, I had tried not to strain; but, well, it was the same old plodding; l didn't mind.

Then unexpectedly he said: "Are you angry about something?"

I was surprised at the question. It seemed irrelevant. "No," I said. "No, nothing that I can think of." Then, without knowing where it came from, I suddenly heard myself saying: "I am angry." I said it in such a changed pitch and with such a tremor that I was shocked at the sound of my own voice.

There was silence. He did not interrupt.

"I am angry, Father, at all the unnecessary suffering and that we the Church are not in there all over the world lightening the burden of the people. When I think of the tens of thousands of prostitutes in Ologanapo in the Philippines who are locked into all of that against their will, and the same all over Asia, and how we could be helping, I feel angry and frustrated. When I think of the hunger and sickness. . . . We have enough for them. We have too much; we don't know what to do with it. We are Dives, and Lazarus is at our gate. We step over his body every day. I feel frustrated and I feel angry."

The director said nothing. He let me continue. When I had quite finished, he opened a New Testament and searched: "He entered the synagogue and a man was there who had a withered hand and they watched him, to see whether he would heal him on the Sabbath, so that they might accuse him. And he said to the man who had the withered hand, 'Come here,' and he said to them, 'Is it lawful on the Sabbath to do good or to do harm, to save life or to kill?' But they were silent. And he looked around them with anger, grieved at their hardness of heart, and said to the man: 'Stretch out your hand.' He stretched it out and his hand was restored."

Angry. Jesus was angry. I needed no more. And he said no more, but gave me the chapter and verse of the passage, and I went back to prayer. But now I confronted Jesus on the promises he had not kept, the people whom he had abandoned, some who had trusted in him, the slowness of the churches in getting together and helping the people. Now I brought my work and life right into the heart of prayer and I demanded to know.

At our evening Mass Sister Elizabeth Moran gave the homily. She took the text from Ephesians where St. Paul trips over his words in an attempt to tell us of the "depth and the height and breadth" of the love of Christ. It surpasses all "knowledge"! Was it because I had at last acknowledged my anger with God? I don't know; but at that moment I had a glimpse of a glimpse of what that love might be, and it remained with me in the following years, filling them with peace in the midst of great anxiety and grief.

Before the course was over some shocking news arrived. The seven peasants who had disappeared a few days after the great rally in Brian Gore's parish of Oringao had been found dead. They had been tortured for days and then hog-tied and shot and buried still alive. They were dug up allegedly on the mayor's *hacienda,* and along with the commander of the Long Range Patrol the mayor was indicted for multiple murder eight days later. Colonel Agudon, the provincial commander, and Bishop Fortich jointly pushed the provincial government to charge whoever they felt were guilty.

The military man who discovered the bodies was Lieutenant Dangup, an old antagonist of the mayor. He and the other local-based military had not been amused when the mayor invited in the Long Range Patrol, a special task force to protect the town. Now the Long Range Patrol, wanting part of the action normally open to the military, had confiscated five trucks of logs which they claimed Dangup had been trying to truck through Kabankalan illegally from the mountains where Dangup had contacts—at least of a logging nature—with the N.P.A.

The mayor was released on bail of 150,000 pesos and took temporary leave of office.

* * *

When Christmas was over I headed back to Negros. News had just come that Bishop Fortich had managed to have the schedule of Pope John Paul's visit to the Philippines altered: in four weeks' time Negros would be receiving the Pope.

Chapter 36

THE PHILIPPINES was all fired up for the Pope's visit. It had been an unexpected coup for Fortich to persuade the organizers to let the Pope stop in Bacolod. Fortich insisted that Negros was special because, he said, it was a "social volcano." The government media were irked by his metaphor, though in fact the volcano was already erupting.

The bishop planned that seminars would be given to all the people before the Pope's arrival, and a group of Filipino priests prepared a seminar which gave the Pope's life story and at the same time the mission of the Church on justice. When I got back to Negros these were about to get under way. Our plan was to try and make sure that all who went to hear the Pope would have done the seminar. Each mini-parish was to give the seminars to its own Christian communities.

There was something besides the Pope's visit on my mind. As soon as I arrived back I was greeted with the news that our cook, Badong, was in prison, accused of rape. His wife and six children were now in need of support, both material and psychological, and it looked as if this was some sort of reprisal against the Church, because the evidence for the case was nonexistent. But someone had to fight the case. Apart from all that, we now had no cook and the cook was a vital part of the *convento* life, seeing that we had almost open house to the whole parish. We would have to find a temporary replacement.

Badong wrote me a heartrending letter from prison. He had been beaten by the other prisoners, his clothes and mat had been taken, he was hungry. I went down to Bacolod to see him in the provincial jail. In all my life I had never seen such a hole: crowds of prisoners locked into what looked like cages; the men half naked, all covered in tattoos of snakes and dragons mixed with images of Christ and the Virgin. Pervading everything there was a stench from the cooking of glue. The cells had no water and only a hole in the ground for a toilet. Many of the young prisoners looked grotesque, with shaven heads and their front teeth fallen out from lack of nourishment. The food must be very bad, I thought, because most Filipinos have magnificent teeth. I slipped some cash to Badong with which he could buy materials to make woodwork artifacts to sell. I promised I would do my best to fight the case. I struggled out of the prison, festooned with prisoners beseeching help in their cases.

The Pope was due to arrive in a couple of weeks. The seminars were going well, and we planned that nine trucks in all would make the 130-kilometer journey down to Bacolod from the parish of Tabugon. But deep down I was apprehensive. Say if the Pope did not speak out strongly. Say if it was so balanced a speech that everything was stressed, thus leaving nothing stressed. Say if he says something that the authorities pick up, as they had so often done before when a plea to priests to keep out of partisan politics was used by the government newspapers as a pretext to castigate us for being involved in human rights and allowed those who were remaining silent about the suffering of the people the excuse that they did not want to get involved in politics.

Immediately preceding the visit of the Pope *Newsweek* carried a stinging article about Negros entitled "Island of Fear." Using Bishop Fortich's description of Negros as a "social volcano," the magazine described in brutal detail the death with torture that had been visited on Alex Garsales and Herman Muleta the previous April and the fear among some landowners that a strong human rights sermon from the Pope could lead to a challenge to their domination on the island.

Many of the people of Tabugon had no place to sleep in Bacolod, so they just spent the night on the grass at their designated spot in the huge "reclamation area" (a site which was being reclaimed from the sea) where the Pope was to speak the next day. I brought two cases of one-year-old and joined them on the grass for a drink with Father Eugene McGeough. I felt the alcohol would act as an internal blanket for everyone. The old Hotel Mallorca, now closed down, opened its doors for one last time and gave us Columbans a bed.

When morning came Bacolod was like a new-born babe, incapable of harming anyone. It is hard to remember a moment like it before. Everyone was celebrating and in festive gear, the city decked with flowers and banners and religious pictures, and the street vendors were ecstatic.

A crowd of three-quarters of a million was awaiting the arrival of the Pope, when who should drive up the center of the reclamation area but the Honorable Imelda Romualdez Marcos, wife of the President, First Lady of the Philippines, Governor of Metromanila and Minister for Human Settlements!

She went straight to the microphone prepared for the Pope and began to speak: "Negros is not an island of fear. It is an island of love. . . ." She was answering that *Newsweek* article.

She disappeared quite as suddenly as she had appeared and was gone almost before the people knew she had been there. All still awaited the Pope. I will never forget the apprehension with which I awaited his word. I felt weak inside, afraid that they would not measure up to the anticipation and suffering of the people and therefore would do more harm than good. From where I sat with the other priests on the platform from which he was to speak, I could see my own people in the crowd with their banners— pathetic things made from old sacks, but their own, painted by themselves. Up near the front I could see where my friend Baby Gonzales had collected all the disabled of Bacolod and had raised a huge banner in Polish, saying, "Welcome Lolek!" (the Pope's pet-name as a boy).

The Pope arrived, standing in the front of a bizarre glassed-in vehicle which the Bishop had helped to design. Fortich himself and the Pope's entourage were in the back. The vehicle stopped below the stage. The Pope alighted and was led up the stairs to the microphone. When the cheering died down he started to speak in a strong clear voice. His opening greeting was in Ilongo. First came preliminary words of goodwill, then he got to the meat of his message. After the first few sentences, I sat back in my chair. I was hardly listening; I was just letting them flow over me. Now I was weak from relief.

". . . Injustice reigns when some nations accumulate riches and live in abundance while other nations cannot offer the majority of the people the basic necessities.

"Injustice reigns when within the same society some groups hold most of the wealth and power while large strata of the population cannot decently provide for the livelihood of their families even through long hours of back-breaking labor in factories or in the fields. . . .

"Injustice reigns when the laws of economic growth and ever greater profit determine social relations, leaving in poverty and destitution those who have only the work of their hands to offer.

"Being aware of such situations, the Church will not hesitate to take up the cause of the poor and to become the voice of those who are not listened to when they speak up, not to demand charity, but to ask for justice. . . ."

On and on it went, interrupted only by wild cheering from the priests, one sentence stronger and more concrete than the next, for example explicitly endorsing the right to unionize, now considered illegal and even subversive in the Philippines. In the context within which the Pope was speaking—before three-quarters of a million workers and peasants, on an island torn apart precisely over these issues of land, wages, unions, and distribution of goods—his talk could not have been stronger. And yet it had nothing that could be called irreconcilable bitterness, because the door was held open for a return of those who had strayed from the truth by enchaining their sisters and brothers.

Then onto the stage came Magdal Muleta and Libing Garsales, the widows of Herman and Alex, men who had been slain because of their membership in the Christian communities. They presented the Pope with a cross on which were written those last words of Alex: "I, Alex Garsales of *barrio* Tan-Awan, offer myself to defend the poor. . . ." Pasted on the cross was a photograph of Alex carrying the cross on the previous Good Friday when he had been the Christ in the Passion, and below it a photograph of the bishop blessing the two small coffins which contained his and Herman's bones.

The two women spoke tearfully to the Pope, in what language I do not know, but he listened carefully to them and bent over to examine the cross. Then he put his hand on their heads to bless them.

As the Pope left, a group of us grabbed the microphone and led the people in songs. We were so happy that it seemed the only thing to do. The Pope had come, nothing had gone wrong—no mishap, no accident, no rudeness, no attempt at assassination—and then that magnificent talk, which turned out to be the best he would give in the Philippines except for when he told Marcos to his face that national security could never justify trampling on human rights.

Our bishop, instead of joining the Pope's entourage to accompany him to the next venue, stayed at home, and all of us priests joined him in the palace to celebrate and recount our little bit of the story.

Suddenly the telephone in the corner rang and the bishop was called over to it. We could see the bishop's face becoming serious. He did not seem to be speaking at all but was listening intently. After he hung up, he walked slowly back to his chair. The call had been from the Marcos strongman in Negros, a sugar magnate, a leader in the political and economic world of sugarland. His message was sharp and clear: "Who prepared the Pope's talk? If that is his message, then there will be war in Negros. And to think we footed the bill for all those decorations!"

The bishop was depressed. All along he had tried to be father to everyone in the diocese. We were the ones who were pushing, and he was always trying to cool us down. On the other hand, he never missed a chance to push the *hacenderos* gently toward reform, giving the example himself with all his social projects. But he had never been angry with them—always patient and understanding. Some planters had remained faithful to him, at the cost of being regarded as subservient, but a great number of them had turned against him. Hence the ugly things said about him on television and elsewhere. He had borne it all in the hope of keeping communications open. Now this message from "Number One" seemed to have torpedoed his delicate policy of dialogue rather than confrontation.

We gathered around him and began to sing. We sang all sorts of songs, trying to cheer him up a bit. Finally we sang "We Shall Overcome": ". . . we'll walk hand in hand some day. . . ." His good spirits returned and he began to share with us the inside story of the visit: his struggle to get Negros included in the first place; his verbal battles with Archbishop Marcinkus, who objected to many things the bishop did; his pride that the Pope had written the talk himself in his own hand. It was an unusual moment of intimacy. He had seen how much we cared for him. We loved him and we were his real strength. He really had become a father to all of us. Not many bishops can say that.

For me the condemnation of the Pope's words by the sugar barons was the sweetest confirmation of my own conviction that the message had been historic.

The *Newsweek* article had put pressure on the authorities and the mayor was returned to prison, this time to the Bacolod provincial jail, where my own cook was also now in residence. The mayor was allowed to live in the warden's house. Of course it would have been unthinkable to put him in one of those awful cells.

Chapter 37

WHILE I had been away in Ireland, the communities had continued to develop with Father Romeo Empestan as acting parish priest. He was the sort of low-key person who allowed people to grow. He could sit in a meeting for hours without speaking other than to ask a clarifying question. He just let the people know he supported them in making their own practical decisions. He felt they must be allowed to make their own mistakes, although he did insist on a quiet evaluation after each activity, in order to expose the mistakes and reinforce the good things.

By the time I came back in January 1981 the number of communities had grown. They had spread up the mountains, across the border, and into the next diocese of Dumaguete. The mayor of the first town on the other side of the mountains had complained, especially about the justice committees of these communities. He was a wealthy man with more than ten thousand hectares of land. He wielded great power in that parish, and the parish priest said the justice committees would be disbanded and he, the priest, would look after justice matters himself!

With their growth in number, the communities were able to begin functioning more effectively as mini-parishes—groups of small Christian communities federated together because they are geographically situated together. Each region or mini-parish could now have its own regional justice committee. If a person had a justice problem the procedure would now be as follows, after discussing the matter with the community:

1. Dialogue with the landowner who is doing this to you. If you cannot come to a fair agreement, then:
2. Ask the justice committee of your Christian community to try. If the landowner still does not listen, then:

3. Confront the landowner with all the justice committees of the mini-parish, and only if that fails do you then:
4. Come to the *convento* where the parish council will deal with it and, if necessary, have recourse to the diocesan legal aid office. If that fails, then:
5. There is still the possibility of active nonviolent pressure through the mobilization of the people.

This was a great improvement on the system we started with, where if the people had problems they brought them straight to the *convento*, so that I was taking on everyone's problems. Now they grew in the process of solving things themselves and I began to realize that the primary purpose of all this was not necessarily to win a particular case but rather to lead the people away from the fatalism which said the problem could not be solved or the feudalism which made it utterly unthinkable to confront the landlord or "big" person with what he or she was doing.

An incident which took place when I first moved to Tabugon will illustrate just how the feudal attitude mentally bound the poor and made them incapable of sticking up for themselves.

Maximo was a poor Cebuano living in the rocky part of Tabugon. His house was burned down by a neighbor, and after a good deal of discussion in which the *convento* was involved, the man who burned the house agreed to pay 150 pesos (about fifteen dollars at that time). The man who burned the house was of more consequence than Maximo and he would normally have got away with no such inquiry. He must have gone to the *barrio* captain when our adjudication did not suit him, because Maximo got a letter summoning him to the captain's house. Maximo complied immediately as if it were a court order.

There at the captain's house, surrounded by all the *barrio* officials, he was browbeaten. He signed a document in English saying he was accepting fifty pesos willingly. Then they gave him only thirty pesos. Finally they did a bit of backslapping and, congratulating each other that the parties had been reconciled, they all had some rum—for which Maximo paid with the thirty pesos.

When Maximo came and told me the story I was tempted to explode because he had signed a document in English—a great way of bamboozling the people—but I could see the shame in his eyes, so I said nothing.

However, a group of parish leaders sat down and point by point went through what had happened to see what we could learn from it. It became clear to us that a great amount of subsequent violence could be avoided at this early stage if people were able to speak up for themselves and answer back, instead of accepting the injustice and going away aggrieved and then possibly seeking a more violent way of getting back.

I felt that one of the simplest, most powerful, and unusual ways of achieving justice was learning to confront the guilty, to speak up and put your case convincingly. That was why it was an important part of the new approach that I have outlined above, and that is why we got an attorney, Francisco Cruz, to come to the parish and give a seminar to the justice committees of the mini-parishes on such simple matters as: What is a summons? How must it be delivered? When are we bound to answer a private letter from a judge?

What had been done to Maximo was being done every day all over the island. A judge would send a private letter, summoning a poor person who, overawed by the letter, would go immediately, borrowing the fare to do so. Then in the judge's office, standing in their bare feet, battered straw hat in hand, the summoned person would meet his antagonist, and a charade would be played out, in which the judge adjudicated the whole matter without a trial, to the detriment of the poorer party.

We trained the people to know their rights, and if they had to meet a judge, a landowner, a *barrio* captain, a lawyer, to discuss the whole thing carefully beforehand. They would even act out the possible reactions of their adversary and in this way get used to absorbing anger. We asked them to sign nothing unless it was in Ilongo and until they had first taken it home to show the community. By doing this we were undermining the feudal mentality which kept so much of the system in place. Victory was in the process more than in the product. In fact, in one sense the process itself was the real product. . . . But too often a bullet cut short that growth-filled process.

I realized that winning was worth very little if the person did not "grow" by standing up and realizing his or her own dignity and potential; nevertheless I realized too that it was important to *intend* to win. It would be a cruel deception to encourage someone to fight a case only because you felt it would help them grow.

Some people would say that what matters is that it is for the good of the community and therefore for the ultimate good of the individual. For myself I suspect that this kind of manipulation entails a spiritual violation which damages our integrity and will ultimately tell in the marathon race we have embarked on.

Anyway, one immediate result of our approach was that many medium-sized landowners who were God Almighty in their area now thought twice before harassing a simple peasant, because the peasant no longer submitted cravenly right away but referred it to his or her community.

The mini-parishes also had education committees. The idea of these committees was to take the weight off the "center" and shift it out to the periphery for catechesis of various sorts—for example, the pre-baptism seminars, the health seminars, and eventually catechesis in the schools.

In my early days catechesis had been the obligation and prerogative of the priest. I took it that way and in Kabankalan had an army of catechists employed by me. I looked after their salaries and arranged with the head teachers about the schedules for teaching. But when I got to Tabugon, I realized I had been going in the wrong direction. If we let it all depend on the priest, when he leaves it all collapses. Making it depend on money ensures that the parish is always strapped for funds and frequently under obligation to those powerful people who provide them. But most of all, by making it depend on outsiders we take away from the people their right to pass on their faith themselves and to grow in the process. It could not be right, I told myself, that someone has to come all the way from Ireland to ensure that Filipino Christians are going to pass on their faith. As it happened, the Filipino priests had come to the same conclusion before me and had started what they called *Ting-og ni Nanay*—"The Voice of *Nanay*" (*Nanay* is an affectionate term for mother)—and they had been asking the mothers to go into the schools and do the teaching. I had taken their lead in this too. No more outside catechists on salaries. Christian communities were to choose the teachers, who would be volunteers, and the *convento* was to facilitate their training. The initial result was of course that the number of first Communions went down dramatically the first year and I was embarrassed when fellow priests would ask about the first Communions. Then in the second year there was the scare about children being kidnapped. But in the third year the communities realized I was not going to come in and teach the children, and they began to elect and choose their teachers, so that by the fourth year the process was quite independent. Religion class was now organized, negotiated, and taught by the communities themselves.

We were making no headway with getting the cook out of prison. Every night his tearful wife, sometimes accompanied by the children, would arrive at the *convento*; and if there was a letter from him, they would all break down. The lawyer to whom the wife had gone was a deadend. Taking advantage of the fact that her husband was in prison and that she had no money to pay for his services, he had tried to proposition her. When she finally told me this, we changed lawyers and managed to get a bail fixed. We paid the bail—several thousand pesos—but when I went down to the city on the day he was supposed to be released, the lawyer told me that the bail bond company had folded because its license had expired. In fact, there was not a single bail bond company at present in Bacolod with a valid license. None of the licenses had been renewed. The money we had paid was gone.

After a few futile hours trying to contact the company, I realized I was out of my depth. I went away carrying the useless release order. How could I go back to Badong's wife and children? I looked again at the order. This whole thing was as crooked as could be. Even when Badong's name was being written on this release order someone must have known that the company's license had already expired.

Now if I could point out to the legal office that we had paid the money in good faith, believing that these people had a license. . . . Or maybe a small alteration of the date on the paper would help, putting his release back to when the company's license was yet unexpired—easily done by typing out a new date, sticking it over the old date, and photocopying the page so that the new date appeared to be part of the original document. Was this wrong? Damn it, the whole thing was a sick joke on this man and his family.

I changed the date and presented myself at the government legal offices which would implement the release order. The office woman took the paper, filled out some forms, and then to my alarm picked the paper up again and scrutinized it in the light. She went out of the office, came back, and raised it again to the light. I became very nervous. She was examining the date. It had, I knew, a faint line around it where I had stuck the new date over and then photocopied it. She went out of the room again. I really began to worry. She was probably going to get a police officer and have me arrested. Why had I allowed myself to be swayed by the thought of the children being without their father? Now I was going to be arrested and disgraced and I would not be able to help anyone. . . .

I waited in suspense for what seemed a very long time. Finally the door opened, the woman reappeared carrying the papers. She made straight for me: "I'm afraid the judge is away and our offices are closed, so we can't deal with this."

"Oh, that's no problem at all," said I, taking back the release order eagerly and leaving hastily, thanking God for that Filipino magic whereby she had been able to find such a gentle formula to cover the statement: "This is a fake and if I wanted I could have you arrested."

After Easter I went to Mindanao to learn to speak Cebuano, in order to show the Cebuanos in the parish that I cared enough to learn their language and be able to say Mass in it. I was very conscious of the use of language as a tool to oppress people. The month's intensive language course was what I needed. It was not so difficult; I had been practicing it a bit, and it was very like Ilongo.

On the boat back to Negros I discovered an old friend, who had a cabin to herself. She was the wife of a *hacendero* whom I liked and she herself helped a lot with the Sa-Maria retreats when I was giving them. They ran their own family farm with justice and the old-style personal concern for the people. We had not met in years and during that time the Church-landlord confrontation had blown up. I knew we would not get a chance like this to talk again. She was a strong, gentle, intelligent person. Beside her on the table I saw her prayer book and her rosary when I came into her cabin after knocking.

After greeting each other and chatting for a while, I told her that I was reading Dom Helder Camara's *The Desert Is Fertile*. "He is dedicated to nonviolence," I said, "and you might like to read it." I also suggested she might like to underline anything she disagreed with or felt was questionable. I said I could come back later and maybe we could chat about it, and about what was going on in Negros. "Because I realize," I said, "that we no longer see things the same way, and this might help as a bridge between us."

She was very happy to fall in with my suggestion.

That night I came back to visit her in her cabin. She had read the book. "Well?" I said.

"Well, this book is not applicable here. You know we have courts which people can bring their cases to." I nodded as I listened. I had been here before. I could feel that wall of non-understanding. Something inside me said: "Leave it alone." Could I recount all I had been through? Had she not lived here much longer than me? Was there any point? She was such a good woman, a woman of personal integrity and a woman who had suffered. If she could not see the connection I was not going to try and force it. Maybe someday she would remember. I made some quiet rejoinders to the effect that I knew of cases where the court did not work, and I left it at that.

She epitomized for me the mystery that hunger, torture, extermination, can be all around and good people do not notice. I was back again to the theme of the Nazi death-camps and the absolute dependence of their existence on the silence of ordinary people. Silence of ordinary people has been the most decisive political act of the twentieth century.

It was precisely this not keeping silent that was the first weapon in the quiver of the small Christian communities—daring at their weekly meetings to discuss the social situation in the light of the Scriptures, daring to confront personally those who were trampling on them, daring to make their private oppression a community concern. In all of this they grew visibly in an understanding of their own dignity and they helped their oppressors to grow in recognizing this dignity too. This was what José Rizal, a great, though much manipulated Filipino hero, surely meant when he said: "There are no tyrants where there are no slaves."

One of the many things I mourned when people resorted to the gun was that it shortcircuited this vital and ennobling growth.

Chapter 38

LARGE green helicopter gunships—late of Vietnam—began to be seen in the Tablas Valley. One helicopter would disgorge its men, while a second would hover overhead, guarding the operation. Mostly the army were not able to get at the N.P.A., so they just killed civilians and dumped the bodies at the door of the town hall, describing this as "an encounter." The logic behind this was that the civilians, the army claimed, had fed or in some way fraternized with the N.P.A. If the civilians could be got to shun them, then the N.P.A. would have no water to swim in. All that to one side, the internal politics of the army made "body count" a factor in gaining promotion. It was also important in the propaganda war. And it was necessary to let the Americans, who were footing the arms bill, know that we were winning.

Apart from this, the army recruits were quite undisciplined, and common thievery, drunkenness, rape were a part of their life-style. For example, on one occasion in the village next to me, *barrio* Tapi, there was a shoot-out among the soldiers over girls they had brought into their camp. Two of the girls and four of the men were killed inside the barracks. This was called an attack by the New People's Army and described as such on the radio. There were shoot-outs between different branches of the armed forces as well.

Army officers were involved in illegal logging and the top brass had moved into big business. The army had been corrupted by the huge amounts of American money that were pouring in. If the N.P.A. had disappeared, they would have had to recreate them, because they needed them as a *raison d'être*. So the killing and "salvaging" went on. "Salvaging" was a word which had appeared to describe one type of military action: They would abduct someone during the night and later on the dead body would be found, frequently with marks of torture. If witnesses came forward to say that the army had taken the person away, they would say that the prisoner had escaped from them so they were not responsible for the death.

It must be to the shame of the media that they so consistently cooperated in this. Take the case of the Langoni Nine. Nine young boys from Langoni, in the parish of Inayawan, returning from voting and on their way to play a basketball match, were abducted and killed by the army. The press release describing this "encounter" was apparently composed *before* the killings took place. The media with some notable exceptions did not question this— and not because they were controlled. Marcos had done something much more effective: he had handed the media over to people who were profiting from the martial law regime; it was in their interests to promote the regime. Censorship was hardly needed after that. There was a little carefully penned, toothless criticism which helped to give a veneer of freedom.

But along with the media there were the public-school teachers. Where I worked the teachers sold out almost in a body. They facilitated the cheating at the voting booths, they taught the new society clap-trap, and they did not protest—only near the end, and then mostly when it was a case of their salaries being in question or their own rights.

Then, of course, there was the quiescent middle class who gained from the passing shallow prosperity, which appeared in certain areas of national life due to the huge bureaucracy Marcos created and the billions borrowed and swilled about. The poor got even poorer and their cries for the most part were not heard by the affluent middle class, who still indulged themselves with the good feeling of giving charity.

Faced with this State violence on the one hand and the compliance and self-regarding apathy on the other, many young middle-class people felt that the only answer was counter-violence. It seemed to be justified at every level. Even on the basis of the Church's teaching it was justified.

Another young man left the *kibbutz* to join the New People's Army. Before he did he asked me to marry him to a young local girl, Faith. Fernando was a Catholic and Faith was a devoutly religious Baptist. She agreed with his decision to leave, and soon after the marriage they both set off to join the revolutionaries. I saw them from time to time, especially whenever they were sick. She had a baby each year, and on one occasion twins. Giving birth was always difficult for her and aggravated by the meager diet and the rough, on-the-run existence they shared, sleeping in the open and carrying a pack on their back and a machine gun on their shoulder. Since each birth was difficult, I would be involved in taking her to a hospital in the lowlands and helping with the medicines. Not to help in this way would have been a betrayal of my priesthood.

One day a deputation came to me from the N.P.A. to ask if I would lend our jeep for an operation. They knew my stand, so I felt that this was some sort of a test. I felt terrible. I did not completely understand what they had in mind by an operation. In this case it involved collecting some people. I refused and wrote them a note saying that "our ways are parallel but not identical, and at this time I cannot see my way to doing what you request." Of course I could have just used a Filipino euphemism and said, "My jeep is in bad condition and will break down" (as in fact was the case). However, I knew the question would not go away, so I reluctantly wrote the note, knowing that those with a strong ideological bent would interpret my words according to the slogan: "Those who are not with us are against us."

Not long after, another deputation came, quite different from the first. It was two young men, brothers, who were in the N.P.A. but who had got news that their father was dying down in the lowlands. They pleaded for help. They wanted to say goodbye to their father and receive his *panu-gu-bilin*—his last words and blessing, a very sacred moment in Ilongo culture. They were surely absent without leave, so they were probably taking a double risk. They asked us to take them as far as the town where their father was dying. I reckoned it would not be fair to send anyone other than myself, and I also reckoned I had a better chance of getting through the checkpoints. So we agreed that I would take them to the rice fields outside the town, arriving as dusk came. I knew they had weapons and noted they each had a grenade, which they put inside the front of their trousers. For them to be caught alive was worse than death because of the torture which was being used. They would have to find their own way back through "hostile" territory.

The journey was without event, other than tense moments when we passed army personnel. The checkpoints were not so much in evidence that day or they were not in operation. I said goodbye to the two men at the outskirts of the town. Across those rice paddies their dying father was waiting.

The dilemma of drawing the line between humanitarian cooperation and military collaboration was becoming more and more difficult. In the case of the N.P.A.'s request for the jeep, I often thought afterward that they had wanted it for a rescue operation for some of their own people and I worried that my not lending it might have meant some lives were not saved. Anyway, there was no escape from the dilemma. In fact the writ of the government did not run in much of the territory next to me, so for all intents and purposes the N.P.A. had become the legitimate government. Certainly Marcos's was not.

In the town of Wicklow in Ireland there is a statue of the "Bould" Father Murphy who in 1798 could no longer stand by and watch the people being capped with molten pitch. He joined the rebellion, as had many before him. A priest is made of flesh and blood and is a human being before he is a priest. And sometimes in the utmost simplicity of soul they can take no more and they join the revolution. This has always been the way, and probably always will be. Many went to the hills and joined the New People's Army but usually not without first growing tired and exhausted and disillusioned with other methods.

My own feeling was that even tactically it was a mistake. They could do a lot more by staying where they were. I also had a dream that if hundreds of priests and Sisters were confronting the system, with all their heart and soul and with alive communities, it could hardly stand. I did not share this dream—it sounded too utopian—but I was beginning to see the results of the Christian communities in my own parish and in the few others which had them at the time. I say "few" because not many parishes actually had the small Christian communities. My dream was that if all parishes had the genuine thing then they would be unstoppable, and I mourned the loss of those dedicated priests who left us to go to the hills.

One day a young Filipino priest from northern Luzon whom I had got to know in Manila came all the way down to Negros to visit me in Tabugon. With him were a Sister and another young man whom I knew well, who had been a seminarian and had just been married. We discussed the grave situation of the people. My priest friend had some tragic stories from his own parish in the north, where the army had tortured even children. We said Mass together. Their dedication and devotion were tangible. After a while I knew their presence there was to invite me to join in a new type of involvement that for them was in line with my professed allegiance to the national struggle.

I felt trusted to be asked, but it was a painful meeting for me. I knew that in a lively discussion the essential logic of their position would emerge. All the conditions required by *Populorum progressio* and common sense were present. My idea of nonviolence as an active weapon for justice must appear to them a pipe dream. It was also clear to me that there had been a moment when they decided to take the risks which would endanger their lives. This moment of "conversion" coupled with the logic of their position and the memory of dear friends killed resulted in a conviction which was surely impregnable.

What was I to say? Should I bring them through the long history of my attachment to nonviolence, when as yet I was unsure if I had made as radical a commitment to it as they had made to the armed struggle? And what success had I to offer? The local examples I could give were so small, was I going to lecture them about things that had happened in other countries? Hardly. What I did was to try to show by the stories I told that a refusal to get involved in the armed struggle did not mean a refusal to get involved in the revolution, and I hinted that eventually the commitment could be as radical as any. On the wall to remind us was a homemade poster with a photo of a young man dying in the arms of his brother. Visible on his chest and stomach were the knife wounds which were draining away his life. Underneath it was written: "*Nato indi ta ikaw malimtan*—We will never forget you."

So I was taking the path of nonviolent action! Did that mean I was condemning their path? If my path was right was theirs wrong? I took refuge in the "charism" idea of Berrigan—nonviolence was a special call, a vocation I could not force on others; it was a gift, a charism whose presence reminded those involved in justified counter-violence of the inherent unacceptability of the means they were forced to use and the fact that these means should be abandoned as soon as possible.

By the time their two days' visit was over they realized I was declining the invitation they had come such a long way to make. By not going into explanations I always left myself open to the accusation of being a coward or loving my life more than the truth. But there seemed no way out for me other than to take the risk that people would think that. But as they said goodbye I knew that in spite of my refusal I was still trusted.

All three are now dead, killed in different circumstances in their attempt to serve the Filipino people. They were devout believers, and though there are communists and Marxists (not the same thing) aplenty among the elite who run the revolution, to say that these were communists is untrue. And to say they were Marxists is incorrect. They wanted to change the social structure. To do this they used the social sciences to which Marx had made historic but limited contributions. They used some of Marx's insights the way vocation directors use some of Freud's. They were aware of the difference between recognizing "classes" in society and fomenting hate between "classes." This they never did. They loved until death.

It is wrong to refer to the revolutionaries simply as "the communists." Behind the Philippine revolution is a long history going back hundreds of years. Its lineage is one of nationalism and a thirst for justice, and the movement is filled with Christians. If it were not, it would be a great indictment of Christianity.

I said that to label the revolutionaries simply as communists is untrue. It is also malicious, because for those of us who know anything about the Stalinist purges or the Cambodian killing fields, an emotive button is pressed which makes dialogue and discussion impossible. But then those who reduce the complicated Philippine situation to a matter of fascists or communists have no need for dialogue. Dialogue implies that we have something to learn; for the true idealogue no new information is necessary. They have the answers before the dialogue begins.

Chapter 39

*O*UR PART of the Tablas Valley was rapidly becoming a no-man's-land. The revolutionaries controlled the inner mountains and the military controlled the lowlands. Each made incursions into the other's territory. In the in-between area where we lived, marauding groups of every stripe grew up. Some were breakaways from the N.P.A.; some were AWOL from the army; others were fanatic religious sects of the *salvatore* type, some of which were being used by the army (a policy of theirs all over the Philippines); and then of course there were individual entrepreneurs, armed with a gun and a Robin Hood vocabulary to justify the stealing and killing they were doing.

Such, it first appeared, was Angelito—"Little Angel." He lived in Amian, one of the hard-to-get-at parts of our parish. He had been involved in two known slayings and was credited with many more. He was said to eat the ears of the victims. Twenty-seven was the number cited, and I had that from one of my own Christian community leaders who had been forced to sit down and watch him eat the ears. There were two or three weak Christian communities in the area. They were in a state of shock and panic. Most of the people in that area were now no longer sleeping in their houses at night. They were sleeping out in the long cogon grass. Everyone had knives, it being a farming community, but Little Angel was said to have a gun, and that was regarded with sacramental awe. I guessed that his gun did not work and pointed out that the two killings that could be proved were done with a knife. But in the cloud of fear that had settled over Amian no one was listening. The fact that Little Angel had a gun was enough to paralyze them, and young men felt that the only remedy was for them to get a gun too.

On one occasion some young men from Amian said that they had seen a group of ten men with guns arriving in their area from Brian Gore's parish across the river. All sorts of contradictory sightings were reported. I tried to corroborate the story through my various contacts but the more I went into it the more it emerged as another scare sparked by the panic being felt in the area over Little Angel, and the sense of defenselessness. One young man beseeched me for a gun. His earnestness amazed me. He seemed to take it for granted that I had one, which of course I did not. Finally, as our argument heated up, I said: "Look, if I thought guns were the answer I wouldn't have come to the Philippines at all. I'd have stayed at home and got a job and sent the extra money to you to buy guns."

But what was the answer? Some were saying: "Leave it to the boys." This when translated meant that the N.P.A. would send someone in to investigate and deliver judgment. The investigators would be young people not without heart and compassion but the trial would take place under the stress of "war." They had no prisons and if the person was found guilty the punishment, when warnings had failed, could hardly be less than death. Prisons for all their inhumanity offer society the possibility of varying degrees of punishment for varying degrees of guilt. Revolutionaries on the run do not have this luxury of options.

I had an even more basic difficulty with the very idea of calling in outsiders to solve the problem. Could not the people come up with something themselves? Once they called in outsiders they became that much more dependent, and we were back to the old need to have someone to look up to and defend us. When some Robin Hood "knocked off" the offender the people could go back to their houses but no one had changed, no one had grown. The tumor had been excised but no antibodies had been developed in the system to stop its recurrence. We would have to do something ourselves. This had been one of the key points in our five-pointed star seminar: that the people of a community would struggle to deal with their own problem.

Our parish council called on Brian for advice because we knew that his communities had been doing just this and, in fact, they had cleared up a much graver *salvatore* situation in their own areas without outside help.

Brian's parish was Oringao, just across the river from Amian. Brian did not have my outlook on nonviolence at that time. He had a commonsense, we-all-have-the-right-to-defend-ourselves outlook, though paradoxically he had much less sympathy with the N.P.A. than I had. But Brian's communities had developed various methods of nonviolent self-defense; they had had to with all the *salvatore* activity. One of the basic principles in Brian's approach was: "We have the numbers; we are like ants. If a few of them come around the place, they are easily brushed away or killed. If a whole nest of them swarms around you, *you* move away." That's how the Oringao people had confronted Rosano.

We all agreed that the Christian community approach is essentially preventive. Strong communities with a good system of communication between them also were the best deterrents to marauders. The problem with Amian was that there were no strong communities, and I noticed myself that those other areas of the parish where the communities were weak were also the areas which had the most problems with night banditry.

Brian sent over his six leaders and they met with our core group and then with the parish council. But first I must explain just how the parish council was organized at this point. It had finally undergone the change I had been angling for this long time. It no longer consisted of the group of seminar-givers who lived in Tabugon. It now consisted of the heads of each of the seven mini-parishes. These people had each been a community leader at one stage but were now president of their own mini-parish council. They brought with them the living experience of their area of Tabugon. The periphery had finally come in from the cold.

Apart from the parish council, which was now truly representative of all the communities, no longer just of Tabugon proper, we at last had a core group. The core group consisted of myself, Junior, Baby Maha, and two women leaders. The core group were to balance me and to give me advice, and to be a sort of steering committee who could make decisions if I was not around and if the parish council could not be gathered.

We had determined to do nothing without the full backing of the Christian communities. Once again I felt that the process was as important as the product. The success would not be only in doing something about Little Angel, but how we did it would obviously be a model for the future. If we failed, on the other hand, he would be shot dead by someone soon after and I was sure that that would solve nothing but only confirm many rogue groups in their worship of the gun.

First Brian's core group met with our core group. Then they came back and met with the full parish council—the presidents and officers of the mini-parishes (this came to about thirty-five people). The discussion went on far into the night and they finally came up with a plan. We would hold a Mass at the house of Little Angel. Though it was way in the back of beyond a thousand people would converge on the place, and while we were there we would ask Little Angel to lay down his arms. Brian's group had done this many times, so they had all the details of how people should travel, what they should do if other groups tried to stop them, what to do if the army appeared, how to avoid panic, how to keep a check on participants to stop infiltration by troublemakers, what if it rained and the rivers rose, and so on.

The final meeting took place without Brian's group. Our core group chaired the meeting and all the details were drawn up. Each mini-parish had to guarantee a certain number of members from each community and they had to be reliable people.

One part of the plan was that there should be a group of strong men who should lead the way and act in some sense as a vanguard for the others; these would be called the twelve apostles. Brian's group had felt that some of these should carry knives, "for clearing the grass," Brian said with a twinkle. I had objected. They objected to my objection. They said everybody in the mountains carries a blade of some sort—it is part of the normal farming culture. We finally agreed that two would carry "bolos"—the sugarcane machete in daily use. We agreed also that Brian's group should *not* come with us. I was the one against their coming. It was a matter of us growing by doing it ourselves. In fact I would willingly not have gone myself precisely for the same reasons, but I knew that there was a whole culture of fear that had set in in the mountain areas. Little Angel was not just feared for his gun and for his gang, whose numbers were said to be legion, but for his spiritual powers. He had a belt of little bottles of oil which would defend him. He could not be penetrated by a bullet, for example, because of these, and he had sold them to his followers. He had other amulets and charms. I should come.

The apostles were to stay in the *convento* the night before and have a last meeting in which they would discuss and plan for unforeseen developments. Careful planning ahead was one of the key themes of Brian's approach. Indeed, it is a key theme of the whole active nonviolence movement. I left them to themselves, but at about midnight I called in to where they were meeting in the parish council hut, curious that the meeting was going on so long, and to my surprise I found them deadlocked on what to do. The question had arisen as to whether they should go ahead with it at all. They were right back to discussing other alternatives. I soon grasped that that strange fear had crept in again, fear of the unknown power of Little Angel. The man who was to be the Peter of the apostles had no heart for it at all. I had underestimated the pervasive fear that Little Angel aroused. He had become myth.

At this late hour, striving to make sure that "Peter" did not lose face, I contrived that he exchange places with Baby Maha, who then became the Peter of the group. I explained that their mandate was not to open questions that had been decided by the whole parish carefully over weeks and many meetings, but to work out the logistics of their own activity as the vanguard. "We all have some fear," I said. "It would be wrong not to be afraid. Fear is a gift from God to protect us, but panic is an evil thing. With the fear we must have courage. But our weapons are not going to be arms.

We are coming with nothing but the truth." And I pointed to the logo on the T-shirts they were wearing—the one Lino had designed for our Christian communities and made in the parish. It was a heart and in the center of the heart there was an open book of Scripture from which rays of light came downward and converged on a machine gun and a sword, both of which were being smashed in two as if struck by a laser beam; underneath was written, "The Word of God is mightier than a two-edged sword." Before I left we prayed together: "Jesus, you promised that you would be with us always till the end of the world. Be with us tomorrow as we walk to the house of Little Angel."

Back in my room I could feel the anxiety in the air. There was one thing I had not said, because I felt they were not ready for it, and that was that I believed that Little Angel was just like the rest of us: not an evil man, but just someone who knew no better and whom no one had ever helped along the way. And I took out my diary and wrote something like this: "I am writing this now because we will forget it when all this is over. There is a terrible fear in the group over Little Angel. Everyone believes he's a devil with all sorts of powers. I feel it will turn out that his gun doesn't work and that he will submit docilely."

I prayed and lay down to wait for dawn when we would start out. Tonight, I said to myself, many people in the communities are lying awake wondering if they should go or not. Some wives are dissuading husbands and some husbands are dissuading wives. They are reviewing their decisions and fighting their fears. But as they overcome their fears they themselves are growing; I can almost feel the people growing!

But I was worried too because if this failed—our first major group attempt at active nonviolence—then people would say there was only one way and that was the gun: the way Rosano had recently been dispatched. And the little groups all over the parish which were so attracted to having guns would shake their heads and say, "There's only one way."

In the morning we set off at a trot. At various points along the way we were joined by groups from the different communities. One of our concerns had been crossing the various rivers if it rained and the level rose. So far it had not rained. I had a little tape recorder with me and recorded what happened along the way.

Finally we got near to Little Angel's house, and some people came to us and said they had seen him at the river washing clothes. This was untrue, but it began to create a certain confusion. We halted while some others went back to the river to check. Should we wait for them? Should the apostles not arrive first? We went on. As we neared the house the tension grew. For a long time now people had avoided even the vicinity of this house like an evil place.

Little Angel was outside his house. He had a large blade in his hand. He was puzzled over the arrival of so many people. I walked up to him. I was trembling. I explained to him that we were coming to say Mass. He surprised me by saying: "Someone said you might come to say Mass so I was about to kill a rooster for you." I said: "Why not come upstairs and have a chat with me first?" We went up together. I tried to conceal my nervousness as I asked him to lay aside the knife, which I then passed out the window to one of the apostles. By this time a huge crowd had gathered outside the house. I then explained to him why we had come.

The tension in the crowd was something terrible. At one stage some people were standing on a bench which broke with a crack like the sound of gunshot: people scattered in all directions in a panic. A couple of the toughest apostles appeared at the door with a "let us at him" look on their faces. I said that they could not touch him because he had agreed to hand over all his weapons. They made a rush at him, but I kept between him and them. It was a charade. It had not been in the original plan, and I felt ashamed of it afterward, but from this distance it is hard to understand the strain and suspense we were all under.

When I had pushed them back he went to an inner room and brought out his knives and amulets and membership forms for what he called the "N.P.A.–Salvatore." And handed them over.

Then we asked him to go to the window and ask his followers to do likewise, because many of his group, when they saw all the people converging on Little Angel's house, had tagged along to see what was going to happen. The crowd gained in courage and began to point out those who belonged to Little Angel's gang, and the apostles collected their weapons and amulets. All in all it amounted to a complete sackful. Then all his followers were rounded up and put in one place and we addressed the crowd as to what should be done.

Now their anger came out as they remembered the killings and how he had terrorized them for so long, and one or two voices began to demand that Little Angel be killed. I explained that that was against our principles and we would become like those we were condemning.

Eventually some in the crowd said he should be exiled from the place. That in fact had been the decision reached by the communities in their own preliminary discussions, so I asked Little Angel if he had any place to go and he said his grandmother had a place in a faraway part of the mountains. It was agreed that he should leave immediately. The rest of the gang were told they could not be members of the Christian community until they had proved themselves.

Then began the Mass of thanksgiving. I explained why I was refusing Communion to Little Angel and his followers and I tried to develop the meaning of being a community from this example.

After the Mass I had an unexpected worry. Little Angel's son Rodrigo, about fourteen years old, had been watching the whole thing, and I felt for the little fellow. I took him aside and told him not to worry, that everything would be all right, and that I would make sure nothing happened to his father. I was concerned about the trauma to the child, watching his father arrested by what to him must have appeared a mob.

Little Angel came home with us, and during the night Junior and Baby spent time pointing out gently but firmly why what he had been doing was wrong. I also spent some time with him. I had my little tape recorder and asked for more details of who was behind him. It became clearer and clearer that he was being used by a certain Jimmy Lopez. I knew Jimmy because I had officiated at his wedding some ten years before. He lived partly in Brian's parish, where he went around among the unlettered peasants enlisting them in what he called the "N.P.A.–Salvatore." He had special forms made out and he charged twenty-six pesos for membership; he also sold amulets that would prevent the wearer from being killed. He had supplied Little Angel with his gun. He controlled Little Angel completely and he probably had similar groups in different parts of the mountain.

The most interesting thing that emerged from my long conversation with Little Angel was the proof for me that Jimmy was working with the army. The army were in fact behind this so-called N.P.A.–Salvatore group. It was a way of discrediting the N.P.A. and gave the army justification for sweeping into our areas which did not have any real N.P.A. presence. Was that why every attempt to have Little Angel arrested had come to nothing? What about the gun? Well, Jimmy Lopez was the one who had given it to him, but recently he had taken it back. Did it work? No, it was broken!

On the wall in the room where Little Angel slept that night we had a huge picture eight feet long by four feet wide, of Christ being scourged. In medieval style the artist, Lino Montebon, had introduced around the central scourging picture vignettes illustrating life in Negros, such as land-grabbing, army atrocities, property speculation, usury, unfair wages, religious hypocrisy, robbery, and rape: there was something for everyone. The picture was done simply and graphically like a carving on a Gothic cathedral and it was meant to teach. Its message was that these things—the land-grabbing, the torture—were the scourging of Christ. The following morning Little Angel spoke spontaneously for the first time. Up to this point he had just been answering questions. He led me over to the picture of the scourging and, pointing at one of the Roman soldiers who held a cat-o'-nine-tails, said: "That's me."

The crowd of ordinary men and women coming all the way to that lonely part of the mountain to protest, the ritual excommunication, fear, the little talks in the night, had made Little Angel think. The simple picture filled with symbols he understood spoke to him, and he used it to speak to us.

Chapter 40

IN MY long interview with Little Angel I had asked why he killed a particular man or threatened another one. It became clear to me that he thought he was doing good! He obeyed orders from others. When those others said that this or that person was "bad," Little Angel was ready to kill. He did not have any clear understanding of the value of human life, of where it belonged in the hierarchy of values. In this he was not unlike other young men, of much greater schooling, who did not question the morality of carpet-bombing, dropping napalm on civilians, or warring over the Falkland Islands. Someone had told them some group of people are "the enemy" and, if necessary, their lives must be forfeited.

Little Angel was a widower, but he had recently acquired a young common-law wife. She must have been only seventeen, and at the time she was pregnant and waiting to give birth. She was staying with her parents and was supposed to be selling a pig so that they could leave the parish and go to a faraway part of the mountain where Little Angel's grandmother had some land, but she was delayed. That delay was fateful.

A few hundred yards away from the *convento* lived a pig-dealer, his wife, and little child. I knew them well. On the second night that Little Angel stayed with us they were all strangled. Their bodies were found in the morning. No one had heard a sound during the night.

The local police, who had refused to do anything about arresting Little Angel for the last couple of years, now arrived to investigate this case. And, having absolutely no lead to go on, they came to the *convento* to take Little Angel. They had to take someone back with them.

When they told me what they wanted, I asked them to wait, and I met with Junior and Baby. What were we to do? Had not Little Angel really accepted some sort of sanctuary here in the *convento*? I had promised his child that I would protect his father. On the other hand, there had been a warrant out for his arrest for a long time. Indeed I had called the police's attention to it several times, complaining that they were doing nothing about it.

Finally we agreed that to refuse to hand Little Angel over would legally amount to complicity in his crimes. But we could make conditions.

We all went back to the police and explained that we were witnesses that Little Angel was nowhere near the place of the present crime—he was in our house the night of the recent murders. They could take him but they would have to guarantee us three things: that he would not be tortured; that he would be released if they found no crime against him; and that they would arrest Jimmy Lopez, who was behind Little Angel's crimes. They agreed and took Little Angel away.

We got the leaders of the mini-parishes together to evaluate the "mass action" as it was called. I was cited as having been too high-profile, and there were other faults as well. But things would never be the same afterward in the Christian communities.

We followed up in another part of the parish by rooting out a gunman who was AWOL from the army, or said he was. After this there were other gunmen and gangs. The result was that individual outlaws like Little Angel disappeared, as did marauding groups. That left the military, because as of this time the N.P.A. did no more than occasionally visit the parish of Tabugon.

The police, the Philippine constabulary, and the armed forces were the three main instruments of government control. The local police were often corrupt but were basically well regarded by the people. (The two who had come up to collect Little Angel kept their promises as best they could. They arrested Jimmy Lopez and made sure that Little Angel was not harmed.) The Philippine armed forces were supposed to be defending the Philippines from aggressors but were now engaged in dropping napalm on their own people. The constabulary were supposed to be in between—more strong-arm than the local police but not as all-out as the army—but in fact the constabulary were very much involved in torture and they used their power to support the local élite in their suppression of labor unions and of anything else that they considered subversive. Their head was Colonel Fidel Ramos.

In the parish of Tabugon we had a military unit called Philcag. They were not supposed to be involved in fighting, but were supposed to be engaged in road-making. They did make roads for the sugar mill, but of course counter-insurgency interested them more than the sugar mill. We planned a special approach to them: pre-emption. Our communities made lots of complaints to them about small abuses as soon as the abuses took place: the beating of a student, the breaking of a girl's watch at a dance, firing shots during the night while drunk. In the last case we had a deputation from a Christian community near the barracks, we complained to the *barrio* captain, I sent a letter, and I gave a sermon on it on Sunday. We found that if the people developed their sense of being able to protest early, *before* things got out of hand, then the military realized they were living among a community who would not take abuse.

When they were out far away from the villages among unschooled peasants, the military went from house to house often stealing their roosters. But in a village where the people were ready to complain and even send letters to higher authorities the military behaved, even if those letters were never attended to. There are rivalries within the army itself, and the military officers did not like those letters going up above, since the complaints might be used against them. The net result was that the Philcag did behave themselves, and within the parish, in those days, they were very rarely guilty of abuse.

In a *barrio* in a nearby parish where there were no Christian communities to protest, the story was quite different. The army in this *barrio* was guilty of killings, torture, and stealing, but there was never a complaint. In fact the *barrio* captain, so craven had the people become, even concocted an obsequious petition asking for that battalion—the 7th I.B.—to stay after they had received their orders to leave.

A deep fear had settled over the area. And one of the main tasks of the Christian community was to subvert this "culture" of fear.

Chapter 41

SIXTEEN parishes of southern Negros organized themselves into the "Christian Community Parish Group." The purpose of this was to help each other in the building of Christian communities. We would meet and recount what was happening in our area and what solutions we were applying to our problems. The sixteen parishes broke into four smaller units for convenience, and our group naturally comprised the four parishes which lay in the valley of the Tablas River inside the Kabankalan Mountains: Candoni, where Donie Hogan had now taken over from Eugene McGeough; Magballo, where Jimmy Martin had taken over from Donie; Tabugon; and Oringao, where Brian was parish priest.

We were all Columbans, and all Irish except for Brian, who was Australian. We began to meet to see how we could cooperate more. It was amazing how four places could be so alike compared to other areas and so different among themselves. Yet we found ground for common action. We would each attend the rallies the others would have, and often we shared the seminars we gave. Donie would put on a drama seminar, or Brian would have an organic farming seminar, or Jimmy would have a protest rally, or I would have the leadership seminar, and members of the other parishes would attend. We would also bring our ideas to the larger meetings of the sixteen.

The new cooperation brought an increase in communication and coordination. A military abuse in one parish would be condemned in the other fifteen soon after. We also found time to relax together. We would travel over to each other's *conventos* with our core group and stay the night. That gave people a chance to meet each other. At Christmas the others would come to Tabugon and I would make sure I had a turkey and all the things to go with it.

One of the many activities the sixteen parishes planned was a leadership course. We realized that we needed something like the course in Mindanao, where I had sent my leaders. Each of the sixteen parishes would be allowed to send two or three candidates. The course would be run by Father Romeo Empestan and Sister Florence. Together we planned what subjects it would include: Scripture, social analysis, group dynamics, liturgy. I was to give the Scripture course. Meantime Donie Hogan was going to put on a drama course in his parish, and I was going to send some candidates over to Candoni. Drama was a very strong way of teaching—more powerful than mere words in communicating an experience—and the medium of symbolic drama and allegory allowed the people to say things which would have been dangerous to say more directly.

I chose Arod to attend this drama course. He was head of the small Christian community in the rocky place he came from, and was one of the few Cebuanos in Tabugon who had finished high school. More than half our leaders were women; a steady young man like Arod was not easy to find. I took him aside one day and we had a beer in the store at the crossing in Tabugon. "Arod," I said, "there aren't many like you. I'm very anxious that you should take a larger role, as that will be a help for our work among the Cebuanos. There's a drama seminar coming up in Candoni given by the leaders there. Would you be able to go?" He had rice-planting to do for his family before the dry season set in, but he would have it done in time and be able to go. We continued chatting, me trying to learn more about him. As our conversation went on I realized that I had hit on a very unusual person, and I said goodbye feeling rich, as I always did when I "discovered" someone in the parish.

Arod went off to the drama seminar, but while he was away his sister Felipa died in childbirth. Arod came back before the seminar was over to take part in the mourning. The death was a double blow to the family because the newborn baby now had no mother.

The leadership course we had planned was approaching, and I felt Arod should be one of those to do it. But that posed a problem. His family, recently bereaved, were against him going away for a month. It was not just that he was needed to help on their little bit of land. It was something instinctive, the need to have the children around them at a time of sorrow. I approached his parents and explained how important it was, and finally they agreed. The course was to open on May 1, 1982. Arod went off with Baby Maha and Balthasar, Junior's younger brother.

I was going to give the scriptural part of the course. I was determined that we would not get bogged down in polemics, that we would not end up missing the wood for the trees, as so often happens when a course concentrates on controversial texts, on Counter-Reformation apologetics, or on arguments for and against violence. Just as the island of Negros was built around the central spine of mountains, so the Old Testament was built around the Exodus experience—God's saving action. If you could imagine one of those peaks bursting out in the fire of power and light and brightening the whole mountain range in the night sky, well, in a similar way at the center of the New Testament was the Resurrection of Jesus throwing light forward and backward on all that had gone before and was coming. Most of all, I now wanted the presence of the risen Jesus to be the center of all the work for justice. I felt that without that spirit we were just well-intentioned social reformers.

My time to speak was coming. I had gone to Batang to photocopy my handouts and I was standing at the Xerox machine when through the window I saw Balthasar, Junior's brother, coming in the gate. I knew something must be up, so I went out to meet him.

"Arod is dead," he said.

"What happened?"

"He was hit by a bus."

I closed my eyes and, after a long pause, I said: "Do his parents know?"

"Not yet. You'll have to tell them."

I sat down, with my head in my hands.

When I looked up, Geoff Revatto, our bursar, was there, holding a glass of brandy: "Take this, Niall. You'll have to go to Kabankalan—if I can help with anything just say it."

On the way to Kabankalan, Balthasar told me the story. Arod had gone home for the thirtieth day after the death of his sister—what in Ireland we call the month's mind. He had stayed up all night, and not to miss the lectures in the morning, had hitched a ride at dawn on a sugar truck going down the mountain. He alighted at the Sa-Maria house. As he crossed the road, just before he reached the other side, an approaching bus, swerving the wrong way in a vain effort to avoid him, struck him. He was killed instantly.

When we arrived at the hospital in Kabankalan they told us that Arod had already been removed to a funeral parlor. I went straight there. Strangely enough I had never been at this place before; it seemed to be still under construction. As I went in the gate I had to pick my way through heaps of gravel and broken-down hearses. The woman who greeted me guided me past various bits of unfinished coffins to a little outhouse at the back. This was the morgue. There, lying in a sink in his underpants, was Arod.

I touched his body. He was still warm. I looked at him for a long time, then knelt and said a prayer.

The woman who ran the funeral home was calm and relaxed. I was glad we were alone as I wanted to discuss several things. In the Philippines embalming is important, not just because of the tropical climate but because of the custom that all the family come home from no matter how far away to have a last look at their loved one. Arod was one of ten brothers and sisters scattered throughout Negros. As we discussed the price of coffins and embalming, the woman quietly worked away at sewing the white lining into a coffin lid. Her children played around her feet.

I went over to the Sa-Maria house to see Sister Florence and Father Romeo Empestan, who were running the leadership course, to get their advice. To my surprise they would not hear of me going to Arod's parents. I must send the Volkswagen up the mountains to Tabugon with a message for them to come down. Those driving the car were to deny any knowledge of anything. Florence and Romeo were adamant about this. The car went off.

The four-hour wait seemed interminable. I waited in the Sa-Maria house till at last I heard the Volks pulling up outside.

As soon as they got in the door Arod's father looked around for Arod. We did not speak, but Florence took his arm and led him and Arod's mother into the office. In stumbling words we broke the news.

It was terrible. Arod's mother collapsed on the floor and began to lament and to talk to Arod as if he were still alive: "Arod, Arod! You asked me for money for a T-shirt and to think I wouldn't give it to you. . . . But we needed it to bury your sister."

Crispin, the father, became enraged. He tore posters off the wall and smashed chairs, and his voice got louder and louder.

At this, his wife picked herself up from the floor. Crossing over, she confronted him and began to strike at his chest with her fists: "You!" she cried. "Is your grief so terrible? Are you being torn apart? How much more I who fed him at my breasts."

Just imagine, we still had not even been to see the body in that awful sink. Gradually we decided to go, and of course the Volks broke down, and we struggled in the blazing sun to get it started. Finally we hired two motor scooters and went off to the funeral home that way. We clambered through the ante-rooms of sand and coffin lids and broken hearses and got to that morgue.

I had asked them not to embalm Arod until his parents and sisters and brothers had seen him. Now his parents fell upon him and embraced him, getting blood on themselves from his wounds. There was no relief from any quarter—nor even a chair or a box to sit on. I just leaned against the wall and sobbed, seeing their inconsolable loss and shocked by the strength of their love.

During the long wait I had at one point thought of saying that at least we could be grateful that Arod had not been paralyzed for life. Thank God I had never said those words. Arod's mother, holding him in her arms, now said: "Oh, Arod. If only you had lived. Even if you had lost your reason, we would have looked after you every day of your life."

In silence Crispin gently touched every bit of Arod's body. Then he stood back squarely, and slowly and deliberately said: "Now I know. There is no God."

The owner of the establishment brought us to a room where we could discuss the embalming. The custom was to do a partial embalming meant to last a certain number of days and priced accordingly. I suggested five days, Crispin wanted ten. His wife settled it with eight. Eight days with the body in the house; eight days of vigil; eight days of visitors day and night.

While we waited for the embalming to be done, I and some of the sons went to the owners of the bus that had killed Arod—the driver had run away—and discussed insurance with them and the police. Now if anyone will be refused entry into heaven—and I am sure that no one finally will— but if anyone runs a danger of not making it, it is surely the people in charge of paying out accident insurance to the poor. That afternoon we began the sticky negotiations that were to go on for months.

We were ready to leave the funeral home and go back to the mountains when the skies opened up and a torrential tropical rain was upon us. The funeral home let rain in everywhere. As we tried to make arrangements for the hearse we had to move from room to room, sloshing through dirty water on the way. The woman in charge explained as indirectly as she could that there was no way their hearse could make it up the mountain road to Tabugon with the road wet like this. I talked with the driver. We had two choices: to chance being stuck all night on a lonely road in torrential rain, surrounded by a sea of mud and with the danger of the coffin sliding out of the back of the hearse (because of the road's gradient), or to stay in that awful funeral home where we could hardly hear ourselves talking with the noise of the rain on the tin roof and a television on all the time, blaring hot rock music. The place was also swarming with children, who ran in and out of the rooms, playing around the coffins and crowding around the television, quite oblivious to what was going on around them. When the rain began, they pulled off their clothes and danced under the spouts. The sight of those carefree children was my only relief.

We decided eventually to go to the Sa-Maria retreat house where Arod had been doing his month's leadership course and to spend the night there. When we got there we discovered that the participants were expecting us. They placed the coffin before the altar and sang a Mass they had prepared. Then along with the family, they kept vigil the whole night in turns.

(Filipinos never leave the dead alone.) I had built that retreat house many years before with its solid stone altar and its walls built with matching stones from a mountain river. The crucifix is special: it was done by Maximo Vicente, one of the best Filipino sculptors. In these familiar surroundings I felt my spirits revive.

During the evening Sister Florence approached me with an envelope from the candidates. It contained one thousand pesos (one hundred dollars). They had met and agreed to cut it off their food allowance. It was a big sum and it meant everyone eating less. They wanted the money to go to the bereaved family to help with the funeral expenses.

When the cavalcade finally set off for the hills I remained behind, deciding not to be present when the rest of the family met the coffin.

Next day I left for Tabugon. The house where the wake was taking place was a few meters away from the *convento,* so though I arrived late at night I went to visit. Of course the house was crowded. I counted some thirty people fast asleep on the floor. Others played cards at the doorstep or under the house as the vigil went on. This is by no means disrespectful; their presence is a comfort to the bereaved. All the time there were a couple of brothers or sisters or maybe cousins hanging over the glass window of the coffin, devouring Arod with their eyes.

I called in on most of the eight days of the vigil and of course I led the prayers on the last day.

A few days after the funeral I was talking to Crispin.

"I'm sure you understand, Padre, how I felt."

"I do, Crispin."

"How is the insurance case going?" he asked.

"Well, you know how these lawyers are."

"Yes I do. I used to have a bit of land over there"—pointing—"but I lost it through their machinations."

"Tio Crispin, that's the work Arod was doing: helping poor people to hang on to their land against officials. That's what he was dedicating his life to."

"I understand. And Padre, you know I said a lot of things, but if I really didn't believe in God you might not be alive today!"

Many little anecdotes came out about Arod when all was over. How the day before he left for his sister's wake he had washed the clothes of Balthasar and Baby because they were in an accident. How he had bought coffee for the others on the truck on the way down that morning, leaving his pocket completely empty. How he had explained to his girlfriend that he wanted to give time first to serving the community. Even the fact that his little gesture of going around to the front of the cab to say thank you to the truck driver had probably delayed him a fatal moment in crossing the road. He was one of the rare people in his area who had finished high school, and that demanded quite a sacrifice. So much did he help at home, plowing with the carabao (water buffalo) and weeding and working in the house, that he had never even managed to see a film.

Chapter 42

ONE EVENING Monsignor Fortich arrived at my *convento* in Tabugon with an unusual companion—an athletic-looking American with spectacles and a moustache. He spoke Ilongo perfectly, without a trace of that special unaspirated "t" which gives most Ilongo-speaking Americans away. It was Professor Alfred McCoy, who had done his doctorate at Yale on certain aspects of the history of the Negros sugar industry and had authored several best-selling books on the drug traffic. At present he was lecturing in southeast Asian history at the University of New South Wales. I think of him as an investigative historian.

Relaxing on my little private balcony, drinking tea with Monsignor Fortich, McCoy began to share with us the results of his most recent research. He had spent a couple of years buried in the archives of Spanish legal documents in Jaro, on the neighboring island of Panay. He was investigating a long-forgotten court case: how Don Teodoro Benedicto had acquired his large land-holdings at the foot of Mount Kanla-on. According to these court records, Don Teodoro had bribed local officials and burned out peasant settlements in order to amass more than eleven thousand hectares of land—the largest single property in Negros. Seven thousand of these hectares were on the slopes of the volcano, Mount Kanla-on.

As McCoy continued, I looked over at Bishop Fortich. He kept his eyes away from mine; he just puffed away on his pipe, expressionless. I knew we were both wondering if McCoy realized just how explosive this discovery was: as McCoy went on to explain to us, this Teodoro Benedicto was the ancestor of Ambassador Roberto Benedicto, now czar of the sugar industry in the Philippines and controller of everything that moved financially on the island of Negros, and antagonist of Monsignor Fortich and the Church.

The bishop was uncharacteristically silent. I pushed McCoy for more. I had an insatiable interest in the history of Negros, but there was very little available to the amateur like me on the questions that really mattered. For years I had wanted to find out what exactly had happened when the sugar industry first came to Negros in the 1850s. I used to ask the old people in the *hacienda* in San Ramon, but the best I could get from them was that long ago some of them had held land themselves in Negros by some title— possibly by virtue of having cleared the land. But when in the second half of the nineteenth century the laws allowing non-natives to acquire land had been introduced, the natives had had to file formal claim to the land they had worked for generations, and this had to be done in Spanish. Most of them were unable to overcome the bureaucratic and language hurdles and so were dispossessed, more or less in the same way that the people in the mountains today were losing their little claims to professionals from the lowlands. McCoy was saying now that some *mestizos*—Chinese-Filipinos— had been so greedy and ruthless in acquiring land in Negros that even their Spanish neighbors had been shocked by their cruelty against the *Indios* (as the native population was called by the Spaniards).

The case of Don Teodoro Benedicto and the slopes of Mount Kanla-on— the volcano from which Monsignor Fortich took his metaphor "social vol- cano"—showed this metaphor to be even more apt than anyone had real- ized. The discovery was made more topical by the fact that Roberto Bene- dicto, the descendant of Don Teodoro and the present head of the sugar industry, had donated the jeeps for one of the most ruthless army task forces in Negros—the Kanla-on Task Force. At this moment they were stationed in the next village to mine and were terrorizing the people, some of whom were not inconceivably the descendants of those dispossessed by Don Teodoro.

Most significant of all, McCoy had unearthed the forgotten origins of the sugar industry in Negros. In the middle of the nineteenth century, the next-door island of Panay had been home to a thriving textile industry centered in the city of Iloilo, which then had a population of seventy thousand—bigger even than Manila at the time.

McCoy had dug up a work by a French scholar, Mallat, who visited the Philippines in the 1840s and published a survey of the archipelago's weav- ing industry. According to Mallat, Iloilo was then renowned throughout the world for its "sinamay" and "pina" textiles. These cotton and pineapple fibers were used for vestments throughout Catholic Christendom and were "impossible to imitate in Europe" because of the cost of production.

Nicolas Loney arrived on the scene about 1850. He was a British vice- consul and agent for the cotton mills of Manchester. He pirated the Iloilo patterns and designs and sent them to Manchester, where they were able to weave them on their steam-driven machines from cheap U.S. cotton at a much less expensive rate. He began to import them into Iloilo, and within a few years the fifty thousand hand looms of Iloilo became still. The queen city of the south was dying.

Loney introduced sugar to take the place of the defunct textile industry, not out of a desire to bring about development but because his ships were going home empty. He needed to fill them. Sugar would do fine and he would arrange loans to the sugar farmers from European financing agencies to buy British equipment. As yet almost untouched, Negros would serve admirably for planting sugar; the natives of Negros were expendable.

Things fell together for Loney because the recently ousted textile entrepreneurs, mainly Chinese *mestizos,* were looking for something to turn to now that their weaving industry had been destroyed. They sent their sons over to "virgin" Negros to start sugar farms. With the entrepreneurs came peasants from Panay, who cleared ground both for the new *mestizo* sugar farms and for themselves. The native Negrenses were driven into the interior for the most part and often exterminated. In parts of Brian Gore's parish and my own, descendants of those natives, called Tumandoks, could still be met from time to time.

As the years passed the peasants from Panay who had cleared land for themselves also lost it to the growing *haciendas.* It was survival of the fittest, and of course inability to speak Spanish made for unfitness, just as today not to be able to speak English is a distinct disadvantage in the struggle of the peasants with the bureaucracy.

Ironically enough, just a few months before McCoy's visit the leading citizens of Iloilo had unveiled a statue of Vice-Consul Nicolas Loney. President Marcos had called him "the father of the sugar industry" and Ambassador Benedicto had called him "the best friend of Negros."

Nicolas Loney, far from being the benefactor of the Philippines, was the callous assassin of the noble city of Iloilo and its great textile trade, and the initiator of the genocide of the native tribes of Negros. Those lines of children's coffins outside our churches stretched back to the man that Ambassador Benedicto was now proclaiming a hero. Nicolas Loney had always been fascinated by Kanla-on volcano. In his thirteenth year in the Visayas he attempted to climb it. While nearing the crater's rim, he was struck down by the malaria that was to kill him—he never got to the top. His statue, erected a hundred years later by those who benefited from the sugar industry, would also be struck down, presumably by those it had dispossessed.

"Surely you're not going to publish this?" we said to McCoy.

"It's on the presses already. It will appear in a volume called *Philippine Social History,* which I am co-editing with Edilberto de Jesus. I can assure you that there's not a syllable in that book that cannot be backed up with careful documentation. I have seen the actual letters of Loney. They are in the British ambassador's archives."

Nevertheless a few months later the Daughters of St. Paul would refuse to stock the book in their bookstore when our superior, Mickey Martin, took a large consignment of them for Negros.

The pulse began to quicken politically in Negros at the end of 1981. The workers in La Carlota sugar factory (which was situated at the foot of Kanla-on between Kabankalan and Bacolod) went on strike and managed to close down the mill. Benedicto was determined not to surrender to union pressure, and the starving workers were asking for help from all over the island. Food was collected from our small Christian communities and the *kibbutz* truck was used to take it to La Carlota. When some of the officials at Dakong-Cogon mill complained to me that we would bring the wrath of Benedicto down on them and ourselves, I explained in all truth that I did not order the *kibbutz* on what to do and what not to do.

When in February 1982 the army was called in to confront the unarmed pickets I remembered some startling things that McCoy had told me about the La Carlota sugar factory in the early days. McCoy was an expert on the whole labor movement since the twenties in Panay and Negros. He had access to thousands of dusty files and memos of half a century before, when La Carlota was struggling to crush labor unrest. Among these documents he found minutes of meetings in which the factory management discussed what to do with the labor leaders. Their decision was there to be read in these long-forgotten minutes. It was startlingly simple: Liquidate them.

As I was leaving for Manila for our pre-chapter convention, things were getting hot at La Carlota and in the following weeks they would reach a climax. The National Federation of Sugar Workers—the N.F.S.W.—had become tantamount to the Church union, not only because it had been started by Father Hector Mauri and sustained by Father Edgar Saguinsin, but because the picket line was like a celebration of the entire Christian community, with food coming in from Christian communities all over the island. Priests like Father Frankie Connon were at the scene all the time, attempting to make sure that whatever happened there was reported to the outside world. Everything was used against the workers . . . hunger, beatings, tear gas, poison chemicals, the fear of death, and the threat of permanent unemployment. At one point it looked as if they would be shot in cold blood. Five hundred soldiers in full battle gear, backed up by three hundred security guards, faced the unarmed strikers, who were merely six hundred in number. If Monsignor Fortich had not arrived, there might well have been bloodshed. I had seen the bishop in Manila the night before when he got the news, and he had rushed back to Negros to do what he could.

Three things resulted from the La Carlota strike. The factory lost millions. The strikers, though they suffered greatly, grew in their sense of their own dignity. In McCoy's words, "They may well have liberated the consciousness of a whole class." And third, the gap between Benedicto, the real head of the sugar industry, and the Church became unbridgeable. Meanwhile, Father Edgar Saguinsin, forced to flee the Philippines because of threats against his life, did his best to tell the rest of the world what was happening.

Chapter 43

EVER SINCE I could remember, Negros had its share of sporadic political assassinations, but right in the middle of the La Carlota confrontation there occurred what will probably be remembered as the most notorious. It happened like this.

The mayor of Kabankalan had returned to his post as mayor some six months before. He did not go to Kabankalan much, nor did he attend his farm. But he was gradually beginning to get back into things. On this day, the day of the La Carlota confrontation, he went from Bacolod to Kabankalan to visit his farm, Santa Isabel. Now there are two roads from Tabugon to Kabankalan—the ordinary road and a new one which I call the "back road." In the hilly triangle formed by those two roads the mayor had a cattle ranch up the mountains, separated from his farm. On this fatal day, March 10, 1982, he and four bodyguards drove out to his farm from Kabankalan town, and then they drove up to see that ranch by the back road. They did not know that on either side of the road, hidden in the cane fields, were ambushers. When they were returning at dusk, not far from the back road entry to Santa Isabel, as they crested a knoll, they were suddenly attacked from both sides by the ambushers. The mayor and his companions were shot dead and the attackers, seventeen in number, escaped across the fields.

I had been attending our pre-chapter convention up in Manila. This was in preparation for the Columban general chapter to be held in Lima, Peru. For two weeks we had been sharing the results of the local meetings we had held in Negros, Mindanao, and Luzon. Three things dominated our discussions: the revolutionary situation now engulfing the whole Philippines; the need to develop a spirituality which would sustain us in these times; and lastly, "Should we go Filipino?" For years we had been proud of the fact that we had built up the local priests wherever we were working and not our own Society of St. Columban. But now we felt the job had been done in the Philippines. In fact the Filipino priests were the finest you could meet anywhere. It was time to ask them to help us in what we saw as our newly focused role of bringing good news to the poor. But such a change would be convulsive unless all the Columbans agreed. So we teased out every aspect of the change before we finally came to an almost unanimous "Yes."

I was exhausted by the whole convention and decided to go up to the mountain city of Baguio for a few days. Baguio is in the Cordillera Mountains, which run down the center of the island of Luzon. It is cool and one of the most beautiful cities I have ever been in, filled with fruit and vegetables and flowers of both tropical and temperate climates and that special Baguio pine tree you don't expect to find so near the equator. The people do skillful carving in wood and handicrafts in brass and gold and silver, and of course there is the native weaving. The market overflows with rare foods like wild honey, strawberries, mushrooms. And Baguio is a center for learning, so the streets are filled with students. It is like a holiday city.

Walking along the street in Baguio City in a carefree mood, I saw the newspaper headlines—"Kabankalan Mayor Ambushed and Killed." I read the story in disbelief.

I had not seen much of the mayor in recent years. But in earlier days he had been helpful to me in building the Sa-Maria house. He had supported my catechists and he insisted on believing that I had helped in his election. I was quite close to the family because his wife had asked me to help in reconciling father and son. I had tried hard to do so. In fact I had been a family counselor for a while. I knew and admired his daughter, and his sister was a dear friend. On one occasion the mayor agreed to do a retreat and I remember once kneeling for an hour before the Blessed Sacrament with the parish priest as we prayed that his retreat would help him. And to me it did seem to have helped him. My last memory of him was at a protest rally which we held in Magballo, organized by Jimmy Martin to protest the rape and killing of the people by the Civilian Home Defense Force (the C.H.D.F.)—that militia which the army created by handing out guns to local thugs. As the people stood up and told their gruesome stories, the mayor listened with mounting anger. When he finally got up to talk to the assembled group, he spoke with passion against the military, even though they were present. I still remember his words: "I myself was a commander during the war with the guerrillas. Our troops sometimes killed civilians. I used to get mad at them and shout, 'Can't you see you are killing your fellow Filipinos?' I've seen this with my own eyes, so I have no trouble in believing the stories of the people here today." And he went and comforted some of the bereaved. Eugene and I went over and thanked him profusely for his support. That had been some three years previously, and it was the last time I saw the mayor alive. Of course many things had happened since then, and I had not witnessed the now-famous confrontation at Oringao.

I returned to the house, went to the chapel, and offered Mass for his soul and for his family, whose suffering seemed never to end.

Chapter 44

AS WORLD War II ended, the Philippines was flooded with tens of thousands of GIs—mostly ordinary young fellows, hardly out of school, little more than civilians with uniforms. They were black and white and brown and had little racial prejudice. They came from a land of plenty and were shocked by what the Japanese had left behind in the Philippines. They took the children in their arms. They played with the kids and shared their gum and chocolate and cigarettes. GI Joe was a good fellow. The Filipinos welcomed him and never forgot his boyish generosity. Their brief stay did more for Filipino/American friendship than a hundred years of State Department public relations.

Of course the goodwill toward the Americans in the Philippines is due to more than that. The American colonial government at the turn of the century had set up a fine public school system throughout the archipelago. It gave a chance of upward mobility to many who did not have it before, but it also successfully introduced the English language strongly enough to tune the Filipino nation forever into American cultural aspirations. The élite were sent to the United States for schooling—the colonized admired the colonizers and wanted to imitate them. The Americans also introduced democracy, and though that democracy was flawed, its myth has nevertheless been a powerful force for good to this day, holding up an ideal to which the present corruption is always contrasted.

When I first came to the Philippines I was surprised by some of the anti-American sentiment of certain columnists. I put it down to sour grapes or the fact that they found it easy to make the U.S. a whipping boy instead of cleaning up the corruption at home. The slogans on the placards—"Down with U.S. Imperialism"—at those early anti-U.S. demonstrations seemed like cant to me, borrowed from the Chinese cultural revolution which was going on at that time. Why could they not apply the same formula the West had applied a hundred and fifty years before when the Industrial Revolution had brought a new era of prosperity to Europe and North America? Surely an increase in exports of raw materials plus the injection of foreign loans could bring about the sort of industrial revolution which had started the West on the road to prosperity. Add a pinch of the Protestant work ethic and cover the whole in a sauce "adapted to Asian circumstances" and the economic pie could be made big enough for everyone to share. Instead we were blaming the United States, the very country which was sending flour and other aid goods.

It is not easy to chart a change of outlook. It comes subtly, now gradually like snow accumulating on a roof, now suddenly like that same snow which has reached the limit of its clinging ability so that the next flurry sends the whole lot tumbling. So my gradual change of perception of the role the U.S. was playing in the Philippines came in different ways: first through reading of Philippine history, second by observing the havoc and hunger brought on by the Marcos regime which owed every day in power to continued American support. Then these two were brought home to me more vividly by individual manifestations of American presence, such as the huge agri-businesses of Dole and Del Monte, which amounted to land reform in reverse, because they made farmers or freeholders into day laborers on what was once their own land. The influence of companies like these on the Marcos government was such that wherever the law needed to be changed to suit them, it was changed—exactly as it had been in colonial times.

Of course, it was not only American companies. Japanese and British companies did the same thing. I was once asked directly to use my influence as a priest to convince the small farmers to sell their land to a new Japanese sugar mill that was setting up across the mountain from me. But then Japan has never claimed to be interested in the huddled masses.

The snow toppled off the roof with a visit to the Prostitute City of Olongapo, which grew up around the U.S. military base. Its children with gonorrhea, its youth using drugs, and the city divided by the GIs themselves into black and white zones. It was a living testament to what I had heard from my fellow Columbans and read about in Philippine history.

Three books which particularly affected my attitude come to mind.

By accident I came across a book called *Filipino Martyrs: By an Eyewitness*, written by a well-known turn-of-the-century Irish writer called Brinsley Sheridan. The book had been out of print since 1900. Sheridan's story was autobiographical. He had been on a visit to the United States and had a great love for the country. The Statue of Liberty summed up how he saw America, especially in the role she had been playing for Ireland. For Irish people America really was the home of the free. On his way back to Europe he passed through the Philippines and arrived just in time for the American-Spanish war in which the U.S. is supposed to have taken the Philippines from Spain. He witnessed it all, and being a journalist he recorded what he saw. Among other things he saw that the popular opinion in the U.S. that the Filipinos were uncivilized pagans incapable of governing themselves was nonsense.

He interviewed General Emilio Aguinaldo, head of the Philippine forces, and was amazed to learn that the Filipinos had themselves already taken most of the territory back from Spain. America was coming in when the war was virtually over. Aguinaldo, though not particularly interested in the poor, was a cultured, capable, and honorable man.

Sheridan witnessed the Battle of Manila. It was over before breakfast, he said, and was basically a face-saving device for the Spaniards. They later sold the already lost Philippines to the United States for $20 million. When Sheridan tried to cable out his story, he was prevented by American censorship. The whole episode so shocked him, precisely because he was an admirer of America, that he wrote his book in protest. His book went out of print and the subsequent Philippine-American war became a well-kept secret as far as succeeding generations were concerned.

The second book was *Little Brown Brother* by Leon Wolff. The catchy title belies careful historical research on the Philippine-American war. Wolff found it necessary to write this book precisely because the schoolbook story of that war reduced it to a few unimportant skirmishes, whereas the reality was a long drawn-out war of ten to fifteen years which cost 250,000 lives. More Filipinos were killed in that war than in World War II, and with brutality and torture of the My Lai variety.

By accident I came across a corroboration of this point in the letters of Mark Twain. Mark Twain was deeply worried over what was going on in the Philippines. Information was not coming through, and with some superb investigative reporting he discovered that reports of U.S. soldiers' heroic deeds in Mindanao were in fact the sanitized version of a terrible massacre of women and children which Twain uncovered and denounced —not an easy thing to do when everyone is hurrahing the troops. Subsequently Twain signed a document condemning the use of torture by American troops against the Filipinos. And the Philippine war was part of the inspiration for his now-famous "War Prayer," so strong a plea that he only allowed it to be published after his death.

And then there was Hernando Abaya's *Betrayal in the Philippines*, which deals with World War II. Abaya describes how on Luzon, the main northern island, the large holders of rice-land in the central area fled to Manila to place themselves under the protection of the Japanese. While their tenants were fighting the Japanese side by side with the Americans, many landowners collaborated with the Japanese. When MacArthur returned, American troops were used to escort the landowners back to their property and to put off the tenants who had taken over. Those peasants were the ones who had given their lives fighting the Japanese. These were the peasants who revolted and became the heart of the Huk communist insurgency in the forties and fifties. As I read Abaya, I could see similar things happening around me now.

As martial law tightened, I actually began to witness the U.S. State Department's support for Marcos. I realized that there was a strand of continuity running right through its policy.

Again and again we priests met representatives from the U.S. embassy. In fact they sought us out. We often ate dinner with them in Manila. Countless times we gave the story of what was really happening, and we lived in the hope that our message would get through. On one occasion, while I was visiting Archbishop Sin, a labor representative from the U.S. embassy was in the palace. He was worried about Father Hector Mauri, the Italian Jesuit who had started the National Federation of Sugar Workers. The archbishop referred him to me, as I was from Negros. Mauri had been reported to the attaché as an activist, an agitator, a troublemaker. All Mauri was looking for was a living wage on the plantations for the workers. Mauri had actually been expelled from communist China, but the significance of that seemed to escape the labor attaché. Mauri's push for labor unions was fired in part by his militant anti-communism; he did not want a repeat of the China experience in the Philippines. It was ironic that those who were doing precisely the things that could preempt communism were the ones suspected of being communist.

We Columbans met frequently in Batang and were able to compare notes over what was happening in other parishes. We also attended the monthly meeting of all the priests where reports were given from all over the province. Likewise we came together from all over the Philippines in Manila in our house in Singalong and were able to hear firsthand accounts of what was going on in Mindanao or in Luzon. Thus to counter positive reports about the N.P.A. from Negros, there were negative reports from parts of Mindanao—about people being executed for stealing chickens, *barrio* captains being shot after "public trial," suspected informers liquidated, agents purged, and taxes, sometimes arbitrarily, levied on the people. But reports about the military were negative from everywhere and the reports about American business and agribusiness were also increasingly negative. Nor were the Australians, the Japanese, or the British exempt.

News was beginning to get out that Marcos was doing a deal with Westinghouse to put up a nuclear plant in Morong, near where we Columbans had a parish for many years now.

Ever since I had read Helen Caldicott's lucid writings on the effects of what is misleadingly called "low-level" radiation, I had been aware of the special dangers of nuclear power even for peaceful purposes, and the news about the nuclear plant a Morong was more disturbing every day. It is a paradigm of U.S. industrial business relations with the Philippines.

The "Monster of Morong," as it is called by Filipinos, was contracted for furtively by Marcos with Westinghouse for more than double the price offered by its major competitor, General Electric. Bidding was short-circuited when Disini, Imelda's cousin, spoke out on behalf of Westinghouse. The proposed plant was to be built on the side of an extinct volcano—forty-five miles from an undersea fault line and therefore vulnerable to both tidal waves and the earthquakes that frequently shake the Philippines.

And no matter what their attitude toward nuclear power was, most thinking people in the Philippines had to be worried that the corruption of the Marcos government made the construction and management of a safe plant very unlikely.

Marcos played the whole thing expertly, appearing to listen to the protests but progressing steadily forward.

The above-the-table commission paid to Herminio Disini—and admitted by Westinghouse—was $17 million. But Jesus Vergara, the former head of Westinghouse's Philippine affiliate, told investigators that Westinghouse paid Disini a commission of at least $50 million, just under four percent of the contract price. Disini gave Marcos about $30 million of that, Vergara said, and split the rest with Vergara and Rodolfo Jacob, the president of Disini's conglomerate. The final cost of the reactor when it was finished was over $2 billion.

After helping Westinghouse win the contract, Disini bought Asia Industries from U.S. Industries and thus became Westinghouse's Philippine distributor. His Summa Insurance Company wrote part of the plant's coverage and, though he had no prior construction experience, Disini formed a consortium of contractors called Power Contractors, Inc., to which Westinghouse awarded major subcontracts on the plant. (I learned these details later in the September 1986 issue of *Fortune International*.)

Disini has left the Philippines and now lives in a turn-of-the-century villa outside of Vienna. The reactor has never gone into operation. The interest on $2 billion now comes to over $100 million a year—almost equivalent to the government's annual health budget.

The question that we were beginning to ask was not how Marcos could inflict such a crushingly expensive, dangerous, and ultimately unessential project on the Philippines, but how the U.S. Import-Export Bank, one of the major creditors, could involve themselves in such a deal. Everyone knew that this was not the will of the Filipino people, who were going to have to pay the money back.

A study published in 1979 by Bello, Hayes, and Zarsky revealed the following facts:

1. Eximbank ignored the findings of the Philippines Energy Development Board that nuclear power was more expensive than other indigenous power sources like coal, geothermal power, and hydropower. At a congressional hearing in 1978 Exim officials were forced to admit that they had not sought comparative costs for other sources of electric energy.

2. Eximbank pushed the project with the awareness that no rigorous site and safety review by a qualified regulatory agency had ever been done, with the result that the plant was to be built in the vicinity of live volcanoes and earthquake faults.

3. Eximbank was aware that such economic and safety studies as were done had been sponsored by the International Atomic Energy Agency (IAEA), an organization whose role is to promote nuclear power, using consulting firms like Burns and Roe, a major nuclear-industry subcontractor. (Burns and Roe was later hired by Westinghouse to help construct the Philippine reactor.)

The concluding remarks of this study shed some light on the reason for the astronomical sums that were being lent to Marcos: "In sum, it is difficult to resist the conclusion that the Philippine nuclear power project was an ill-disguised effort by Eximbank to bail out a desperate Westinghouse."

Banking circles were aware that much of the money being lent to the Philippines was coming back to the United States to buy property for the Marcos family and their friends. They were also aware that, as the loans they approved grew, the real income of the bottom third of the population declined. My brother used to send me the Barclay Bank investors' three-month report on the Philippines and Taiwan, and the figures were there for anyone to see. This leads to a significant conclusion.

There was never any way that Marcos could have gone into the nuclear venture, the eighteen luxury hotels, the San Juanico bridge, the cultural center, the folk arts theatre, some nine hundred crony corporations . . . to mention but a few of the schemes, without the full cooperation and blessing and final approval of the more than three hundred major banks who financed these projects. Many of those who signed the vital papers are devout believing Christians. I strongly believe that the apparently beneficent act of giving loans to Third World countries can have devastating consequences on the poor of those countries. This is the case in the Philippines and those who signed the papers wittingly or unwittingly have been involved in an immoral act of monumental proportions. The signing of those papers was in fact the signing of the death warrants of untold numbers of Filipinos—to realize this is to realize what is meant by "integrating life and religion."

The reaction to the insurgency, which resulted indirectly from these loans, had been a massive buildup of the military, to be financed by crushing new loans.

As for my earlier idea that what had helped the West during the Industrial Revolution would help the Philippines, over the years I was gradually disabused of that notion. In the Industrial Revolution a little capital gave work to a lot of people because the machines were labor intensive. Today's industrial technology was capital intensive; a huge injection of industrial capital succeeded in giving work to only a few. The emphasis should have been put on improving food farming and on labor-intensive, middle-level industries for a start.

As for exporting primary products, my experience with the cooperative farms which we had started taught me something about that. The laborers in the cane fields did the same amount of work for less and less because the price of sugar was decided in the buying countries and not in the selling countries, whereas the price of the tractors and fertilizers we bought was decided in the selling countries and not in the buying countries. We lost both ways. When we started the farm, a hundred tons of sugarcane cut and loaded could earn enough to buy a small tractor. But now you would have to cut and load four times that amount. It was a treadmill on which you had to run faster and faster to stay still.

Molasses is a by-product of sugar. The members of the *kibbutz* had put all the money from their molasses in a special bank account cosigned by me for use as an educational fund for the children. After eight years they had twenty thousand pesos in the bank. But overnight the peso was devalued almost fifty percent as a result of pressure from the International Monetary Fund and the fruit of their sweat of eight years was halved, while foreign companies in the Philippines holding dollars found themselves with double what they had the night before. When they looked out of the window that morning, everything was sale price.

Moreover, the money we had borrowed to expand the *kibbutz* cooperative was generously given to us without any interest to pay, but we did agree to pay it back in sterling, never realizing that sterling would relentlessly gain so much on the peso. Our debt eventually became impossible, no matter how hard the members worked.

Examined carefully in its origins and in its results, the long economic and political relationship between the U.S. and the Philippines had been to the benefit of the U.S. and the local élite who controlled the Philippines, but to the ruin of the ordinary people.

I still found cant and slogans repugnant. They seemed to control people more than enlighten them and favored the sort of black-and-white thinking which ideology revels in. That local élite was willing to sell out to anyone, not just America; as far as they were concerned the Philippines was for sale. Japan for one was now doing as much "trade" with the Philippines as the U.S.

Nevertheless I had to accept the reality behind the anti-U.S. slogans. Without the United States the Marcos regime would tumble. The State Department was justifying its exposed position by saying: "The devil you know is better than the devil you don't know." But some felt they were really saying: "He may be a devil, but he's our devil."

Filipinos make a clear distinction between the people and the State Department. They like America and Americans, and given a chance many Filipinos would pull up their stakes and move to the U.S. in the morning. On the other hand, not to be critically aware of the role that U.S. business and banking is playing in the Philippines is to promote it. We always come back to those death camps and the silent consenters.

Chapter 45

I GOT BACK to Tabugon from Manila in time for Easter 1982 and the *Flores de Mayo* (the Flowers of May), which is a very beautiful tradition in the Philippines. The children come to their little chapel each day and make offerings of flowers to Our Lady. This is done to the accompaniment of song and even dance. Every year people make a vow to organize the *Flores,* and neighbors try and supply a little food for the children, especially on the last day, when Mary is crowned. For hungry children this is a happy time. Because the first *kibbutz* was called Kibbutz Santa Maria, its members took on the obligation of organizing the *Flores.* But nearby Christian communities also held their own *Flores.*

It was the night of May 31, the last night of the *Flores.* The *kibbutz* finished their religious ceremony early and prepared for a dance. A nearby community had no dance, but had planned to have porridge for every child in their area. They were proud of their feat in doing this from almost nothing, and the hungry children were excited.

Unbeknownst to the children, however, the Task Force Kanla-on were on the prowl. Some say they had heard the music and were aiming to go to the *kibbutz.* Anyway, they arrived outside the house where the children were being fed. The soldiers had walkie-talkies and Armalite machine guns. They announced that they were the N.P.A. and then began to shoot. Thirteen-year-old Romulo Martisano had his spoon of porridge up to his mouth and was shot dead in that position. Three other children were hit. The soldiers then ran back to their camp at Tapi, the village next to Tabugon.

Our justice committee immediately went out and examined the place, took photographs of the holes in the walls, and registered a complaint with the provincial commander, who claimed he had no jurisdiction over that group. Three priests including myself were there for the Mass and blessing of the coffin, but no one from the village of Tapi came, not even the *barrio* captain. After the Mass I went to see the *barrio* captain and asked her why she had not attended. She said that she felt she had to be neutral. I said that being neutral was a myth, that it was a vote for the violence. Either you were against it vocally or for it by your silence, and that if a priest like me or a *barrio* captain like her did not side with the people against such butchery we should not be a priest or *barrio* captain at all.

Later when that battalion had pulled out of the area an old woman, a Mrs. Orchida, came forward with her story. One night the task force had pulled up outside their house and "borrowed" their son Carlito. For a few days he was seen in the task force camp, but then he disappeared. She went back repeatedly to look for her son, but they said that he had asked permission to urinate and had escaped to join the N.P.A. But now that the task force was gone, her family went into the abandoned barracks and there they dug up an oblong section of the ground about the length of a man that looked freshly turned. There they found the body of Carlito her son. Father Dodo Dejilla got the provincial coroner, Doctor Lavada, to come. He determined that Carlito's skull had been cracked, three of his ribs were broken, and there were scars on his back. In the grave lying beside the body had been a brutal-looking whip with nuts and bits of metal tied at the end of it. Doctor Lavada discovered that there was dust and dirt in Carlito's trachea, and in his opinion Carlito had been buried while still alive.

We brought the whole case to the Church-military liaison committee. The meeting was televised. Of course there was no redress, but the provincial commander, turning toward the television cameras, handed a one-hundred-peso bill to Mrs. Orchida. I shall never forget the look of confusion and anguish on her face. The onlooking people were disgusted at such a grotesque gesture. Afterward they said it implied that a life was worth a hundred pesos.

A letter I wrote home catches the atmosphere at that time:

Dear Mom and Dad,
It is very late and not really the time to be writing as I have a Mass at six in the morning, but if I let the time pass I won't get the chance again for a while and then I'm going down to Batang for a couple of days so I will get a chance to post this letter.
The army are active around here again. Until last week they did not come into this parish. But in the next parish they carried on what can only be described as Vietnam-style counter-insurgency exercises, using pairs of helicopters to strafe the ground and then drop in troopers.
Well, last week the bishop was up here for a meeting in the sugar mill. The chief of the constabulary appeared and, with a disarming schoolboy

face, told us all about his frustrated desires to be a priest. (Army men here are always telling people about their brothers, uncles, etc., who are priests, and about how they served Mass!) He also gave us a lecture on the way he insists that his men never take anything without paying for it. Especially chickens. The bishop puffed away on his cigar and I looked at him, earnestly trying to join in the charade, afraid that if I allowed my real thoughts play I might utter something like "Liar!" at him and so do more harm than good. At the very moment he was talking to us his men were making a raid in the parish. If I had only known!

Finally we did get the details (the following morning). I found that they had taken in five men and tortured them, and done two things consistently as they went from house to house in this forlorn part of the parish: they had stolen the chickens and fighting cocks (the latter are worth a lot); and they had consistently condemned me. They also told the people that I was a member of the N.P.A.

You can imagine how the families feel, losing their men. Some of the people had (homemade) guns—I think the soldiers found four in all—but they had these to protect themselves against bandits. And these bandits were controlled by the army, as I explained in another letter this time last year.

My car overturned. Only Alex was in it, and he was going at a great speed. It went for twenty yards on its roof, and then righted itself. I arrived a few minutes later, sharing a ride with Mickey Martin. We saw my wrecked car with no one around. My heart leapt, as I dreaded another death. But Alex had miraculously come out of it with not a scratch, thought the bodywork of the car was in smithereens.

A new priest has joined me, a Filipino. He will be chaplain in the sugar *central,* and that will leave me full-time in the parish, leaving everyone happier.

What I did not say in the letter was that right after the army raid, which took place in the area where Little Angel used to be active and where there was no N.P.A. presence at all, we went around and got full details of the raid from the people, taking down the exact words of the army men at each house. Their main target seemed to be the Christian communities, because they threatened to burn the chapels and to cut off the head of the priest. If they had asked they would have known that I was against violence, but I know now that they were not worried about me being for or against violence. They were worried about any talk about human rights or justice, because both those things are seen as subversive and are probably more so in the long run if accompanied by nonviolence, because it makes it so much harder for them to combat.

We carefully documented everything they did, feeling somehow that it would be useful later because the military always flatly denied that anything had happened—and this works unless you can produce evidence.

I did not know that the same troops had done quite a tour of the Tablas Valley, humiliating people wherever they went—making old people in the market do push-ups, for example. Well, they arrived at Tagucon, where there is a Christian community attached to Brian Gore's parish, and picked up one of the members of the community, ostensibly because he was wearing an old fatigue jacket. This he had bought in the marketplace at the secondhand clothes stall for eighteen pesos. It had on it a badge of the sixtieth battalion. The task force tore the badge off his jacket.

"Put it in your mouth," they said. He put it in his mouth.

"Chew it," they said, pointing a rifle at him. He began to chew.

"Swallow it."

At that, Geronimo Perez, one of the core group of the Oringao Christian communities, who had been watching, as terrified as anyone else, stepped forward and protested. They turned from their wretched victim and arrested Geronimo immediately.

The next morning they arrested Brian himself, who had just arrived back from his vacation in Australia, and accused him of having a gun and four bullets and subversive documents in the house. These of course had been planted by them the night before. They had only been waiting for him to arrive back.

Brian was released that day. Even so, it was a sign that things were going to get worse. The bishop demanded a meeting with the military. Up in Tabugon I was blissfully unaware of the whole proceedings. In fact I was fast asleep at *siesta* two days later when a knock came, and I was handed a note from Donie Hogan saying that there was an urgent meeting between Church and military in Dancallan, the next town south of Kabankalan, and to come immediately.

Since the Volks had been smashed up we were using the old Ford Fiera and were just in the middle of painting it. Alex took off the wrappings, and we set off for Dancallan along a back road—a journey of about thirty kilometers.

While we were traveling this back road a furious storm broke out of the heavens. I had never seen the like of it before. Lightning and thunder cracking and roaring around us amid a deluge of rain. Of course our vehicle let in all the rain and we were drenched. I thought we had better take shelter in case we were hit by the lightning. So we stopped at a poor shack. . . . Enter strangers in the middle of storm from nowhere, like in a melodrama. Inside an old woman and a young man were huddled on the floor, trying to avoid those parts of the shack where the rain was coming in.

It was dark and empty and utterly miserable. These accidental glimpses of just how the people were living always touched me deeply.

When the storm had abated a little, we left those huddled figures behind and set off, only to discover that further down the road, a kilometer away, the ground was dry. We were told later that we had been safer in the car than anywhere else because the tires were insulating us against the electric storm.

We arrived at 4:30 at Dancallan with the meeting already in progress. The tables were arranged in a horseshoe. The bishop and the colonel were at the center table, the priests at flanking tables to the right and the military at tables to the left. Brian had just recounted his story and the bishop was speaking. He was saying that the military had broken the agreement that they would not detain priests without prior knowledge of the bishop. He also said that there had been talk about sending the army up the Candoni road because the N.P.A. had burned a grain truck. He did not think troops were the answer. The problem was that the grain dealers were cheating the people.

Then I asked permission to speak. I took a notebook from my pocket and began to read word for word what the Task Force Kanla-on had said and done house by house throughout the Amian part of the parish. The soldiers grew uneasy. The exact quotations, the detailed petty thefts, were in their own way more damning than the arrest, because in the arrest of Brian they were claiming that he had a weapon and therefore it was a political matter, whereas here were cases which showed that those same troops were just thugs and common thieves.

The colonel coughed and said that he would arrange for payment for those roosters if I could get the list. It was the same colonel who had given the one hundred pesos to Mrs. Orchida.

We ended the meeting and I had a chance for the first time to speak to Lieutenant Gallo, the leader of the task force. Something told me it was a time for a bit of conciliation. I said simply that I was willing to sit down with him anytime, that if he had complaints about the Christian communities why not just come to me and tell me; but I asked him what sort of a priest I would be if I did not complain when his men did something wrong.

I rushed off home again because I had a Mass the next morning and because we had Doctor Sylvia de la Paz, the wife of Doctor Bobby de la Paz, arriving to give some training to our barefoot doctors. Doctor Bobby had spent his life serving the rural poor and training them to help themselves medically, using the same techniques as Doctor Jimmy Tan. He had been gunned down in his clinic on the island of Samar. Sylvia, his wife, who came from a professional family in Bacolod, had been able to speak to the Bacolod professional classes in their own language and show that Bobby's killing was done by the security forces—the people who should have been protecting him.

A few days later the authorities issued a proper warrant of arrest for Brian and the six lay leaders who formed his core group. The charge was subversion and illegal possession of firearms. It would all be done with legal correctness this time. We all accompanied Brian to the prison in the town of Kabankalan, and as they closed the gates the crowd sang *"Ngaa nagasubung sini?"* ("Why has our land come to this?")

The next day the bishop called for a diocese-wide Mass in front of the town hall of Kabankalan. They came from everywhere. The rain was bucketing down, but the bishop insisted on going ahead with the Mass.

His opening words were: "Even the heavens weep to see what is being done to our people. . . ." It was strange how as the years went by the simple fact of taking the side of the people had gradually changed all of us, and most of all the bishop.

For the three days that Brian and his six companions were inside the prison, the members of his Christian communities flowed down from the mountains. Since the male leaders had gone to prison, their wives took over and organized the parish. And, though continually harassed by the military who tried to prevent them, they walked all the way down from the mountains, many in bare feet, and fasted in front of the prison.

Then something very beautiful happened. The townspeople of Kabankalan came with food to feed the members of the communities. Apart from having no money, they really wanted to fast—the townspeople had seen that they were not eating, but did not realize that they were trying to fast. The peasants did not know what to do. They wanted to fast, but it is completely against Filipino culture to refuse a gift of food. So I am sure that they ate what was put before them. In its own way it was a symbolic reconciliation between the townspeople and the peasants, for these peasants had been victims of some of those who were now giving them food.

On the third day there was a tense court hearing at which the prosecution tried to have Brian moved to another island away from where he would have people supporting him, and in fact Benedicto's helicopter was ready waiting to accomplish the transfer. However, Attorney Francisco Cruz, the diocesan lawyer, put the case so well that as he made his clinching point the crowd in the courtroom clapped, and the clapping was echoed by cheers from Brian's people who were praying outside the courthouse. The judge could not refuse bail.

Next time there would be a different and a tougher judge.

We all marched to the prison to collect the six lay leaders and Brian. With them we walked back to the church, which was fuller than at Easter time as we prayed and sang together in thanksgiving. I was thanking God for something else, too. Sixteen years ago I had made my first trip to the interior of what was then a forested mountain. I had been the first priest to go there in fifty years. I had seen much worse things since, but never forgot the hungry children I had met in the shacks along the way. Now the area was filled with the Christian communities of Brian's parish, and I knew that if those children had lived they were surely among these poor but dignified and determined people rejoicing here today.

Chapter 46

*I*N *THE* fall of 1982 the farmers in Candoni went on strike to protest the low price they were receiving for their corn. Our people made the journey over to Candoni to support them. Father Bennett in Sipalay had a prayer rally to protest the army killings there, and our people walked thirty kilometers over the mountains to join the rally. The Church-military liaison held a meeting in Magballo, and our people went there to show solidarity. Brian's *fiesta* came in Oringao, and again the parish leaders from all the communities walked the long journey to join with the Christian communities there. And of course several truck loads came down from Tabugon for that Mass before the town hall in Kabankalan. In many cases these journeys were tough and demanded sacrifice, as the people had no money with them, just a little rice wrapped in a banana leaf, and there was always danger from the Civilian Home Defense Force and the other military units. But we now saw this active support for other suffering people as an essential part of being a Christian community. It would be fatal to let ourselves become wrapped up only in the world of our own personal rights. We must be open to the needs of our sisters and brothers in the surrounding parishes. If we were not, our communities would turn in upon themselves and stagnate.

The taller a tree grows, the deeper and stronger its roots need to be. The more active our communities became, the more I felt we needed contemplation and prayer. But on the face of it it seemed as if this activism would make prayer all the more difficult, if not impossible.

Let me explain. In the mission seminary where I trained, we had a life of prayer which essentially followed a monastic tradition that has been carried down from the fourth century: silence, prayer, study, sacrifice. Then of course there was the Irish Celtic tradition of penance which was in the air we breathed. I am talking about 1960. We rose at six in silence. We prayed till 7:45 A.M., and then had breakfast in silence, with reading of the martyrology and the Scriptures. Class from nine till noon, when we had spiritual reading for thirty minutes. Silence at lunch with spiritual reading. An hour and a half recreation. Three o'clock, study. At 5:45 P.M., rosary. Six, supper; we could talk at supper. Seven, visit to the Blessed Sacrament and back to study. Nine, night prayers, Benediction of the Blessed Sacrament, private prayers. Then the "great silence" till 8:15 the following morning. In all there were only three and a half hours in which we spoke during the day. We attended three retreats each year and the whole course started with the Ignatian exercises—almost thirty days of complete silence. And that was the way it was, more or less, in all seminaries throughout the world.

However, the Columbans also had their own tradition. Common sense and moderation were the key words. No private penance. No more prayer than was laid down. No studying during recreation. An abhorrence of visions, private revelations, or spiritual excess; and a deep suspicion of the emotions. The demands of hospitality or sickness melted the rules of the house.

To me going through my youthful conversion, I found not the rules but the moderation irksome. Each of us had a spiritual director. I chose Father Ronan McGrath, who epitomized this tradition of moderation, common sense, quiet piety, and a game of golf. He kept a rein on my enthusiasm. When I proposed joining the Cistercian monks—a strict monastic order— on the basis that I might as well be hung for a sheep as for a lamb, he sat back and said: "Yes, some of our men have done that, and in fact two of them have become abbots. It's a very special vocation. But then again, if everyone became a monk, who'd go to the missions?" I learned that many of the students during their first fervor proposed going to the Cistercians.

The seven years of prayer and discipline caused me no stress. In the theology of the time this was the way to holiness, and if that was what it took, that was fine by me. I was very happy all those years.

In my last year I read Hans Küng's book *The Council, Reform and Reunion*. The thesis was very simple. The forms of prayer and the liturgical forms and even the doctrinal formulations were not all of equal age and venerability. Some in fact were as recent as the First Vatican Council. There had been changes going on right through the ages—changes, that is, in form but not in essence. Why not therefore, if the upcoming Council aimed at reunion of the churches and renewal of our own, change those forms and formulations standing in the way of unity and renewal? The thesis was clarity itself. My seven years were nearly up. I had been happy during them, but I accepted the heart of the Küng thesis, so now I felt a lot of things must change and I started asking for these changes immediately. I was able to look back now with a critical eye on our "formation."

Posted to foreign lands the "faithful" Columban priest tried to keep to the regimen of prayer he had learned in the seminary. Indeed, so did I. And we tended to lay down the same as the ideal for the Christians whom we catechized. If the prayer patterns of the Sa-Maria retreat were examined, in spite of all the inculturation, they would closely match what I had learned in the seminary.

One result of the imposition of a quasi-monastic prayer-life on the faithful was that a Filipino priest had to learn Latin through English to be able to read his breviary. One of my memories of Beijing is the Chinese priest from the national church saying his breviary in Latin. Over the years I produced many different prayerbooks for the people, but they all reflect that prayer-life of the seminary in Ireland, reflecting in its turn the tradition of the monastery.

This tradition would not have lasted so long if it did not have a lot to offer, but taken out of its natural habitat, the monastery, it had disadvantages. It gave rise to formalism—the need to get all these prayers "in." A priest who anticipated a very heavy day of traveling would say his night prayers in the morning in case he could not get them in later. Many said their morning prayers the night before. There used to be a story going around about two Columbans who, driving across the United States, found it coming up to midnight. They had not said their breviary, but were still far from home. They stopped the car, left the headlights on, and both got out and sat on the road, their backs against the front bumper. Taking out their breviaries, they began to read away. A passing truck stopped and the driver leaned out saying: "Anything wrong? Can I help?"

"No, we're just reading."

"Gee, that must be some book!" And he pulled away.

Any priest remembering those times knows that the story had to be true. Another trick was to read your breviary from eleven till midnight, and then read on till you finished the one for the next day. Or if you were scrupulous, you could pull from your wallet a little graph and map, and reckon just what time "real" midnight was in this particular place. Maybe you still had twenty minutes to spare. In Ireland it was not real midnight till 1:20 A.M. in the summer.

The Council introduced a whole new spirit, which was more human, more relaxed, and in a way more demanding, because it shunned the "obligation" approach. Many older priests found it impossible to change the habits of a lifetime. Sadly, when the obligation was lifted, many younger priests dropped it altogether. It was common to hear people say, in defense of dropping all the previous obligations, *"Laborare est orare"*—"To work is to pray." Or, "Good human relationships are prayer." So formal prayer took a beating.

In the early days it was always a struggle to get prayer a genuine place on the agenda at the stress-filled meetings of the sixteen parishes. I felt badly about this. I felt that to deal with so much tension and death and torture and uncertainty we needed far more than before to call to mind the presence of Jesus risen and present among us, and surely that is what Christian prayer is about.

Eventually Tabugon came to be the group usually assigned to prepare the prayers. This peeved me, as I felt that prayer should be a natural priority without our group having to push it. However, I learned to accept this arrangement, realizing that each group brought a different gift to the gathering. If ours was to be prayer, so be it.

Of course one of the reasons why some priests, and lay leaders too, eventually turned against prayer was that we witnessed so much talk of prayer and praising of God by the very people who had their foot firmly on the neck of the poor. It was always an embarrassment to me, who wanted to see more prayer, when such people were the ones to propose it! I felt that a lot of talk about prayer, yoked with little justice, was the best formula for producing atheism in the next generation.

Another cause for downplaying prayer was a certain way of using social analysis. When you analyzed the varying classes of society, you began to see the significance of the underlying patterns in social behavior. The joy of discovering a key to the oppression around us made some reduce all reality to the interplay of economic forces and class struggle. It became for them the master key to explain everything. If some fact did not fit the paradigm, it was ignored or reinterpreted.

If all reality could be explained by identifiable human and economic factors, then where is there room for prayer? Prayer will simply cloud the issue. If God can change things, why should we work to change them when we can just pray to God to change them? Human beings have no longer got the wheel in their hands; they are at the mercy of the capricious will of God. Religion then is the opium they administer to themselves to console themselves in this vale of tears over which they think they have no control; religion could also be seen as the opium the "real" controllers of society administer to the masses to keep them happy and subservient.

It is easy to dismiss this kind of thinking as turn-of-the-century Marxism, but it found plenty of examples to justify itself right in the semi-feudalism of Negros. Had I not often heard the people, when I asked why their child had died, say: "It is the will of God"? Had I not witnessed myself the fact that so many landowners wanted religion for their people provided it was harmless and domesticating?

However, we were presenting something quite different, in fact the very opposite: a "good news" that was socially explosive and very demanding. It had to be accompanied by more prayer, not less. But the monastic spirituality did not meet our needs, it was too tied to schedules and a quiet peaceful life.

We needed a spirituality suited to our hectic situation, and so through the years we began to build it up, piece by piece. Our prayers had to be triggered not by the clock or the church bells, but by events. If a group came to the *convento* to discuss some problem in their community, we would frequently finish by praying together for help or in thanksgiving, like the spontaneous gathering in the church after Brian and his leaders were released. If we attempted to fix it by the clock, we were too frequently frustrated because we had very little control over the events of life. Poor people do not have such control, and we were living more now by their rhythm.

The Scriptures began to play a larger role in our prayers, especially the passages concerning the Exodus—the escape from Egypt, the crossing of the Red Sea. We rediscovered that Jesus built the Mass around precisely that event, for the first "Last Supper" had taken place at the feast of Passover, the celebration of the liberation of the people from slavery and from Pharaoh. The Mass now was the celebration of our liberation from sin and all its consequences—including the unjust structures that brought injustice and hunger to our mountain.

Our penance and sacrifice now grew out of the struggle for justice. There was no need to invent penances. There was the asceticism of endless meetings, the penance of the long walks in the blazing sun, and the fasting and frugality that were the normal accompaniment to living close to the poor.

We also found ourselves giving a second hearing to "popular religiosity," having a greater respect for the devotions of the people—the processions, the Way of the Cross, the rosary, the novenas, and the *Flores de Mayo*. These we sometimes revised to bring them into line with the Vatican Council and to remove that fatalism which suggests that God is honored in our inactivity. For example, the pastoral council of Bacolod under Monsignor Iledan had rewritten the *Flores de Mayo*, keeping the beautiful ceremonies of the flowers for Mary, but adding readings and songs which challenged us to struggle for a society as beautiful as the ceremony. They rewrote the Stations of the Cross, emphasizing Christ's identification with the sufferings of the people. In the same spirit the Redemptorists rewrote their famous novena—a novena my friend on the seafront in Manila never missed—removing anything like fatalism from it and putting in strong emphasis on social justice.

Cutting across all the various individual practices, our newly emerging spirituality above all was "paschal." It took me years to understand that word. By "paschal" I mean that it was a return to the way practiced by Jesus, a confronting of the evil structures, a saying to Pilate: "Why do you strike me?" A saying to the powers that be: "By what authority do you do this?" A saying to the military: "Is it lawful to cure or to kill?" and a taking of the consequences. The whole structure of government was death-dealing, and the people were challenging and confronting this. As a result, for many of us there was the temptation to call in legions of angels to help us. We too had our agony in the garden. And for many thousands and thousands there were the scourging, the torture, the death.

I had first arrived in the Philippines during the Vatican Council, talking about the Resurrection and Easter Sunday. But when I got close enough to hear them, the people were telling me of the Crucifixion and Good Friday. Slowly I realized that one was the door to the other, and Alex and Herman had walked through that door. Their spirituality was truly paschal—a *passover* from death to what we believed with trembling hope was life.

From the day I left our seminary at Dalgan Park I missed the great Gregorian liturgy. I missed the solemn chant, I missed the "complaints" and the "Hagios Athanatos" of Holy Week, I missed the "Alleluias" of Easter, I missed that solemn "Te Deum" when other words could no longer express how I felt about God. I missed the moments after Communion. I missed the satisfaction of lying down knowing that all due prayers had been said and sacrifices done. And as for my noble vision of chastity and poverty, I had learned my own weakness since. In a way those days could never return. And for a time I felt aggrieved with the Lord that in my attempt to serve I seemed to have forfeited the consolation and self-satisfaction which made that service joyful.

Now as our new spirituality emerged, I felt that the words which God addresses to Francis Thompson in the "Hound of Heaven" could also be addressed to me:

> All which I took from thee I did but take
> Not for thy harms
> But just that thou mightst seek it in My arms,
> All which thy child's mistake fancies as lost
> I have stored for thee at home.

It is strange, but one of the reasons for monasticism in the fourth century was precisely to rediscover the spiritual experience of the days when the Christians were persecuted and hiding in the catacombs. The persecution of those early days forced the disciples to be witnesses to Jesus. The fourth-century Christians chose the monastic life as a voluntary witness—a way of imitating the sufferings of those early disciples. The spirituality they developed in the monasteries had a profound effect on the life of the Church. Strong echoes of it were in the training we received in our seminary and in the spirituality we had been proposing to the people. But the poor people in the Christian communities by confronting the authorities had gone back not in symbol but in reality to the early Church. They were beginning to live again the days of the catacombs and the life of Jesus himself. Their penance and sacrifice were written into their lives. They had *integrated* their spirituality—precisely what we had been trying to do. We had thought to catechize them, and now they were evangelizing us.

Chapter 47

IN THE parish of Sipalay on the coast, south of Kaban-kalan, there had been a great many army atrocities. Terry Bennett, the parish priest, decided to hold a prayer rally at which the whole parish would be told what was being done to the peasants. Brian's harassment and arrest cast a shadow over the plans. Terry was worried that the rally might backfire and unleash more army brutality. On the other hand, silence would encourage them. One night, he woke up in a sweat, trembling with fear over what could happen. Finally, after much prayer and agonizing, Terry decided that the rally would go ahead. The Christian communities in the sixteen parishes were to pick people who would go to show support. In Tabugon the parish council decided that we would go on foot, though it would mean walking thirty kilometers over rough terrain in the tropical heat.

The *kibbutz* truck took us the twenty kilometers to Bactolon in the hills beyond Candoni. There we disembarked and were joined by the Candoni people for the thirty-kilometer journey over the hills to Sipalay. It was a brutal march, and after a precarious journey through a dank swamp it was made worse by rain, because then we began to slither and slide.

We had started just after dawn. We reached the large Sipalay River at dusk, and holding onto one another we crossed it safely. Darkness had fallen and it was maybe eight at night when our cavalcade, now swelled to some four thousand men, women, and children holding makeshift lamps made from bottles, cloth, and kerosene, was halted by a group of soldiers.

They had obviously been waiting for us. I and Donie Hogan, then parish priest of Candoni, and the Redemptorist Pat Horgan found ourselves confronting the captain of the troop. He had a two-way radio and was in contact with Sipalay town. The soldiers were nervous. A voice over the radio said not to let the people pass. I explained to the captain that many of the women were carrying little children and that keeping them out in the cold was dangerous. Also others of the women were pregnant (surely a fair guess) and any disturbance would have a negative effect on them. His first sign of relenting was when he said he must search everyone. I was in favor of this as a means of him saving face. I did not believe they could search four thousand people at this hour of the night. Donie felt it was dangerous to consent to the search; say if they did find something. . . .

Finally, while we were still arguing, the commander arrived, and as Pat Horgan and I began talking with him, without warning Donie took out his camera and took a flash photo of the three of us. The commander must have realized that whatever he did now was going to be recorded for the newspapers, because he countermanded the order of the man below him, and so after making a few face-saving demands, he allowed the people to pass. The alternative would have been to force four thousand people to stay out in the night and to take the responsibility if anything happened (a thing that would not have caused the officer to lose any sleep if there were no witnesses—the basic army philosophy always being that poor peasants are expendable).

We resumed the march. By the time we reached the cement road leading into Sipalay, I was hardly able to lift my feet. Someone tried to start up a song, but no sound would come out of my mouth. I needed to conserve all the energy I could. The last three miles seemed interminable. It was not the first time I had arrived at Sipalay at an odd hour: seventeen years ago I had arrived at 2:00 A.M. But I could never have foreseen this.

As we passed through the town on our way to the *convento* and school, the people of the town, terrified by the recent killings, heard the pad of thousands of bare feet; they knew who it was, and, standing silently in the dark of their doorways, they wept.

Next day was the Mass. Inside the school grounds thousands more people joined us from other places, though not so many from Sipalay itself: they were afraid. But the wives of those who had been killed or had disappeared were not afraid, or if they were they overcame it and got up and told the crowd what had happened to them. All around, outside the compound, soldiers were in evidence and a couple of helicopters swooped around overhead. From the town hall some troops kept an eye on us with binoculars, and of course everything was taped. But the women spoke on.

Then Father Dodo Dejilla gave a sermon which would have taken the paint off the walls of a church. I could see Terry wincing. He had hoped for something a little lower-key. After all, he was the one who had to deal with the authorities in Sipalay. But if he was nervous about them, they were equally nervous about him ever since the day they had dumped some bodies outside the town hall and left them there to rot. Terry had gone over and, dressed in his soutane, knelt down with arms outstretched and prayed there for several hours, in reparation, he said, for the insult to human dignity which the army had committed and the town officials condoned. For the people of the town that silent white-robed figure kneeling in the tropical sun was equivalent to an Old Testament prophet pointing the finger of anathema at the powerful ones. The point was all the stronger because Terry was known not to be sympathetic to the N.P.A.

I was scared that on the journey back our group from Tabugon, who had the farthest to travel, would get caught in the darkness and rain in that swamp. So we left ahead of the others as the Mass ended, missing the dramatic prayer for reconciliation which Terry led. We saw a truck and asked the owner if we could hire it as far as the river; this would save us ten miles, and the road went that far. He said yes, and that he would take no payment. When we left him, he gave us bread from his truck. The people of the town may not have attended, but they were in sympathy with us. Typical of many of the middle class all over the Philippines, they would come secretly in the night like Nicodemus. Someday we hoped they would confront Pilate openly in the day.

The reasons for the walking were manifold. We had in fact gradually developed a sort of theology of walking. We learned it to a great extent from Brian's group in Oringao. First, it meant that you were not relying on transport and money for fares: it was self-reliant. Then the journey itself brought the people together and helped members of Christian communities to get to know each other on the way. And it also had the unexpected effect of giving people a sense of control over their lives. Poor people live locked into a place. They do little traveling for pleasure or knowledge. Once they had forded the river and discovered a way to walk to Brian's *fiesta*, they knew that they could do it again. They began to know the location of these places in relation to their own. The fact that they made the journey to Sipalay gave them a sense of not being locked into one place; they realized that if necessary they could "escape." In subsequent discussions about going places they would often say: "We can walk it. It's not as far as Sipalay." They knew the way through the wilderness. They had made the surrounding land their own.

But there was another reason. All the talks, sermons, and seminars on what was happening around us were not equal to a journey like this to hear personally of the "martyrdom" of their sisters and brothers all over the mountain. They began to see that they were not alone and that there was a pattern in what was happening. Up to this they had quailed at the thought of soldiers. Now they were prepared to pass their camp or checkpoint or meet them on the way. Every time the leaders and priests convinced people to stand up and give evidence they had deep misgivings, knowing that it was possible that there would be more military reprisals on the families of those who witnessed. But some people had to stand up and break the spell of fear. The sight of others doing this gave them courage.

When the communities chose who would go on these walks I knew that there was much discussion and fear, and people who volunteered did not do so without long dialogue and argument with themselves and their families. Each person deciding to come marked the crossing of a personal Rubicon.

One of the secrets of training people in active nonviolence is to give them the chance to do things which are within their present capacity but which stretch their courage even a little. Walking did just this. To embark on one of those long walks and show solidarity with the people of another parish was a way of confronting the authorities which was legal. Many people were reborn to a sense of their own dignity on those long walks. Secretly I hoped that they would also begin to glimpse the possibilities latent in active nonviolence. And for myself, I was beginning to realize that the journey was as important as the destination.

We were now nearly six years into our small Christian communities experiment. Well, the first two years had really been a transition period. I had never dealt drastically with the old forms of parish life: they held their own wisdom. So I had tried to build the new within the shell of the old. But by now, though my ideas of active nonviolence were still only in embryo, I was convinced that the small Christian communities were the right womb for that embryo to grow in.

One incident more than any other woke me to the fact that the Christian communities were beginning to open their petals. We planned a penitential service for the leaders of all the communities and prepared it very carefully with the new parish council—the heads of each mini-parish. It would take place at night. There would be songs followed by readings, then representatives of different sectors of society would read a list of sins which were typical of their group. The emphasis would be on those faults which damaged the community and on the good things we had failed to do. Then the whole assembly would sing the "Kyrie eleison" after each of the "confessions." Individuals would be free to confess before the community should they wish. After that I would give a common penance to the whole community and then absolution. We would sing the "Our Father" together, holding hands, and finish with an embrace of reconciliation. Many tears used to flow at this time and genuine reconciliations took place. Should anyone wish private confession, I was there afterward.

It took the parish council a few hours to prepare all this, but finally it was ready.

Now it happened that in the early afternoon of the appointed date Jimmy Martin from Magballo came to see me and asked if I would go back to his parish with him for a visit. I kept saying: "Jimmy, sit down a few minutes and we'll have something to drink." He wanted to hurry, but something was telling me that I should wait, although I could not remember what. Finally off I went with him, and only when I awoke the following morning in Jimmy's *convento* did I suddenly recall that I should have been leading the penitential service the night before. I got up and left immediately while Jimmy was still sleeping, found a sugar truck, and made my way back to Tabugon. I felt ashamed: all the preparation we had put into it; all the people meeting for a confession service and then going home disappointed when the celebrant did not turn up. The long journey in the dark.

As I walked into the *convento* I expected to be greeted with a chorus of "Where were you?" But no one said a thing. That made me even more nervous.

After a while I asked outright if the people were annoyed that I had not turned up. No, they had simply gone ahead on their own.

"You mean they held the service without the priest?"

"Yes, except for the two visiting nuns. When they saw you wouldn't be there they went home. Then the people went ahead and held it. . . . It was very good."

No one at all remarked afterward that I had not been there. People were taking responsibility for their own lives.

The whole shape of the parish had changed far more than I had anticipated. Within the parish, some sixty small Christian communities made up six or seven mini-parishes. The boundaries changed with the addition of new communities. Each community saw itself as a sharing community responsible for the sick, the oppressed, the lonely, the dying, the children in their community. When they prayed together on Sunday they brought these concerns vividly into the prayer of the community. When they left the chapel it was frequently to go straight to tackle some new problem that had been brought to their notice at the assembly: to help plow the field of a man who had T.B., to collect clothes for a family whose house had been burned, to investigate rumors of a child being maltreated. And they themselves instructed their children for first Communion. If there was another community with a problem, someone would be reporting and asking for volunteers to help in a rally or a long walk. And sometimes there was someone to be corrected—a youth who was being tempted to loiter around with half-time bandits, for example.

This was all a far cry from a few years before when a priest would visit once a year at which time people would fill the church with the past year's unbaptized babies in their arms. The babies would be baptized without any instruction for the family, in a ceremony which held very little meaning for the people. Afterward the priest would be invited to the biggest house around, usually the cement house with the tin roof, where he would dine alone. And if it were not for the Spanish novenas which some people had for times of death, the people would not gather for group prayer again till the following year. Religion was reduced to the sacraments and the sacraments were reduced to religious rites which it was dangerous not to have but which were not related to the toilsome life of the fields and the fight to survive. In fact, the "neutrality" of the sacraments acted as a blessing on the unjust status quo. This is why it was so necessary to allow the sacraments to regain their real strength and not to let them become deodorants on a corrupt society.

Baptism now was a challenge to confront the society with the truth. We avoided anything that would present baptism as a superstitious rite to preserve one from the wrath of God. It was preceded by a seminar given by the local leaders and not at the *convento* but in a designated place in their own mini-parish.

Confirmation now was a personal and public acceptance, for those who were willing to make it, of the challenge accepted vicariously at baptism through one's sponsors and parents. It was not for everyone assembled at a mass ceremony, with much signing of papers and collecting of money from would-be candidates in the next election. I recall on one past occasion a candidate for mayor sponsoring one thousand confirmations!

Marriage was little changed, except that there was a seminar beforehand, and the first- and second-class marriage ceremonies—euphemistically called "special" and "ordinary" but blatantly reflecting and strengthening class divisions—were gone.

Extreme unction was now called "the sacrament of the sick." Not just the name had changed. With a parish of close to sixteen thousand people it was usually impossible for me to make more than one too-hasty visit to anoint a sick person with the holy oils, but often they would linger on for days or weeks afterward. Now the community looked after the sick, bringing them Communion regularly and holding prayer services around the bed as often as the sick person requested it. In their last days they were surrounded by special care and affection, and if I was away when death came, the people knew how to read the last blessings and sprinkle the holy water to consecrate the grave.

Confession had not changed as much as I wished. I did not normally favor group absolution, introduced at the time of the Council; it was too mechanical and legalistic. Personal confession is a human need, and I hoped that, as the notion of sin widened to include a sense of responsibility and guilt for the suffering and hunger around us, confession would regain its inner power. But it was an uphill battle.

As for Mass, in our parish it used to be a purely personal devotion. Now it was a vivid challenge to the corrupt society we lived in. The bread and wine become Flesh and Blood reminded us all of Alex and Herman and so many others who had given their lives so that the passover would become a reality for everyone.

The parish council was different too. It was not a coterie of comfortably well-off people from the town making decisions to back their own financial interests. It was not a group of well-meaning leaders from the town, trying to guess what was good for the peasants. It was not a clique of ideologues manipulating the people into what they, having seen the light, saw as the only solution. It was the elected leaders of the outlying Christian communities who were serving their own people and knew exactly what the hopes, fears, and aspirations of their communities were.

Nor did the priest rule alone, apart from the parish council. The sixteen parishes had agreed that the priest should have a core group who would decide with him, or on their own in an emergency when he was away. It had become second nature to me to consult with them. In Brian's case it was the core group who had run the parish when he went home for his last furlough, and it was the wives of the core group who had taken over the parish when he and the core group were put in jail. We priests are usually strong-willed individuals, too strong at times. We all had the problem of learning to share power. It is an art, a discipline, a sacrifice, a heroic act of trust.

In Tabugon the core group was Junior and Baby Maha and three others. I struggled against my own individualism to allow them to make as many decisions as possible. It paid off because when trouble struck the parish they were able to take over.

The health program was no longer a handout program with me like Santa Claus distributing medicines or trying to persuade the well-off to spare some money to look after their own workers. The barefoot doctors and nurse's aides were trying to teach the people themselves the elements of preventive medicine and to use the local herbs, though in a crisis the core group was always prepared to endorse a patient to Mommy Paz Torres in Bacolod Provincial Hospital or to Mila in Kabankalan Hospital.

These programs frequently broke down and did not work, but that did not worry me because I knew we were going in the right direction, and no matter how slowly you move, if it is in the right direction, then every inch is something gained. Like the grass, the people kept growing, even while I slept—especially while I slept!

I no longer paid an army of catechists, collecting the money from the wealthy or from abroad. The people chose and supported the catechists themselves. What help I gave was in their training and in producing the books they needed.

Social justice was not just another parish office with the words "Social Justice" written on the door and inside someone behind a desk with filing cabinets. It was the touchstone of the Christianity of each community. Without it everything else was considered void. And it was not a cold justice, looking for a theoretical egalitarianism; it was a justice which looked for reconciliation, knowing that the human being who ceased to oppress gained as much as the person who ceased to be the victim of opression. This justice sought not the mathematical equality of statistics, but the caring equality of sisters and brothers convinced by the love of God.

"Active nonviolence" was not much talked about. I did not push it as such; I knew its time would come. I preferred to wait patiently till it came from the people, but *they* already practiced it through daring to discuss their problems and analyze the causes, through learning to break the sacred silence which made so much oppression possible, and through one mobilization after another, making small social gains but huge human gains for those involved. They gradually realized there was more than one way to combat the Goliath of organized oppression which the government had become.

Money did not flow out of the *convento*. All the local leaders and seminar-givers worked voluntarily, and in the *convento* we tried to live a family life, praying and eating together with those who helped in the *convento*. They went to school and when they came home they helped to fetch and carry.

The lessening of the association of the sacraments with money went hand in hand with encouraging the people to support me with rice and food and to pay for the gasoline should they wish to use the jeep for a *fiesta* or a sick person. The *convento* was not run as efficiently as a parish plant with many different offices and paid officials with special hours, but it was a family and a community, a microcosm of what we dreamt of for the whole parish.

We had no traditional parish organizations for a very good reason: I had never started them. Many of these organizations are formed precisely to give people a channel for implementing their desire to help others in one way or another. But if the parish is a family of sharing communities, then by their very nature these communities are involved all day and every day in helping those in need within the community. Sharing is a way of life, not an "extracurricular activity." It is *the* way of being a disciple, and other organizations, with some exceptions, are superfluous. Such organizations usually are centered on the parish church, thus working against the decentralization which the Christian communities are all about. For the same reason centralized parish celebrations were kept to a minimum. No daily public Mass. No schedule of novenas or First Fridays which only the people in Tabugon proper could attend. Even the Sunday Mass was not always at the *centro,* at Tabugon, where I lived, but was rotated from place to place to take the emphasis off the village of Tabugon.

Of course we did have many parish activities when all the communities got together—for example, when the bishop came, or when we went in solidarity to help each other—but we did not want the small Christian communities to feel that they were peripheral or that more "grace" was available to those who lived physically nearer to the priest. I wanted them to know that their little community—with its thatched shack for a church, the daily sharing, and their heartfelt prayers together—*is* the Church.

The parish did not work totally on its own but in coordination with the four other mountains parishes, with the group of sixteen parishes, and with the diocesan pastoral council, which eventually made the small Christian communities the keystone of the diocesan pastoral plan.

But probably the most profound change occurred without me realizing it: a change in myself, a new understanding of what it is to be a disciple of Jesus, and therefore a new understanding of what it means to be a priest. In the early days I had seen myself as a model for the other Christians. I could not live up to that, and for a while I was depressed at my own weakness, but somewhere along the line I realized that I was not the model. I was not meant to be the arch-Christian. There were so many real saints around the communities if I would only open my eyes and see—people like Padot and Arod. My task was to discover them, recognize them, learn from them, and help others to learn from them. I would say to myself, going into a new place: "There are some rare and beautiful plants here. My job is to lift the stones and discover them so that the whole community can share them."

It was a great relief to accept that I was the same as everyone else but with a different role to play. Anyway, how could I look God in the face and say: "I have more faith than anyone in the parish"? The truth is that we are not priests because we have more faith or gifts than others. We are priests to discover and uncover the faith of others and learn from it and help it to flower and be shared with others. The people will do the evangelizing. We just have to remove the barriers before them and encourage them in their mission. It now became a joy to discover and thank God for the faith of the people, a faith they obviously had "in spite of" me.

The spirituality of superiority does not only affect priests and ministers. It affects all Christians who go in search of an overindividualistic "perfection," who interpret "Be you perfect" in a Greek rather than a Hebrew sense, who see perfection exclusively as me becoming virtuous and shining so brightly that the radiance of my virtue affects others. One is reminded of the famous nuns of Port Royale who were reputed to be as pure as angels but as proud as devils. If, however, perfection is seen as "compassion," then in our striving to be compassionate we will be taught willy-nilly by each other. And just as we see that our life of service has made us very *imperfect* and we are beating our breast and saying "Lord, be merciful to me a sinner," we will receive without ever knowing it that elusive thing called holiness.

Having finally accepted that I was an instrument and not a source of grace, I could now lie down at night knowing that in every corner of that mountain parish the natural goodness of people was being unleashed and blessed, and the idyllic vision of the communities of the Acts of the Apostles was finding some reflection because the sick and the old and the young and the lonely were being cared for. And I remembered that curious Gospel passage about John the Baptist. While in prison John got worried as to whether the Messiah really had come. Had he made a mistake? He sent messengers to ask Jesus whether he really was the Messiah. Jesus did not answer directly; he just said: "Look around you. The blind see, the lame walk, the sick are cured, and the poor have the good news preached to them."

One day soon after the Church-military liaison meeting at Dancallan, I was asked to say Mass in a new community which was so far in the mountains that it was slightly across the border of the diocese into the next diocese of Oriental Negros. I was in the middle of the Mass—in fact at the homily—when over the half-walls of the chapel I noticed we were surrounded by soldiers in fatigues, carrying machine guns at the semi-ready.

A great tension came into the little assembly, and I went quite blank. What had I said last? Was I talking about army abuses and cooperating with them? I could not remember anything, I had received such a shock. Noticing that most of the congregation were women, I started the homily anew: "I notice that most of you here today are women. You know, at the first Mass on Calvary only the women remained to stand by Jesus. And standing there they were surrounded by Roman soldiers, armed Roman soldiers who saw them as sympathizers with the criminal who had been stirring up the people. To remain there meant great courage for those women because in fact the men had all fled. But they stayed there. . . ." I began to get stuck and repeated myself: "They stayed there even though they were afraid of the soldiers. . . ." I concluded the sermon abruptly and as I resumed the Mass I looked up. The soldiers had come in closer, and they continued advancing very slowly right through the Mass until, by the time the Mass was over and I was about to do the baptisms, they were almost looking over the half-walls.

I started the baptism service. When I came to the point where I would ask them if they renounced injustice, torture, militarism, I paused. I looked up at the soldiers. I opened my mouth and I heard myself saying: "Do you renounce Satan? And all his works? And all his pomps?"

It seemed obvious that they wanted to arrest me, but they were uncertain about something and not sure of the reaction of the people who surrounded me in a large bunch when we left the church and went over to a house to have a meal. The troops then surrounded the house, and only when I was leaving did the captain come up to me and finally confront me. Only now I noticed that he too was nervous.

"Are you Father Bryan?" he said.

"Which Father Bryan?" I said.

"So there are two Father Bryans?" he said, a bit perplexed.

"Well, actually there are four," I said, remembering a few others from bygone days and hoping I was not confusing him. He let me go.

The thing which bothered me most on the way home was my sudden changing of the baptism formula. Why had I not stuck to the one we had agreed on? Was I afraid? Certainly. Why? Because it was clear that baptism as we understood it in the Christian communities had become subversive. But was that not the way it was meant to be? Was that not the way in apostolic times when Saul arrested the Christians or when they lived in the catacombs and refused to join the army? Should genuine Christianity not be subversive of any society which will not allow us to live as the sisters and brothers we really are?

Chapter 48

LEO WAS in trouble. Leo was the leader of one of the mini-parishes. He had come up the ranks having started as a leader of one Christian community in whose area our friend Trinio's farm was situated. Trinio had now fully recovered and one day had threatened Leo with a gun.

Now a new problem had arisen. A largish area of land, nearly fifty hectares, was foreclosed by the bank. There were many small sharecroppers on it, all members of the local Christian community. The sharecroppers should by law be allowed the first option of buying it on a long-term basis, but a local landlord coveted it. He warned the sharecroppers to get off and he began to plough up the land. But Leo moved quickly. He and the sharecroppers went to the diocesan lawyer, Frank Cruz, and got assistance. The agrarian court decided in favor of the sharecroppers, a rare occurrence; but then the opposition was not expecting the sharecroppers to appear with the new social action director, Baby Gordoncillo.

So far the victory was only on paper because the next thing that happened was that a group of soldiers from the local town, drinking companions of the landlord, went to Leo's house and picked him up and brought him to their headquarters in Dancallan, several times threatening to kill him on the way. The message was clear—withdraw from the land of our friend. Leo was trembling when he was eventually released . . . he worried, too, about his pregnant wife and the children at home, one of whom was profoundly deaf.

The community carefully planned the next move. Leo hid his wife and children away and stayed at the *convento*. A complaint to the army would do no good—they would be investigating themselves. But there was an upcoming Church-military liaison meeting in Kabankalan. It was to be public and we were to bring forward complaints. Halfway through the meeting, when many cases of army abuse had been brought up, including that of Carlito Orchida, who had been buried at the army barracks in Tapi, and the provincial commander was longing for a breather, Leo stepped up on the stage and presented to the colonel the rare agrarian decision in favor of the sharecroppers and said that some people would like to block its implementation. Leo carefully made no reference to who those "some people" were. Desperately looking for a chance to appear pro-people, the colonel brought Leo up beside him, put his arm on his shoulder, faced the cameras, and magnanimously announced that this decision was proof of the wonderful things that were happening in the Philippines . . . land reform. He read out the decision, grandly ordered its immediate execution, and threatened anyone who would stand in the way. Apart from radio and television there were other reporters, so Leo had it all in black and white and it appeared on television that night. The army backed off.

Of the hundreds of land cases that was one of the only ones that the communities in Negros "won." I put "won" in quotes because even those few winning cases were often not implemented.

Around this time, Trinio experienced a change of heart. The local Christian community had confronted him head on over his pointing the gun at Leo. It was the first time they had confronted him. But then Leo's community at Casoy was more self-assured than the Pinamulakan communities where Trinio used to go to stir up trouble before, especially since they had won the land case. The result was that Trinio suddenly realized he ought to change. He apologized publicly, explained he had been drunk, and asked to join the community. They insisted that he do a retreat and only then could he attend the prayers, but not as a member. And they demanded that he submit to a complete review of all the things he had done by all the members, even by members of the nearby communities of Pinamulakan.

Trinio submitted. Quite a group gathered in a little hut beside the *convento,* and one by one they went through all his crimes, including the fact that he was said to have left various young women pregnant.

In my opinion he came across as genuinely trying to change. He admitted wherever he was wrong and asked for forgiveness. He clarified wherever there was confusion and denied what he said were false accusations (I happened to have discovered privately that the holster found outside Luding's house was actually Luding's and Trinio had not been involved in that one). I found him convincing. . . . The group agreed that he should give up his gun and become a trial member.

Soon after, when Trinio was walking along a lonely path in Pinamulakan, someone jumped out of the bushes, pointed a gun at him, fired and fled. He missed but Trinio was very shaken. Trinio saw the man and from the description I had a good idea who it was. Now I tell this story because it illustrates the two ways of approaching the problem. Our way was to confront and discuss; that's what Casoy did. In Pinamulakan they were afraid to discuss; they preferred a method which was quicker. I thought I sensed a hint of an underlying belief that Trinio *could not* change. Because of his class? In this case a simplistic understanding of Marx could mask an ancient tradition of revenge killing.

Trinio came to me. He said he had promised to give up the gun and was willing to do so right now, but since the attack on his life, he really felt in danger at night. By this time he was living quietly with his wife and child.

"You live alone in a lonely place. Let things remain as they are till I have a chance to see that man who made the attack."

I made inquiries about the man whom I suspected; he owed me several favors. But he had fled. My inquiries were answered by a strange note. It intended to imply the authority of the N.P.A., which I am sure it had not. Between the lines I could read the fear of those behind it—that the failed attempt on Trinio's life coupled with a successful attempt by us to rehabilitate him would cast a shadow on their methods. Another note told me, slightly ominously, to stop inquiring. I never got a chance to go any further. Trinio was shot dead some time later.

Chapter 49

IT WAS now eight months since the killing of our mayor and his four companions on the back road to Tabugon.

There were two theories as to who did it. First the N.P.A. A mimeographed issue of the N.P.A. newspaper called *Paghimakas* (*Struggle*) appeared fourteen days after the killing claiming that the N.P.A. did it by way of "execution." There were pen-and-ink drawings showing how it was done. The "newspaper" looked genuine. And after a quick investigation the army declared that it was the N.P.A. that did it.

The second theory was that the army did it. Many people in Kabankalan held to this, especially among the *hacenderos*. They pointed out how close the army H.Q. was to the point of ambush—two kilometers—and they claimed that the local school had been mysteriously closed early on that day to make sure there would be no homegoing children on the road. They pointed out that the mayor had been at odds with certain army men who were smuggling logs from the mountains through Kabankalan. Others wondered if the Long Range Patrol was not afraid that the mayor would eventually point to them as the killers of those seven peasants who had been buried alive on his farm certainly without his knowledge, since on the night of the killing he was in the house of his daughter.

The theorizing had died down when eighteen months later out of the blue a bombshell was dropped. The army investigator discovered the "real" murderers. I heard about it like this.

The woman next door to the *convento* used to sell vegetables at the crossing to support her family. Her husband had been a guerrilla fighting the Japanese during the war and had lost an eye and an arm, but never got onto the coveted veterans' pension list. At the crossing she overheard a radio announcement saying that I and Father Gore and Father Dangan and

Father Gore's six core group members were being indicted for the murder of the mayor and his four companions.

She immediately sent word to me, so I hurried down to the market to get it from her own mouth. I was stunned and decided to check it out right away.

A young man from Manila, Vicente, had been acting as our cook for the last few months since our cook was in prison. I asked him to go to the town hall in Kabankalan and try to find out if there was any such accusation.

Meantime all we could do was listen to the radio for more news. But the news did not come on at any fixed time—they did not seem to use clocks—so the only thing was to keep all the stations on all the time, which caused a great cacophony in the house.

No further broadcast was made of the accusation that day, but in the evening Vicente the cook returned and said that he had learned in the town hall that not only was the accusation for real but right now they were looking for witnesses and willing to pay them. Unbeknownst to me, he himself had agreed to be a witness and to say that he was along with me and the others when we were killing the mayor! With that sort of witness up their sleeve, no wonder the military were able to announce to all the news agencies that they had the evidence and that it was only a matter of time.

The next few months were filled with tension. Lying awake at night, quite unaware of the role the cook would play, I weighed the seriousness of our situation. It could mean sudden deportation. It could mean a show trial. There had been many of these recently. I thought especially of the case of Father Kangleon, whom I myself had seen speaking on television with glazed eyes, telling us that he was a communist. Unknown to us at that time, he had been tortured and sexually harassed, and of course they finally killed him.

Just then there was a carefully orchestrated campaign to denigrate the Church and especially the small Christian communities, with such newspaper headlines as "Priests Plan to Kill Their Bishops," "Two Bishops, Nineteen Priests, Linked to Dissidents." And on the same day that the headline "Murder Complaint Poised vs. Fathers Gore and O'Brien" appeared, Marcos was reported to have ordered a national manhunt for "117 Radical Religious." The interesting thing about our case was that it was immediately released to the international press. Also, unlike the other cases, we were not accused of subversion of any kind, just of plain straightforward multiple murder. The motive to be suggested was clearly revenge against a mayor who they claimed had thwarted us.

Why had they gone after me and Brian when both of us had clearly shunned violence? It reminded me of what I had said to Exor the night I was persuading him to give up his idea of procuring guns: "Look, Exor, if you are good at chess and your opponent is good at draughts, why play his game? Play chess. The army wants you to play their game, which is arms. If you get guns, they get bigger guns. If you get bigger guns, they get bombs and napalm." By accusing us of killing the mayor and his companions it seemed to be now that they were revealing how necessary it was to show that we were violent people in order to justify their own violence and, most of all, to impugn the credibility of the Church, particularly Monsignor Fortich, who continually told the world what was happening in Negros. But there was still another reason.

Colonel Kintinar, a military political analyst whose job was to keep tabs on the Church and who was alleged to have been involved in the torture of Father Kangleon, had recently produced a major study of the Church in which he said: "The most dangerous form of threat from the religious radicals is their creation of the so-called basic Christian communities."

The next shock was when we discovered that the military were busy training a whole roster of false witnesses. We did not know this until one of these witnesses escaped and told us that he had been forced to sign a document implicating us. The document he had signed was number eighteen, and he had seen the name on number seventeen: that of Vicente, my cook, who by now had left us. This was the first we knew about Vicente being a witness, and I immediately realized that things were even more serious than I had thought. What documents had he picked up in the house? How far back had he been recruited?

And what if we were tried and accused and condemned to death, like the three priests whose statues were now outside the cathedral in Manila; their necks broken by the Spanish garotte. That seemed farfetched, and no one was about to discuss it. I did not want to think about it, but I forced myself to do so, so that I could make a decision knowing just what the worst possible scenario was. And the worst possible scenario was death. What then?

I let my mind wander over all the sadness I had witnessed. I thought of Nora being dragged from hotel to hotel while she was dying, of Clarita asking me to give advice to Nanding when she was gone, of me asking Lina to hang on, of Vilma tortured by the army, of so much hunger alongside so much plenty, of Nato being glad that his death was bringing the people together. Then I thought of all the lost and unknown deaths of hunger in the mountains, not far from the sight of plenty, and of the graves of idealistic young people like Ofelia Cana, the daughter of my catechist in Sipalay, who had joined the N.P.A. for no other purpose than to try and stop the suffering. I said to myself: "Well, if it should come to the worst, I've had a great life. Few people can have been as happy as me. I have people who love me. What more do I want? If it should come to that, what harm if it would in some way help to ease the burden of so many who are suffering?"

Then I would say to myself: "But what if at the last moment I were to panic? What if when the sentence had been proclaimed I lost my nerve? What if when I was on the brink of darkness I was to step back? How would I endure the shame?" My imagination was in danger of running away with me. Then I remembered the words of Jesus in Saint Matthew: "When they deliver you up, do not be anxious how you are to speak or what you are to say; for what you are to say will be given to you in that hour." And I turned over and went to sleep peacefully.

With this hanging over us I wanted to have everything in order in case the end came suddenly. Brian and I met and agreed that we would not take advantage of the opportunity to flee, which was obviously being given us by the delay. And we would use the accusation as much as we could to bring about what we called "the coming of the kingdom," a phrase which summed up everything we had been trying to do.

The months of waiting for the sword to fall dragged on and on. I continued with the communities with a new urgency. It was agreed that Terry Bennett from Sipalay would take my place. The leaders all knew him, as they had walked across the mountain to attend his prayer rally. I could not have asked for anyone better. Terry was not only a deeply spiritual person but was fully aware that spirituality involved actively working to change the structures of society. Unfortunately, Terry would not be arriving until May. It was now March.

Our ex-cook was now living in the army headquarters and was frequently seen with army people, trying to recruit witnesses. Attempts to contact members of his family were foiled because they had all been spirited away somewhere. One night I heard that his father, Vicente Senior, had returned to Tabugon to collect some things but was going to leave the following morning. It would be my last chance to see the old man and try and get him to get through to his son that he was being used and would eventually be destroyed by the army when they no longer needed him.

When I got the news about Vicente Senior being in Tabugon, I was down in Kabankalan and it was nighttime. Some of my friends warned me not to go that night. Traveling at night was dangerous, but I knew that getting a message through to Vicente was important. He would be the star witness because he was going to claim to have joined in killing the mayor with me and Father Gore and the six lay leaders. In a sense it was a last chance for him too. I wanted to tell the old man that it was not too late. We would help his son to start again.

So Alex and I set out. We decided to take the shortcut—the back road past the spot where the mayor and his companions had been killed. At that hour you would see no one on the roads, except possibly a sugar truck deciding to mill in the lowlands.

When we were well past that unhappy spot we came upon an unusual sight: a van stopped in the middle of the road with its lights on and its doors open. It almost blocked the middle of the road, and we slowed down to edge past, expecting a greeting or a nod, but the two men who sat in the front seat made no sign to us.

For a few minutes after we had passed them neither of us spoke.

Finally I said: "Did you see that they had machine guns on their laps?"

"Yes."

After a moment's silence he added: "Did you notice the antenna?"

"Yes. I was wondering: Is it a two-way radio?"

"It is."

"Are you thinking the same thing I am?"

"Yes. I'm thinking it's only a foolish priest who would continue the journey on a night like this."

"And tonight is the anniversary of the mayor's death. It was this day last year he was murdered."

"They may be in contact with someone further up the road."

"That's what I was thinking. But we can't go back. Let's look for somewhere to stay along the way."

But there were no houses along that lonely road. The further we went without seeing a house, the more serious the situation seemed to me. Finally I saw what looked like a *quartel,* or barracks for *sacadas,* slightly in off the road. There were no lights. We pulled in, quite anxious by now, peering along the road in front of us for a sign of anything moving.

I called out: "*Tag-balay* [Anyone at home]?" (Which is what you say when you come to a house like that.) I knew that one of our Christian communities reached almost as far as this, though we were not in Tabugon parish yet. I knew too that the people would be scared, as so many people were called out of their houses at night and "salvaged" by the army or *salvatore* groups in this very way. That was what happened to Carlito Orchida, and to Alex and Herman.

"*Tag-balay.* This is Father O'Brien from Tabugon. Can you let me stay the night?"

A woman's voice answered: "We know you, Father. We're opening up."

The downstairs door was opened and we were let in. Alex meantime had concealed the Ford Fiera as best he could behind some stunted trees.

The woman and her husband slept downstairs. She led us upstairs into a long room, and there in the moonlight we could see lying on the floor a long row of bodies: *sacadas,* fast asleep after the day's toil in the fields. Their cane-knives were piled around the place. Some had a blanket, some had not. None had pillows. A few ragged jackets were hanging on pegs.

Alex and I lay down among them. I felt the tension ease. We were safe at last, protected by the *sacadas'* presence. I lay on the bamboo floor, my eyes wide open, thinking.

The mysterious *sacadas*. We had always hoped in some way to help them, but had never succeeded. I had heard the swish of their cane-knives in the early morning when it was too dark to see them. I had once stopped the Christmas Mass on the plantation when I heard that the *sacadas* were not able to come because they were cutting cane, and had only resumed it when they arrived. I had once been called to a dying *sacada* in his barracks. And I had heard of a *sacada* and his wife who in their despair had committed suicide with all their children. A few had strayed in to do the Sa-Maria retreat, but really we had had no contact with them. They were the lost people, the untouchables. Even our Christian communities had made no contact with them. They were silhouettes in the cane fields, seen through the window of a speeding car on the way to Bacolod and the lights. I thought of them as people I should be helping but felt helpless to do so. Now, lying there in the night, they were helping me, maybe even saving my life. I stopped listening for the sound of a hostile motor coming along the road and fell into a fitful sleep.

It was still pitch dark when we heard stirrings. The *sacadas* were rising. Some were gathering stacks to boil water to make *sarasara* (a sort of coffee made from roasted corn). As dawn broke they gathered their things to go to the fields. They had slept in their working clothes, so they left as they were.

We hastened away to Tabugon as soon as it was bright, and went straight to the house of Vicente Senior. He had left on the 4:00 A.M. bus.

Easter 1983 was approaching—my last Easter in Tabugon. I had always attempted to make the Easter vigil the highpoint of the liturgical year because, as I tenuously understood the Resurrection, it was the center of everything for us as disciples. But somehow it used to get lost in the welter of other religious bric-à-brac. On Easter night I wanted to rediscover for myself and with the people the joy and shock of the early Christians when they realized that "He is alive." But at the same time I did not want to lose anything of the rich tradition which had grown up over the centuries. So it was a liturgy that had to be planned with great care.

First came a little play with scriptural readings to set the scene in Old Testament times: the slavery in Egypt, the escape from Pharaoh, the crossing of the Red Sea. We acted these rather than read them. Then suddenly out of the darkness the Easter fire, and the Easter candle, with the "Exultet," that primitive cry of praise for the gift of fire and light with its echoes of some pre-Christian liturgy. Then with the flame we blessed the new Easter water and baptized the adults who had been preparing.

This was my chance once again to show the connection between becoming a disciple and the call to confront the Pharaohs of our time. Then all the congregation would renew their baptismal vows with the same radical formulas of renunciation of torture and militarization and war and the structures of war. As I sprinkled the people with the Easter water, I walked down the center aisle to the door where people had spread out on a table all the precious seeds which they had stored for planting; these I sprinkled too, with a prayer for an abundant crop.

Then the Mass, the new Passover, began. No penitential service: straight into the ancient alleluias and the gospel of the Resurrection. What a wonderful hope, especially for the poor and lonely people in the mountains, who when they lose each other, know that they lose everything. And I would think of the old woman and the boy shivering in that hungry shack. And thinking too of the unmarked graves of those who had chosen a different path, I would speak of the hope—the daring hope—that we would see and love again those whom we had loved and lost. For it seemed impossible to me that God, having given us so much, would refuse to complete the gift and give us all.

And could we not say that ultimately faith is not a belief in doctrines or religions but a conviction that the deep heart of the universe beats with living goodness?

Coming out of the church on that last Easter Sunday morning, Stephana fell into step beside me. I could see that she had something on her mind. She was a teacher. Almost none of the teachers went to Mass in Tabugon, partly because they were afraid to be associated with the Church. The teachers to a great extent had sold out to the martial law regime. They were an important pillar in its construction and they had hardly murmured. Some decided to keep their distance from the priests and from the Church. Among the less privileged people there had been a great increase in attendance at worship in the Tabugon parish—I reckoned from two hundred men, women, and children when I first came to two thousand adults not counting children—that is, if you were to add up those attending Sunday worship throughout the Christian communities. But nearly all of these people were small farmers, peasants, or workers . . . in fact there had been a falling off among the teachers and the middle class, or else they went to church in the lowlands to someplace which did not "disturb" them.

Now when Stephana approached I knew that something had happened.

"Father, I have not been going to church for twenty years. . . . Am I still a Christian?"

"Yes, Stephana, I suppose you could say you have come home."

"But the Church had changed. This is not the Church I left."

"Well, the Church is struggling to become itself," I said. But I suppose I was really saying: "The Church too is coming home!"

"Something has happened to me . . ."

"I understand."

I could see that things had fallen together for Stephana and she had had that "glimpse of a glimpse." And I knew that the next few weeks were important. She would want to read. If she read individualistic, devotion-oriented books, she would set out on a journey of spiritual capitalism, piling up grace on grace, polishing her virtue, and seeking to recapture the joyful experience of this moment again and again, so that it would become an end in itself, religion equaling spiritual consolation and the world a constant distraction from, and interruption of, this pursuit. But if, right now from the beginning, she saw that being a disciple meant a journey *into* the human race to help reveal that we are sisters and brothers, then a truer holiness would be found.

I went into the *convento* and came out carrying Penny Lernoux's *Cry of the People.*

The next time I saw Stephana she said to me: "Reading that book has shown me why I left the Church."

In a way Stephana was the only "convert" from the middle class in all those years in Tabugon. And she immediately set to the unenviable task of starting a small Christian community among her friends and fellow teachers. Before, Stephana had done a rare thing for a Filipina: she had actually rejected the Church, though she had not been able to put a finger on why. Reading Penny Lernoux's exposé on the Church in Latin America and its journey from domination to service put a name on it for Stephana. Now she was starting over, but this time she knew she could not be a disciple without participating in the human struggle for liberation. I wondered how my nonbelieving friend of the *Golden Bough,* whose wife Stephana was, was going to take it all.

Not long after Easter, a young man came to the *convento.* He said he would like to go to the diocesan seminary. I looked at him. He reminded me of someone. After a few questions, I realized he had no illusions about what being a priest was. I asked him about how often he went to Mass. Surprisingly he had rarely been to Mass in his life because he came from a faraway place. But, he said, they had a Christian community, and he led the Sunday service. At this I perked up.

"What did you say your name was?"
"Crispin."
"No, your surname."
"Rallo."
"Any relation to Arod?"
"I'm his younger brother."
"You could be a great priest."
But first I would have to see his parents.

Chapter 50

THE MINI-PARISH of Inapoy had planned a big *fiesta*. All thirteen of its Christian communities were to assemble for the Feast of San Isidoro, and I and the new parish priest, Terry Bennett, and Father Brian Gore and his leaders, were invited. We gathered in their little *plaza* with more than a thousand members present. We priests were on the wooden stage and I was at the microphone, when suddenly a green helicopter gunship appeared in the sky. It seemed at first to pass by, but then abruptly it turned and came toward us, almost as if to dash us off the platform. From its open side a large gun was leveled at us. The helicopter screamed to a halt, flinging dirt and dust at everyone, and out jumped a group of soldiers in fatigues with machine guns, headed by the provincial commander carrying his own silver machine gun, given to him by a U.S. army colonel. We were under arrest.

We spent that night in the Kabankalan jail. Father Itik Dangan was charged with the same crime and jailed with us. Our cell was a small cement room with a barred window high up and a gate. The nine of us— myself, Brian Gore, Itik Dangan, and Brian's six lay leaders—stretched out on the floor side by side. Lying down was not that easy as there was barely room for us to stretch out our legs without putting a foot in some other body's mouth. I was the last to sleep. I lay awake, thinking in the fetid heat, careful not to move too much. A deep peace had come over me. I did not worry about the morning and I may even have slept for a couple of hours.

Next morning visitors from Kabankalan began to come in, bringing us food and encouragement. We would need it, but not for the reasons they supposed.

We did not mind the cramped space, or that we had to rattle the gate if we wanted to get out to use the bathroom facilities, or the hard floor, or even the mosquitoes. We were worried about something very different: we were determined to stick together and we guessed that there would be an attempt to separate us priests from the lay leaders.

It was the Church and our fellow priests who seemed to understand least how we felt. They were so stunned by our imprisonment that some of them wanted us out at any cost, for our own sake, even if that meant leaving the lay leaders in. And this was precisely what we had agreed together would not happen. We did not even have to work out the reasons. Everything we had been saying and doing said that we should undergo this together.

Fearing the worst, we sent a note to Manila, where negotiations were going on between the cardinal, the government, and others, saying that whatever the negotiations we wanted all to be treated in the same way.

In the afternoon, however, Major Yulo brought a telegram from President Marcos granting us priests house arrest on certain conditions. We refused it out of hand. As the pressure was increased, we said we would do nothing till we saw the bishop, who was in Manila working on the negotiations. We prepared our arguments very carefully. We felt that, in agreeing to take us out without our lay companions, the Church people would be falling into a trap. We would end up in a limbo with the double opprobrium of being accused of murder and of having obtained special treatment above our companions, showing that our lay leaders were in fact not really our brothers when it came to the crunch. Tactically, too, it was a wrong move. The case would drag on for years because there would be no pressure on the government, and to those who felt the Church was not sincere in her involvement in social issues, this would be proof that they were right.

At midnight our superiors arrived. There was no doubt in my mind that they were not there to dialogue. The decision had been made, though not by them, and they wanted us to accept it. I felt anger and frustration. We were being given a choice: to divide the Church or to leave our friends behind. I had to remind myself again and again: He is risen. Why am I not trusting?

I will never forget that night. Tensed up, we waited for the arrival of the bishop from Manila. The bishop got to the prison around midnight, as we were finishing the heavy discussion with our superiors. We were ready with our arguments. We had even worked out our strategy. But we had one weak spot: we had spent years in the communities practicing dialogue as opposed to debate, and dialogue means you *do* listen to what the other party has to say. No matter how right you feel, you keep a corner of your mind open for the "remote" possibility that at least you could modify your position.

The bishop appeared at the cell, and before a word was spoken he had already fired a shot, because to our surprise he looked worn out and tired.

Even his soutane seemed worn. We sat on the floor of the prison around him, he on the only chair, with his skullcap askew, giving him the air of someone who needed our sympathy. I often wondered afterward if on some level he had planned it that way.

When he spoke, it was quietly and with the concern of a father. He said: "Give me a chance to explain. You are all in for multiple murder." He said the last two words slowly and deliberately to try and let the seriousness of the crime sink in. "This is an unbailable crime! There's no way that bail can be obtained for such a crime, but if I can get three of you out and under house arrest, that will make it clear to the world that no one takes the crimes seriously—which will undermine the very unbailability of the crime. Then they would not be able to refuse bail, and in fact we could institute bail hearings within ten days."

"But what of the safety of the lay leaders? Won't they be in greater danger without us beside them?"

There was a silence. We had planned this question carefully.

After a moment, the bishop answered quietly: "If anything happens to the lay leaders, then I will resign as Bishop of Bacolod."

He had made no mention of a divided Church and a jubilant military, or the weakening of the cardinal's position should we refuse what he had won in hard negotiation. (Later we were to learn that the cardinal had even threatened Marcos with the suspension of all Masses in the Philippines.)

We looked at each other, and finally I said: "Monsignor, we'll do nothing to humiliate you. But maybe it should be left to the lay leaders to make the decision."

Brian and Itik nodded in agreement, and all eyes were turned toward the leaders.

The leaders looked at each other, and the answer could be read on their faces. "*Sigue* [Okay], Monsignor," they said. "We accept."

To my dying day I will always believe that in itself the decision was wrong. But in fact it worked out all right because, taking everything into account, the Church was not ready at that point to accept or value or profit from our way. Eight months later, however, the Church had changed, had grown, and was ready to see its priests in prison and for the right reasons. And those eight harrowing intervening months were an essential ingredient in bringing about that change—a change which was itself ultimately more important for the poor than if the "right" decision had been made in the beginning.

In May 1983 the bail hearing opened in the court of Kabankalan. The judge had been changed! By this time world media, especially in Australia, had caught on.

The prosecution began to produce their witnesses. From the start it was clear that they had been very carefully trained. Where they were weak, the public prosecutor came to their aid, unimpeded by the judge. Attempts by our lawyers to object or to cross-question the witnesses were continually stymied by the same powerful combination. Then their star witness appeared: Vicente, my ex-cook. His story was that he had accompanied us and witnessed the killing of the mayor and even participated earlier in the planning. It was I, he said, who had counseled killing all the companions of the mayor.

We sat in the dock listening. Any temptation I had to laugh was tempered by the sight of the reporters earnestly writing down every word. It was one of those occasions in life when you say: "Is this really happening?"

He was then asked by the prosecutor to point out those who had accompanied him on the ambush. He walked over to the nine of us and, stretching out his arm, he pointed his finger deliberately, naming each one of us. Someone photographed him in this dramatic posture. His face is fixed in the frozen smirk of a wax figure. It is one of the saddest photographs I have ever seen.

Why did he do it? There may be a clue in some investigations we did. We could never contact his family because they had all disappeared, but eventually I managed through a seminarian to contact a brother. My contact knocked at the door: "Is this the house of the Silva family?"

"Yes."

"Are you the brother of Vicente?"

"I am Vicente."

"What, are you the young man who is involved with the court case?"

"I am his brother."

"But he is Vicente."

"Yes. So am I. But I am older. Our father's name is Vicente. He called us both Vicente."

What must be the struggle of a young man to find his identity when he is born into the world to discover that he exists only as a shadow. His name has already been taken. Surely he has to forge an identity of his own. That interpretation fit in with a remark he had made to some young women in Tabugon, that soon he would be famous.

Vicente, as the star witness, got to travel with the prosecutor and became the batman of certain army men. He lived at army headquarters.

The other witnesses also stayed near army headquarters, but they did not fare so well. They looked frightened and browbeaten. The crowd in the court was nearly always hostile to the State witnesses. Their antipathy could be felt in the air, and there were constant murmurs and outright cheers when a witness made a *faux pas*. Those witnesses were only pawns. They looked like trapped rabbits, and though I shared in the joy whenever they made a mistake I also felt for them. These were the very people we wanted to help.

I did not feel that way about the army people or the judge. I felt that they were callously using anyone who came their way, and they cared nothing about what was happening to the wives and children of these men, or that they would be liquidated afterward, as seemed very likely.

My first day on the witness stand approached and I realized that recalling what had happened was not that easy. Michael Martin would continually say: "You have no problem. Just say the truth." In fact it was not that simple. I sat down with the members of the household to discuss who had actually been in the *convento* on the night of the mayor's death. All remembered that Vicente had been there that night and had actually cooked the dinner, but all their stories were slightly different. The witnesses for the prosecution, on the other hand, had no such problem. Their stories were learned pat, and when asked any awkward questions they replied immediately: "I don't remember." No matter how banal the answer seemed, it was legal and they got away with it.

Since my evidence was so strong, our defense produced only me as a witness. I explained with much documentation that I had been absent from Negros during the killing.

We expected that bail would be granted in a few days, but the court responded by delaying the decision for bail. Delay followed delay, week followed week, and month followed month. The reasons given for the delay, for example, that the stenographer's notes were not ready, were obviously more tactical than real.

For Brian, Itik, and me things were now looking bad. And we were feeling bad. Our companions were in prison and we were under house arrest, so that our movements were curtailed. Even going to see them meant all sorts of permits from the provincial commander. In prison they were visited by an army colonel and accused of killing Jimmy Lopez and threatened with torture. It seemed to us that the nightmare scenario which we feared in agreeing to be released ahead of our colleagues was now being acted out.

The months dragged on. Terry had taken over as parish priest in Tabugon, and I was installed in Batang with two guards. After a while one disappeared and the other became quite agreeable to short journeys, so I could give talks in the local schools, as I was officially in charge of recruiting young men for our seminary. It must have been a bizarre sight: me giving a talk to the students on becoming a Columban missionary, while my armed guard stood near.

Whenever I could, I got permission to go and see our lay leaders, who had now been transferred to the prison in Bacolod. There we discussed what we should do. The beginning of a plan was taking form in our minds: we must find a way of joining our companions again. But how?

Meanwhile on the national scene, things were heating up. Benigno (Ninoy) Aquino, Marcos's only credible rival, was threatening to return from his exile in the United States. Aquino had spent seven years in a Marcos prison and was a capable and charismatic leader. On August 21 1983, he boarded a commercial airliner at Taipeh, Taiwan, bound for the Philippines. Thousands of supporters sporting yellow, the welcome home color, were waiting for him at Manila International Airport. But when the plane landed, it was immediately boarded by armed military guards who led Ninoy away. A few seconds later shots rang out, and Ninoy was dead on the tarmac.

The shock and outrage of Filipinos from all walks of life was unparallelled. For Brian and myself and Itik, it was the final confirmation that we were dealing with a totally ruthless regime and we could not afford to leave our leaders alone in prison.

For me the moment of decision came from a strange source. The last court hearing had been in July. It was now November 1983 and the court said that the stenographic notes were still not ready so the judge could not make a decision. Then I received sad news. A close friend of mine, Sister Nanette, a Carmelite nun who had helped organize the barefoot doctor program on the island of Mindanao, had set out from Mindanao by boat to go to the island of Cebu. Friends had wanted her to fly because the sea was rough. She refused, saying she could not go off and get a plane, leaving the lay leaders who were traveling with her to go by boat. One of those lay leaders was Boy, also a dear friend of mine.

Shortly after leaving port, the ship started to take on water through a hole in the hull. The cargo began to shift and people began to put on lifebelts. The crew told them to take them off, and when the boat finally capsized many people had to jump into the sea without lifebelts. Many others were trapped inside and went down with the boat. There were Filipino nuns on board. They gave their lifebelts to others, and held hands and prayed: that was the last that was seen of them. Hundreds were lost, including Boy and Nanette. Nanette had recently renewed her religious vows at the funeral of Diego, a young pastoral worker like Nato who had been killed. About that occasion she had written: "I stood near his dead body, and, crying from anger and sorrow because of such a brutal killing, I prayed: 'My God, I want to go with these people all the way in their suffering, whatever may happen to me.'" Her offering, like Nato's, had now been taken up.

I was deeply shaken by the deaths of Nanette and Boy, and it revived the urgency of our own dilemma. I spoke to Brian and Itik, and they agreed that the time was ripe to hand in our privilege of house arrest and join our leaders, who all this time had been in that fetid hole called Bacolod Provincial Jail.

But how would the bishop react? We planned it carefully. We sent a telegram to President Marcos, and Brian and Itik slipped their guards. I brought mine with me, and we drove to the bishop's house. It was three in the afternoon. He was still at *siesta*. We waited impatiently, putting our ear to the door to hear if the shower was going. Finally we heard it, and a few minutes later we entered.

One of the greatest gifts a priest can have is a bishop who is *simpatico*. Bishop Fortich was this, and for that reason we did not want to hurt his feelings or go against him. However, we now felt we must join the others. The telegram had already been sent. What if he disagreed?

He welcomed us and told us to pull up three chairs. He guessed it was something important. We had decided that it would be Itik who would break the news, but I almost regretted that because it took Itik an age to get the words out. He went round and round, till finally he abruptly said: "Monsignor, we are going back to jail." The bishop puffed his pipe and smiled: "You're probably doing the right thing." We were overcome with emotion and we all leapt up and threw our arms about him. It was such a relief that an end was in sight to the shame of us being out and our companions being in.

Chapter 51

BACOLOD Provincial Jail is an old Spanish prison which was built a hundred years ago. Inside its high walls are six hundred prisoners, two hundred of them in the high-security section which consists of ten cells built around a small prison yard. It was in Cell 7 that the nine of us, now dubbed the Negros Nine by the media, spent the last six months of my first twenty years in the Philippines.

The conditions of the prison are difficult to describe. What you first saw on entering the prison yard was its open sewer carrying human waste and the many ducks (which belonged to the wife of a guard) feeding there. (You had to pick your way carefully across that yard.) The next thing you saw was the pleading faces of the prisoners jammed against the bars as they called out for help. Brian used to say that the authorities had provided four walls and a roof, guards, and nothing else.

There was a food ration: five sardines two inches long and two and a half cups of rice; that was it for the whole day. On our first night inside we caught a rat in our cell. We were about to kill it when a deputation from Cell 1 came, asking if they could have it. I wondered what they could want it for. I soon knew. They killed it, skinned it, cooked it, and ate it immediately. It was obviously a treat. The rats they caught themselves were the only meat they had. Luckily rats were plentiful. They liked to come out at night to the open sewer which ran through the yard.

At night the prisoners, mainly young people and nearly all in for murder like ourselves, cried out with hunger. They would pawn what clothes they had to buy some food from the store run by the wife of one of the guards. The prices there were higher than outside. At other times they could sell their blood, and the guards would get a percentage for arranging the deal.

Tuberculosis was rampant in the cells, and sleeping on the cold cement floor aggravated it. Most prisoners had disfiguring skin diseases, and some had asthma or epilepsy. If they managed to get to the hospital, they were chained by the foot to the end of the hospital bed. Many young men were missing their front teeth because of the chronic lack of vitamins. With macabre tattoos covering their bodies, and the missing teeth and either outlandish donated clothes or almost none at all, they looked ghoulish and dehumanized and old before their time. Their ribs stood out like those of the specters seen in old newsreels of Nazi concentration camps.

There were no toilets, just a hole in the floor, in public view, and only one faucet for the whole high-security section. And through it all there was a nauseating smell of glue being boiled inside the cells to make handicrafts which might bring in a little money for food.

There was the suffocating smoke coming from the fires lighted on the cell floors for glue or cooking. The smoke had no outlet other than the narrow slit windows. The smoky gloom was penetrated sharply by one glaring light bulb left on night and day. There were no containers for people's things, which were hung around the wall in plastic bags or stored in some pathetic cardboard box—all a person possessed.

Sometimes in desperation prisoners would gash themselves with a secreted knife. In one case a prisoner, after gashing himself, with the blood flowing down his body, tied himself up to the gate as if crucified. We all thought he was mocking, but later when I thought about it I realized that this was not so. He was deadly serious. In his frustration he was telling us and the world: "I am crucified." He was only eighteen and had already spent much of his youth in prison.

Different things got to different people. One of our leaders became depressed, sinking slowly into lethargy. Itik would get mad at the sense of being incarcerated. For me, I found the endless noise and the lack of privacy difficult. I was always the last to go to sleep, usually at one in the morning. As I tried to write in my diary, I would become aware that the others had all fallen asleep but that maybe three transistor radios were still going in that small cell. Usually I would walk over quietly and turn them off, but sometimes I would just lie down with them blaring, accepting the fact that lying quietly with closed eyes was a form of rest.

Most of the other prisoners were in for murder. On examination (I sent a questionnaire around to the prisoners) we learned that there were roughly five categories: those who were in for a killing committed during armed robbery; those who had been paid by others to kill; those who had killed in self-defense; those who had killed in revenge; and, possibly the largest group, those who were in for something they did not do.

Many of the self-defense cases resulted from the fact that the police did nothing to protect the people outside the towns, and the retaliation cases resulted in large part from the fact that there was absolutely nothing to be hoped for from the courts.

The true nature of the court system revealed itself in the prison. The prisoners were sometimes assigned state attorneys, and the prisoners dubbed these "Attorney Carabao" or "Attorney Guilty." They said the first question the attorney asked was: "Do you own a carabao?" If so, the animal could be sold to pay expenses. Otherwise they would say: "Plead guilty, then when your time is up you will be let out." In actual fact a great number of the cases were never tried and the prisoners were just allowed out when they had finished the time they would have done if they had been found guilty.

There was one man there named Boy Herbalario. He had been in for most of ten years. The first five of these were while his case was being tried. When the proceedings closed, there being no jury system in the Philippines, the judge said she would deliberate and deliver her judgment in due time. Five years had now passed and she had not yet delivered judgment.

A little boy called Ronie, though only aged thirteen, was in for murder. His father, an amputee, had been attacked by a gang of thugs. Ronie had a catapult and a sharpened nail with a jagged point. He fired it to defend his father's life. The attackers fled, but the one who was hit by Ronie's "Indian target" died subsequently in hospital. Ronie, at that time only twelve, was imprisoned for murder, along with his father.

A lad in the next cell, Winnie, was punished by the court for not attending a court session, although the fault was the prison's, since they had not taken him to court. Another boy had epilepsy, and the judge would not hear the case unless he had a guarantee that the boy would not have an attack in court. In some cases the judge had died and no one had reassigned the case. In another case an old man was accused of a murder it was impossible for him to have committed, because he had been serving a sentence in prison in Manila at the time; but they had brought him down from Manila and only now discovered that they had made a mistake. Meantime his sentence in Manila was up. Brian brought the case to the warden, who said he could not release the man; he could only be released from Manila, where he was still officially incarcerated, but he could not go to Manila because it was six months till the next prison ship left!

The boat to Montinlupa, the huge prison in Manila, was dreaded by everyone. In the days before it was due, a special atmosphere would creep into the prison, a smell of death. To come back from Montinlupa alive was an achievement. As the day of departure drew near, the prisoners who were marked for going would begin to collect little things together: soap, a towel, a hidden knife surely.

Most of the prisoners were from poor families. No, not most, all were from wretchedly poor families. There was not one who was from the middle classes. (There was one son of an important man in Bacolod, but he had been put in by his father and had his own special house with servants.) Since the prisoners were so poor, their parents found it difficult to get the fares to come to see them, but then if they heard that their boy was to be shipped to Manila, they would put together what they could to come and say a last goodbye, sometimes walking a long distance, and bringing some vegetables as a farewell gift for the journey. That was a pathetic sight. Then as the moment came the designated prisoners were rounded up and chained together, leg to leg. Many broke down in tears as they begged us to remember them. Was it that they felt that they were going to their death and there was some warmth in the thought that they would at least live on in the memory of someone who cared?

What they feared most about the journey were the guards, some of whom would be accompanying the human cargo and who would take the opportunity to get revenge on any prisoner who had not been sufficiently submissive and kill him on the way. The investigation into acts carried out by the guards was always nil. The guards were investigated by other guards, just as was done throughout the armed forces. Nothing ever came of it.

Indeed right outside our cell door the prisoners would point to the spot where a couple of years before a fellow prisoner had been beaten to death by the guards. When he was buried his name was changed. This was not just hearsay: I collected all the evidence, even from the hospital.

At midday I would take my *siesta* in Cell 9, away from the noise of our own cell where we had a lot of visitors. In Cell 9 I heard the personal stories of so many prisoners; almost every one of these stories was tragic and unjust. Like that of Romulo, who was eighteen. Coming home from plowing one day, he saw blood spilling out under the door of the house. Inside he found his pregnant mother dead. The house was empty. His father and uncle had chased after the perpetrators and killed them. Now his father and uncle were in prison, and Romulo too. He was the eldest boy, and tears came to his eyes as he talked about his younger brother and sisters with no one to look after them—"scattered" was the word he used. There was no one to watch their carabao or the plants. And why had it happened? The attackers had wanted their land, though they already had plenty.

After a while I no longer asked people their stories. They were too harrowing and I felt helpless to do anything about it. And there were so many. Grown men crying, not out of self-pity but out of compassion for people they could no longer support.

We asked the warden permission to start a program to help those prisoners who had no lawyer. He agreed, since less prisoners meant less strain on the already too small budget. Finally Brian got what we called the "barefoot lawyers" off the ground. We had discovered a man named Ben who, though he had only finished high school, had learned a lot of the legal jargon. He was able to type up necessary legal papers himself and then present them to a judge or a prosecutor or a public notary to sign. He had got many prisoners out.

On Sundays we were allowed to offer Mass in the prison yard. Those guards who attended were sympathetic to us. After Mass we would ask the prisoners to bring their cases. Many had already done the maximum term for what they had never committed anyway. The Columbans provided Ben with a secretary and funds to make the journey to the home courts of the prisoners. Now I was able to refer to Ben the prisoners whose stories I had heard.

Brian and Itik did a lot of organizing in the prison, distributing food that was brought to us, and organizing handicrafts to make our fellow prisoners independent of handouts. And I took over in health matters because of my experience with the barefoot doctors program and in bringing out the health book.

We formed three teams, one priest and two lay leaders in each team, and we shared the cooking and the cleaning in our cell. We divided up the other cells among us, and if we had extra time we would give it to them. We in fact had very little extra time because of course we were also fighting our own court case, which involved over a hundred witnesses.

Chapter 52

WE WERE driven to the courthouse in a jeep, at times with an impressive guard, which I did not object to because I felt that anything could happen on the way . . . and as we discovered later those fears were not idle. A top army man had been made an offer—which fortunately he *was* able to refuse!

Unlike the others, I found the court proceedings much harder to take than the prison cell. It was not being on the witness stand I minded, but watching our other witnesses being humiliated by the prosecution, undergoing this for us. Again and again they were browbeaten into testifying in English when they had the right to testify in Ilongo. On one occasion Lydio, one of Brian's lay leaders, was on the witness stand. We were in the dock. He stated that he had been in school on the day the mayor was killed, and he was being quizzed now on the timetable of the school. In the middle of the cross-examination, during an unguarded moment, the state prosecutor snatched Lydio's letter out of the hand of our lawyer (this was a letter Lydio had sent to our lawyer showing the complicated layout of his class schedule). Using this document, the prosecutor began to quiz Lydio with questions implying that Lydio had learned false answers by heart and this was a list of the prearranged answers. Our lawyer meanwhile was stunned by the action of the prosecutor. I could not take it any more. I stood up in the dock and shouted at the prosecutor: "Can we take your private notes and read them?" The judge hammered me down, but as he did so our lawyer snatched Lydio's letter back.

The court case went on interminably. We were under an extra tension because of a gratuitous statement made by the judge when he had refused us bail. It read: "By and large . . . the evidence presented by the prosecution induces the belief that the accused have committed the offense charged [multiple murder] unless otherwise overcome by competent evidence, *of which at the moment there is none.*" And then he added by way of threat: "In case of conviction, *the imposition of capital punishment may well be justified*"! The statement that we had shown no evidence was made in the face of my own clear testimony that I was not even on the island of Negros at the time the mayor was killed. All that evidence was to count for nothing and that had been our ace!

The threat of the death penalty had made the Irish and Australian newspeople doubly interested and, of course, it revived my initial fears. I was glad that early on I had pictured the worst scenario and prepared myself for it, though I was ashamed to share my thoughts with others because they sounded so melodramatic.

As the media interest grew, the court and prison were besieged with reporters. Growing pressure to end the charade from the Australian and Irish governments, as well as the public, was apparently to no avail. Then an opportunity suddenly presented itself. America's President Reagan announced a visit to Ireland. It was a pre-election visit in the manner of Nixon's and was planned for June 4, 1984. This was a chance for us. Fifty-two congresspersons signed a petition for our release and the pressure on President Reagan from Ireland was soon so great that it threatened to overshadow the visit.

At almost the same moment as Reagan touched down on the tarmac in Ireland, Bishop Fortich received a telephone call saying that President Ferdinand Marcos was offering us all pardon!

Gathered in the cell, we were all silent when the news reached us. We had been right about the U.S. connection. But it was no consolation. I knew the lay leaders were thinking now of their wives and children. I looked at Brian. After a moment, direct as usual, he said straight out: "There's no way that we can accept that." Everyone began to nod . . . relieved that we were not going to go through an agonizing debate. "Pardon implies guilt," Brian added. We knew—we had discussed it so often.

Our refusal of the pardon was not the end of that initiative. The Australian reporters brought it up at one of Marcos's *Meet the Press* T.V. conferences some time later. They asked him outright if "the door was still open for negotiation." The answer was roundabout, but it was "Yes." And negotiations began.

I found the court hearings more and more excruciating and began to dread them. I would ask the judge permission to go out to the toilet. A guard would accompany me down to the bathroom on the floor below. I would dawdle coming back, and even walk up and down in the corridor, but always when I got back it seemed to be still going on, and always I felt the same tension in my stomach and anger when our witnesses were tricked into contradicting themselves. This was not hard to do. They were trying to remember things that happened two years before and they were conscientious. The prosecution witnesses, on the other hand, had learned a story and just had to stick to it.

For me the legal system came to seem more and more obscene. In a sense it was the most sacred institution of the State, and it was being turned into a charade by its very guardians. Since the law was the only door the people had to justice, to take it away was to force them to take up arms as a last resort, and this was what was happening all over the country. These judges and prosecutors and certain lawyers were the real subversives.

I say the legal system is a sacred thing because it is one of the great achievements of the human race. It took seven hundred years for our present system to evolve, if you take the Magna Carta as its symbolic beginning. Every little advance—the right to a defense, the jury system, the right to remain silent, the rules governing witnesses, the right not to incriminate yourself, the outlawing of torture—took decades and centuries to achieve with great pain and sacrifice and much slipping back. Its survival depends on the integrity of those set to guard it. Now it was being shamelessly violated, and for me this was a true sacrilege.

All the more so because, for those of us who had made the commitment to active nonviolence, the legal system was one of the great weapons upon which we relied. Few human endeavors have done more to prevent violence than good judicial structures and honest and brave judges. And it is wrong to point the finger solely at the Philippines. Brian and I were receiving huge amounts of mail. (In all we must have received ten thousand letters and cards.) Among the letters we received detailed accounts of court cases in Australia and Ireland where due process of law was being short-circuited, and this sometimes in the name of stopping violence—but it could only add to it in the long run.

There are many lawyers with sensitive consciences, but there are too many who build a wall around their legal life and will not ask themselves about the moral consequences of the side they are taking. On one occasion a woman landowner in the parish had sacked a laborer, Lucio Ramos, for joining the N.F.S.W. labor union. (Before we got the free diocesan lawyer, she would have imprisoned him.) I knew the laborer well because his twelve-year-old child, Anselmo, had osteomyelitis; his bones oozed pus, and he had lain on the floor of their hut for three years now. I had managed to get the boy into hospital with Mommy Paz. Then his father was sacked.

We backed the father, and the case went to the National Labor Relations Court, the N.L.R.C. A "neutral" judge dealt with the case. It did not take long. The judge spelt out the case. Lucio Ramos had been working on

Hacienda Tingub for eight years. By law he was allowed to join a union, though not allowed to strike. Why had he been sacked? The lawyer representing Hacienda Tingub said: "Your Honor, this man has never worked on Hacienda Tingub." Lucio could not believe his ears. He said: "But I've been there for eight years, and for many years even before that." "Well, Your Honor," said the lawyer, "his name is not in the books, which I have here." The judge examined the book. "Case dismissed," he said, and banged the table.

We stood up. Lucio was almost in tears. He needed the work desperately with his small son in hospital. I was exasperated. The lawyer approached me with outstretched hand: "Let's shake, Father O'Brien. This is just a day's work." I could not bring my hand to shake his: "I don't believe it is just a day's work. That's what the people who built the gas chambers said." He was now angry: "Oh, I see, you are one of those subversive priests." And we both walked down the corridor, unable to talk to each other.

Now my own fate was being decided in another court. It had become a place of anguish for me, but early on it had given me an experience of deep joy which still sustained me. It happened when I first sat in the witness chair in the courthouse of Kabankalan, during the early stages of the trial, more than a year ago. My own cook had just "given witness" that he had been with me at the ambush. Things looked bad and I knew I was fighting for our lives. There from my perch on the high witness chair, I could look down over the balcony at the whole town. It was as if I saw the last twenty years passing before me. I could see the steps of the church where I had sat the first day I arrived, the bell tower with the cracked bell whose tolling had accompanied so many friends to their graves, the school where at Christmas I had dressed as Santa Claus for the children, the ancient acacia trees under which we had held our rallies and Masses and demonstrations. Now I saw the throng of peasants standing patiently below the courthouse, praying for us, and as I thought of how many of them had walked from the mountains in bare feet, fasting, I suddenly realized we *were* guilty of a subversion more profound than those who had trumped up this murder charge could yet imagine.

And suddenly my youthful self with that passion to belong to God, a passion I seemed to have lost amid my human weakness and the cares of the journey, was standing beside me smiling.

Chapter 53

ONE DAY in prison I needed to mend a tear in my trousers. Someone told me that there was a "tailor" in Cell 12 who did these jobs. During the morning sunning period in the yard I went to Cell 12, a large cell with thirty prisoners in it.

"Who is the tailor?" I asked.

They pointed out a man at work in a corner of the gloomy cell. I went over, carrying the trousers. Sitting there sewing was Little Angel.

You could call it a happy reunion. I was glad that it was now perfectly obvious that I was sincere when I had told him on the day he was taken away that it was not part of the original plan. He told me that he and Jimmy Lopez had been taken from the police headquarters to the constabulary headquarters and had been interrogated there. He had admitted one murder and participation in another, and said how Jimmy had been his boss. Jimmy admitted to having controlled him, but said that the real mastermind was Father O'Brien. Jimmy himself was an operative of the constabulary, so his answer was probably for Little Angel's benefit or for the minor officials who were standing around. Anyway, they released Jimmy and kept Little Angel. Jimmy was knifed to death shortly afterward.

Little Angel was asked to testify against me. That did not materialize. They probably felt he was too naive. But a fair share of the witnesses who did testify against us had, like Little Angel, criminal records. So apparently it was established procedure to look for false witnesses among criminals. There was a carrot and a stick, and then of course they could easily be killed off later on the basis of their previous crimes. Coordination among the various branches of the armed forces is never good, and it must never have occurred to the writers of the script against us that we would ever be in the same cells as people they had tried to bring into the cast and then unloaded.

In the prison we met many prisoners who had been tortured. One in the next cell had had a catheter put up his penis in the presence of the chief of police. We also met two prisoners who were tortured and asked to implicate us. One was only in for stealing, so he felt that it was not such a bargain to exchange that for admitting to having killed the mayor with us. The worst example of torture in our case occurred when my old friend Fernando was taken in by the Philcag—the road-builders—in Tabugon. He was given the third degree and asked to sign a document saying that Brian and I were members of the N.P.A. The fact that he escaped with his life was a minor miracle. Faith recorded all the details of his torture and sent them to me. Pliers had been used on his fingernails. What was frightening was not the commonplace brutality inflicted on the prisoners; one can understand that while not condoning it. What was frightening was that torture had become a regular part of military practice. Normally it is uncommon in the Philippines. All of us were agreed that Filipinos as a race are extraordinarily free from sadism and its variations. Why had they now turned to torture, and who had instructed them in its uses?

Cell 8, where we had started, was so small that we had continually to step over one another. There was not even room to sit in a circle and offer Mass. We asked the prisoners in Cell 7 to swap with us. We were surprised at how quickly they agreed to give us their roomier cell. We soon discovered why: the sun shone in all day. The heat was unbearable and it was impossible to wear regular vestments without being soaked in sweat within minutes. So the Carmelite Sisters made some Mass stoles for us, with the words "Be not afraid. It is I" and a very special design sewn on them. One of the guards lent us a table and around it we held our Eucharist. We also prayed the Psalms from the Ilongo breviary which I had published just shortly before. Prayer became very important right through the ordeal. The Christian communities had taught us this ease in praying together. Our own training had been in a more individualistic style.

Apart from Mass we used to pray the Psalms together. It was so easy to pray them now. We could see immediately that the psalmist wrote from conditions very similar to ours. All this about being falsely accused, pursued by enemies, ensnared, hungry, sick and abandoned, forgotten, was literally true, word for word, of so many of the prisoners here. I began to understand one reason why the poor and oppressed find it so easy to accept the word of the Scriptures—the words so often come from an experience identical to theirs. The scriptural experience spoke to our experience. It had the ring of truth. And I began to see how difficult it was for those who had never been oppressed to comprehend, and if they had never even mixed with the poor and oppressed, then understanding and accepting might indeed be as difficult as for a camel to pass through the eye of a needle.

Gradually as we discussed the Scriptures we began to see how so many of them were actually written from a prison of one sort or another: the captivity epistles of Saint Paul; the prophetic writings written in the forced exile of Babylonia; even back to the Pentateuch, with its story of captivity and slavery in Egypt. In fact the Scriptures could almost be called prison literature. From prison they made sense.

Reading the breviary in the yard one morning, I was struck by a line in a commentary of St. Augustine on Psalm 11. It read: "The Father sent His Son into the world to defend the poor." Just imagine, I thought, St. Augustine, one of the great theologians of the Church, saying in the fifth century that the whole purpose of the Incarnation was to defend the poor! And I felt that I knew exactly what he meant.

Into the prison came all sorts of Christian groups. One was named unpretentiously "Visitors in Prison Aid" and was led by a marvelous woman called Manggi. Manggi might be described as a Bacolod matron from the landowning class. And though she had twelve children of her own, she and her friends found time to come in and do what they could for the prisoners, with no religious strings attached. And when prisoners were transferred to that hellhole in Manila, she followed them there too. I have met so many women like Manggi in the Philippines that it leads me to believe the theory that the Philippines was once a matrilineal society.

Other more evangelical groups also came to the prison. They constantly tried to "convert" the prisoners and took no interest in their cases. They presumed they were "lost souls" and poured on the emotion and guilt. Their aim was to make the prisoners accept Christ as their personal Savior—a comfortable domesticating Savior. These groups were flooding the Philippines at this time and received much encouragement from the Marcos government and from prison administrations everywhere.

One American evangelist came into our cell to convert us. We received him cordially and he asked to pray with us. We obliged. After a few moments he began to get worked up: it seemed that he presumed we were guilty and was begging us to repent. He was almost in a trance as he prayed for the Holy Spirit to touch Brian's hard heart. He was getting set to "lay hands" on Brian, and I sensed that Brian was just ready to haul off and belt him, so I interrupted with a couple of hasty "Amens," raised him to his feet, and thanked him before he got any further.

It was the prisoners who truly taught us about spirituality. Two points in particular come to mind. The people of Bacolod brought us in so much food that we had lots to share. But the other prisoners never grasped or grabbed.

They sat down and quietly shared whatever we passed on, even in extreme conditions of hunger.

Often they would approach and ask for help. The phrase they would use if we refused was: *"Diin ang imo kalooy?"*—"Where is your compassion?" At first this annoyed me, but then I began to realize that compassion is an essential element of faith and what they were saying to me was: "Can't you for a moment get inside my skin and look out through my eyes? Can't you see how low I am just now? Can't you see that I am your brother?" And of course that is what it's all about.

Always at work on something, Itik and Brian organized a petition for an increase in the food allowance. At that time the allowance stood at three pesos a day per person; with eighteen pesos to the dollar, that was less than twenty U.S. cents a day, which explained the necessity of eating rats. We had to refrain from putting down rat poison lest we poison our fellow prisoners who ate the rats. And we went ahead with the petition. We felt that the very exercise of uniting the prisoners and motivating them to protest was in itself, in the word beloved of Latin American theologians, *conscientizing:* it raised their level of awareness of their own ability to change things—something that was sorely lacking. So we petitioned for a food allowance of ten pesos, and finally got four and a half pesos—an increase of fifty percent. The prisoners were jubilant.

On the first morning of the new allowance, the cook, a woman guard, came over to our cell glowing. She knew that there was always suspicion as to how she spent the allowance, and she knew that this particular raise was carried in the local papers. She was at pains to prove that she had really spent all the extra money on the food and she pointed out that the fish had doubled in size. Which was true.

Visitors usually brought us in newspapers, and just around this time we learned of the U.S. government's huge appropriation for the Strategic Defense Initiative—Star Wars. Almost immediately, the value of the dollar went up, reflecting the withdrawal of so much cash from the U.S. dollar pool. And the Philippines, among other Third World countries, found itself faced with increased interest payments on its vast dollar debt—then standing at around $25 billion. It was unable to pay. The International Monetary Fund agreed to a rescheduling of the loan, but forced a devaluation of the peso. Prices all around rose.

Once again the cook paid us a visit. This time she was very apologetic. She said she had not touched any of the allowance for herself but that the prices of everything had gone up and that was why the fish had returned to their former minuscule size. It was not her fault, she said. It was the mysterious rise in prices. Everyone in the prison went to sleep hungrier that night, but no one knew the real reason why.

One of the things that startled us in the prison was learning about the hired killings. Frequently the hireling ended up in prison and the hirer went off to the United States or continued safely in office.

In the special punishment cell, the *bartolina,* which we referred to as "the black hole of Calcutta," there was at that time a prisoner whom I got to know. His name was Sergio Herbolario (not to be confused with Boy Herbolario). I felt that most of the other prisoners were in for reasons which were essentially unjust. Sergio, however, was a killer. Over the months I gave him anything we had to read, and he told me his story. He had been a hired killer, working for politicians. We talked a lot about the value of life and human dignity. Eventually, when I thought his attitudes had changed, I suggested that he make his confession and begin to receive the Eucharist. He agreed, and I put him through a long period of preparation which he willingly underwent. After the Sunday Mass in the yard I would go to his cell and bring him Communion.

Sergio wrote out his whole life-story and gave it to me. Two hundred handwritten pages. It is his *confessio* and change of heart. Reading it, I was deeply moved at how even his life of killing had had an origin in the way he had been treated, though it was the furthest thing from his mind to write an *apologia.* At the end of the book he wrote: "Father O'Brien, don't be afraid to publish this. Every word of it is true."

Sergio changed so much in the prison that the other prisoners elected him as head of their new organization, which Brian had initiated to safeguard their rights. Though the food had dwindled to its original quantity, the prisoners had grown in the process of standing up for their rights, and the difference became visible. Subsequently, when we were no longer there, they did the unthinkable: they held a protest. Sergio as the leader was taken out of the cell by the guards, brought over to the warden's office, beaten, and shot to death.

One night, while we were singing "Happy Birthday" to Father Dangan, the guards who had been drinking got angry. They came to order two of the prisoners, Nene and Moldez, out and to do something to them. Moldez of Cell 8 came out, but Nene of Cell 9 refused, and his cell mates backed him. We heard the guards cock their rifles. The prisoners reacted by smashing the light bulb in each cell as protection. The guards fired into the air. The prisoners rushed up barricades and attached the electric wire of the lights to the cell gates, thus electrifying all the gates. The prison cells were now in darkness, because for some reason the floodlight which normally lit the yard had gone out. Ours was the only light still on. An eerie silence settled over the prison.

We were still recovering from the scare, in fact I was trembling as I filled in my diary, and the others were in quiet conversation analyzing what had happened (except for Itik, who had lain down because his blood pressure had risen), when suddenly we became aware that in utter silence the yard had filled up with at least a hundred soldiers. In the gloom we could see glints of stray light reflecting off their riot shields and helmets. We could see the gleam of their machine guns and an ominous white band on each head so that they could distinguish each other when the shooting started.

A huge floodlight was rolled in and trained on the darkened cells. They had water cannon and tear gas. We could hear Colonel Geolingo's voice calling to Cell 9 to hand over Nene.

Brian called through the gates to the colonel, telling him that the prisoners were not at fault. I added that since a prisoner had been killed by the guards they were naturally reluctant to surrender themselves.

The colonel ordered our gate to be unlocked. Meantime Itik's blood pressure had risen so high that he was completely incapacitated. The colonel asked me and Brian to tell the prisoners to take down the barricades and he would withdraw. He was obviously embarrassed by our presence. If there was killing, it would be reported to the press through us.

I went over to Cell 9 and spoke through the bars: "Nene," I said, "he says that if you take down the barricades they'll withdraw."

"We won't take them down unless they return Moldez."

I had completely forgotten about Moldez. Here was Nene and his group now putting their lives on the line for him.

I went back to the colonel, shaking a little. I said: "Colonel, they won't take them down unless Moldez is returned. They are afraid for his life . . . because of the other prisoner who was killed," I added.

"Where's Moldez?" asked the colonel.

There was some scurrying around and Moldez was produced.

"Tomorrow I'll have this thing investigated, and if there is any more trouble, I'll come back and use tear gas," said the colonel, and he left with his troops.

The next day during the "sunning hour" I saw Nene sitting despondently on the step outside Cell 9, his head in his hands. "What are you thinking about?" I asked, "the words of Teresita Tayum?" (She was the wife of a guard and had said that Nene would "get it" once the priests left.)

"No. I am thinking of the guards," he said in a low voice which betrayed hate.

I said that I too felt bad about the guards. We had been close to death; but that when all was said and done the guards and the warden were victims like us. The way I felt was that they were our brothers, and that if I ever allowed myself to hate them, my twenty years in the Philippines would be wasted. Nene nodded and smiled. Then I added, "You know, Nene, when you refused to take down the barricade last night unless Moldez was released, you were putting your life on the line. I don't know that I would have been able to do that."

The shared fear of those days brought about a new solidarity in the prison. We felt as close as blood brothers to our fellow prisoners, and they felt that way toward us.

The whole episode left me weak. There had almost been a massacre. In all probability if we had not been there it would have taken place. To think that the city streets were just outside the walls—rows of houses with good people in them reading books and looking at television; religious houses of nuns and priests; charismatic prayer circles; devout Christians of every persuasion—and no one knew what was going on behind these walls. People passed by each day and did not know that Boy Herbolario was here for ten years without his trial being finished, that young children were in here for murder who should be home with their mothers and playing with their little sisters and brothers, that a prisoner was beaten to death then buried under a false name and his family not even informed, that prisoners were selling their blood to keep alive. I was reminded of the scene in *Zorba the Greek* when the widow is stoned to death outside the church while the sound of the "Kyrie eleison" drifts out from the worshippers within, in some perverse way by their ignorance blessing the murderous act.

So all over the Philippines deaths inflicted by hunger, by unattended illness, and at the hands of men were taking place while the music of the towns and cities played on.

Near the end of his Gospel that wise Rabbi, Matthew, decided he must sum up simply all Jesus had been saying about loving God and being a disciple, indeed about being human. Strangely enough his criterion is not religion or ideology or even belief in God. His criterion is simply this: I was hungry and you gave me not to eat.

When I ponder these words I think that it is not cherubim with flaming swords who will guard the Gates of Paradise, but the famished children of Negros who will stand there with their sad eyes reminding me of how they died.

Chapter 54

LIFE WENT on in the prison and the court. Only recently had I become aware that there was a women's cell. It was in the outer yard near the gate. There were only about ten women there compared to the six hundred male prisoners. Some of the women had babies with them.

One day a new woman prisoner arrived from Manila. She had just finished twelve years in a mental asylum there. Originally she had been detained for killing her husband's lover. I was introduced to her by some of the women prisoners. I suppose they wanted me to help her. Her face showed signs of great suffering, and it seemed that only now was her depression lifting. I was afraid to ask any questions—too much horror lay behind those eyes. She addressed me in Tagalog, which she had apparently learned in the asylum . . . a nightmare of a place where naked inmates hang in cages. When she learned that I was a priest, she insisted on singing religious songs that she had learned in the asylum. She sang them with a terrible fervor till tears were running down her face. I stood listening reverently and visibly approving. But inside I was in anguish. As I looked at her, a once beautiful person, overdressed for the prison, in ill-fitting clothes and out-of-place makeup, I thought of that awful asylum, of the long years and the cages. I wondered where her children were now. I dared not dwell further on it and took my leave firmly.

It was now July, the middle of the hot season, and the cells were like furnaces. I would wait till the tap was free, fill a plastic bucket with water, soak my towel in it, and rub it all over myself . . . then lie down limply with the damp towel in my hand and intermittently wipe the perspiration from my forehead and my face. Yet I was at peace.

News of the negotiations begun by the Australian reporters reached us all the time. We had had so many false hopes dashed that we had become wary. So when news of yet another offer came, we listened attentively but tried not to get excited by what we called "the false hope syndrome." This was the best offer yet. The case to be dropped against us . . . our innocence guaranteed, the safety and innocence of our companions guaranteed. One condition: We must leave the Philippines.

The night the news came, Brian and I walked up and down the yard. It was time to face a topic both of us had been avoiding. The door was now open to an acceptable solution. Pardon would not be part of the final formula, but we would certainly have to leave the Philippines. We both agreed that we would prefer to see the thing through to the end; however, we could not ignore the fact that we were not the only ones involved. There were others . . . others with wives and children. I was haunted by the possibility that the judge would suddenly declare us innocent and the other six guilty. Anything was possible after the weird bail statement. I thought too of the remark made by one of the Australian reporters: "Are you fellows trying to make martyrs of yourselves?"

If leaving was the price we had to pay for the safety of the others, then that was how it would have to be. We tried to console ourselves that we would be able to come back someday. But we had no illusions.

We lapsed into silence, our thoughts drifting back over the years. We had both gone to the seminary when we were hardly more than boys and after ordination we had come straight to the Philippines. In a way we had grown up here; it would be hard leaving.

One day we drove to the court in the guarded van for the last time. This was now around the fiftieth hearing. The judge read the judgment impassively: "The evidence of the defense tends to weaken the evidence of the prosecution," he said. All of us were free. None of us in the dock applauded. There was no public mention of banishment, though that was down in black and white and we had signed to that effect the night before.

Continually saying goodbye has turned out to be the hardest thing about being a priest in the Society of St. Columban. This promised to be a special test. Those who were very close friends kept their distance, knowing that with all the fuss there just was not the space to say the sort of goodbye they and I would have liked. But two goodbyes stand out.

First, the prison. As the news of our possible release spread, all the things in our cell and our belongings down to the last piece of extra clothing were "booked" by various prisoners. We gave our wooden settles to those who had T.B., afraid that in the scramble after we left they would never get them. We wore shorts in the prison because of the terrible heat. I kept mine on till the last moment before I changed into long trousers to go to the court . . . the fellow prisoner who had booked the shorts followed me around all the morning to make sure no one else got them.

When we returned from the court to be thumbprinted for the prison records and collect our things, our cell was bare, not a nail or a fitting or even a piece of string left . . . nothing but the Irish newspapers we had pasted on the walls. We went from cell to cell to say goodbye. Nene and Moldez and Junior and Boy Herbalario were all pressed up against the bars. Now the tattooed bodies no longer looked frightening; we didn't even notice them. It was their eyes. So many. And nothing we could do. But inside I was saying . . . someday we will do something.

The second goodbye was to my parish. Of course the bishop came and there was a Mass and much show. There were too many people and I was numbed. When I was changing after the Mass on my little private balcony, where I used to read the Psalms and bits of Irish poetry in the evening, a man suddenly appeared.

He was from an outlying Christian community. He was in his bare feet. Those feet had never worn shoes. He held in his hand a plastic bag of new rice. For the poor, rice is life, and new rice is grace. I knew that he had planted and weeded and harrowed and harvested this rice himself, and maybe we had helped him to hold onto that little bit of land. His eyes were shining with pride and affection. He held out the rice to me, and I took it.

Epilogue

IT WAS now time for my long postponed studies which I took up in Rome. While in Rome I received news of the slaying of my Italian friend Father Tullio Favali, who had often visited me in prison. A very gentle man, he was gunned down by the Civilian Home Defense Force while coming to the aid of a harassed family. Soon after I got news from the *kibbutz* cooperative. Putut, a long-time member, had been snatched away by the army as he went to a rally on human rights day. He was never found again. His seven-year-old child, Noel, wrote to me to help find his "Daddy."

As the end neared, I was finishing my studies in New York when I got a letter from Faith. Fernando had been captured by the army, tortured, and then beheaded. Still in hiding, Faith was expecting her sixth baby.

At that time, too, news came first of a massacre of 29 civilians in Escalante in northern Negros, then the murder of my friend Father Pites Bernardo, the beheading of Father Nilo Valerio, and the abduction in broad daylight by the military of Father Rudy Romano, never to be seen again. It was with great tension that we watched the denouement of Cory Aquino's challenge to Marcos.

Next to Manila, New York was probably one of the best places to be those last few days. Every major T.V. channel had its own team out in Manila and around the provinces, and we had a front seat for what was happening.

The people had come out into the streets of Manila to confront the Marcos army, which was advancing on a small breakaway group of soldiers. All day and all night the people held their vigil, but especially at night, when they trembled fearing that the helicopters and the tanks would come . . . and they did come. At dawn the tanks rolled and when they came, a group of women, swallowing their fear instead of running away, ran toward the approaching tanks, surrounding them immediately, and bringing them to a halt. An acquaintance of a friend recounted how he was sitting on the ground and heard the tanks start up again. He wanted to run, but the two nuns beside him were not moving; the old Filipino machismo got to him . . . he was ashamed to move though he was weak with fear when the tanks finally stopped a yard from them.

How often this happened during those days; confrontation after confrontation of unarmed people facing heavily armed military. On the T.V. screen we saw the people holding hands and praying and singing the Our Father, using their precious statues of the Virgin Mary to guard the entrance to the streets.

Some military men said that when they looked in the crosshair of their guns, they thought they could see their mothers and wives and children in the crowd. Many people told how when the helicopters came they trembled below waiting for bombs or napalm to be dropped on them. Up above, the helicopter pilots were receiving their orders:

"Have you fired?"

"Not yet, sir," they kept replying, "we are still positioning." And when they looked in the crosshair of their guns they too had the illusion that they were seeing their own sisters and brothers . . . and they couldn't pull the triggers.

Many ambiguities surround the fall of Marcos. Many groups played their part visibly or invisibly, and many others prepared the way though they were not there at the denouement; their shallow graves mark every mountain in the Philippines. But no one can take away that "fast fierce hour and sweet" from the ordinary men, women, and students and the most marginalized of all, the squatters of Manila, who put their bodies on the line and became a wall of flesh holding back a wall of steel.

For myself there was a special joy. As they held their vigil on the streets of Manila during those days, I joined them faraway in prayer and watched the T.V. round the clock—shortwave radio, too, in hand—following the ebb and flow with anger or elation; anger at the fraud and violence unleashed on the people, elation when the women counting votes walked out en masse, and deep unspeakable joy when I saw the young and the old kneel in the streets as human barricades against the tanks. The nonviolence that I had kept so much in my heart, not daring to speak the word till they, the people, spoke it to me, was spoken now in actions far more real than anything I could have said.

* * *

While they danced with joy in Manila my thoughts went to Negros. The *sacadas* still cutting and loading the cane . . . would there be dancing in the streets for them? Would there now be hope on the plantations for Nora's grandchildren? Would the long lines for the soup kitchens go away? My companions in the prison, were they still in those dank holes? Would Boy Herbolario be released now after ten years in jail without a verdict? Would Putut appear from some dark place and burst in joyfully upon little Noel and the family? Could Faith emerge from hiding to search for food? Would there be an end to the 17 years' war, and would the boys in the mountains be home for Christmas? Would the grave of Fernando and like graves throughout the mountains be forgotten, or would they bloom with flowers? And our little Christian communities, how fared they now?

Another letter in the post with a Filipino stamp. I didn't recognize the writing. I opened it and glanced quickly at the signature. It was from Felipe Untal, head of the small Christian communities of Inapoy when I left. It had been at the *fiesta* in Inapoy that we were arrested in front of Felipe and all of the people. I remembered the panic in their eyes and I remembered, too, my last words to them: We are proud of you. I am proud because I know that no one is lonely or hungry or sick, but you care for them; *and that is the sign that He is alive: so be not afraid.*

Now I read the letter. Padre, it said, the feast of San Isidoro is approaching. The people of the communities of Inapoy have asked me to write to you. We are proud because through our sacrifices and suffering we have overcome in spite of all the dangers and threats. We did it ourselves. Come back and celebrate our feast with us . . . and if you can't come, you must send us a tape of your message and we will play it at our Mass.

It is they who have a message for me and it is the one they have tried to teach me for so long: God is the fullness of life. Where human beings are deprived of live, struggling for life, crying out for life . . . God is there.

SELECTED BIBLIOGRAPHY

Abaya, Hernando J. *Betrayal in the Philippines*, with a new introduction by Renato Constantino. Quezon City: Malaya Books, 1970 (original edition, 1946).

Bonner, Raymond. *Waltzing with the Dictator: The Marcos's and the Making of American Policy*. New York: Times Books, 1987.

Bello, Walden, Peter Hayes, and Lyuba Zarsky. "500-Mile Island: The Philippine Nuclear Reactor Deal." *Pacific Research*, First Quarter, 1979 (whole issue).

Blair, Emma Helen, and James Alexander Robinson, eds. *Sources of Philippine History*, 52 vols. Cleveland, Ohio: The A.H. Clark Co., 1903–9.

Brown, Raymond E., S.S. *The Community of the Beloved Disciple*. New York: Paulist Press, 1979

Caldicott, Helen. *Missile Envy: The Arms Race and Nuclear War*. New York: William Morrow, 1984.

Claver, Francisco F., S.J. "Non-violence: The Imperative of Faith?" Unpublished lecture.

Coblentz, Stanton A. *From Arrow to Atom Bomb: The Psychological History of War*. New York: Beechhurst Press, 1953.

Cornell, Thomas C., and James H. Forest, eds. *A Penny a Copy: Readings from the Catholic Worker*. New York: Macmillan, 1969.

de la Torre, Ed, S.V.D. *Touching Ground: Taking Root*. London: CIIR, 1986.

Dorr, Donal. *Option for the Poor: A Hundred Years of Vatican Social Teaching*. Dublin: Gill & Macmillan, 1983.

Dumaine, Brian. "The $2.2 Billion Nuclear Fiasco." *Fortune International*, September 1986.

Emmanuel, Jorge. "Terror in Paradise." *The Diliman Review*, July–October 1985 (whole issue).

Emmanuel, Jorge, and Burgos, G.C. A *Disaster in the Making: The Bataan–Westinghouse Nuclear Reactor: The Technical Controversy, Social Impact, History, and the Alternatives*. Durham, N.C.: Friends of the Filipino People, 1982.

Flannery, Austin, ed. *Vatican Council 2: The Conciliar and Post Conciliar Documents*, 2 vols. Northport, N.Y.: Costello Publishing Company, 1984.

Foner, Philip S. *Mark Twain: Social Critic*. New York: International Publishers, 1958.

Freire, Paolo. *The Pedagogy of the Oppressed*. New York: Herder & Herder, 1970.

Gremillon, Joseph, ed. *The Gospel of Peace and Justice: Catholic Social Teaching since Pope John*. New York: Orbis, 1975.

Hechanova, Louis G., CssR. *The Gospel and Struggle*. London: CIIR, 1986.

Hitz, P., CssR. *To Preach the Gospel,* translated by Rosemary Sheed. New York: Sheed & Ward, 1963 (original French edition, 1954).

Jecena, Arsenio, S.J. "The Sacadas of Sugarland," in *Liberation in Sugarland, Manila, 1971.*

Kung, Hans. *The Council, Reform and Reunion*. London: Sheed & Ward, 1962.

Las Casas, Bartolome de. *In Defense of the Indians,* translated by Stafford Poole, C.M. DeKalb, Ill.: Northern Illinois University Press, 1967 (translated from a ca. 1552 Latin ms.).

Lernoux, Penny. *Cry of the People*. Garden City, N.Y.: Doubleday, 1980.

Lernoux, Penny. *In Banks We Trust*. Garden City, N.Y.: Anchor Press/Doubleday, 1984.

McCoy, Alfred. *Baylan: Animist Religion and Philippine Peasant Ideology*. Manila: Philippine Quarterly of Society and Culture, 1983.

McCoy, Alfred W. *Priests on Trial*. Victoria, Australia: Penguin, 1984.

McCoy, Alfred W., and Ed C. de Jesus, eds. *Philippine Social History: Global Trade and Local Transformation*. Sydney: George Allen and Unwin, 1982.

Martinez Cuesta, Angel, OAR. *Historia de la Isla de Negros, Filipinas: 1565–1896*. Madrid: Raycar, S.A., 1974.

O'Brien, Niall. *Seeds of Injustice*. Dublin: O'Brien Press, 1985.

O'Fiaich, Tomas. *Columbanus: In His Own Words*. Dublin: Veritas House, 1974.

Sharp, Gene. *The Politics of Nonviolent Action*, 3 vols. Boston, Mass.: Porter Sargent Publishers, 1973.

Sheridan, Brinsley. *Filipino Martyrs: By an Eyewitness*. New York: John Lane, 1900.

Twain, Mark. *The War Prayer*. New York: Harper & Row, 1968.

Werner, David. *Where There Is No Doctor*. Palo Alto, Calif.: The Hesperian Foundation, 1968.

Wolf, Leon. *Little Brown Brother*. Manila: Erewohn, 1968.